# MORAY:
# PROVINCE AND PEOPLE

Edited by
**W. D. H. Sellar**

Published in Scotland by
The Scottish Society for Northern Studies
c/o School of Scottish Studies
University of Edinburgh
27 George Square
Edinburgh
EH8 9LD

ISBN 0 9505994 6 8

The Scottish Society for Northern Studies gratefully acknowledges financial assistance in the publication of this volume as a whole from:

MORAY DISTRICT

and towards the publication of chapters three and four from:

THE UNIVERSITY OF MANCHESTER
and
GRAMPIAN REGION

Cover: Composite engraving of Sueno's Stone from Stuart's *Sculptured Stones of
Scotland* (1856, 1867) superimposed on Gordon of Straloch's map of Moray.

Text set throughout in Monotype Times New Roman.

Typeset from author-generated discs by BPCC-AUP Glasgow Ltd
and printed by BPCC-AUP Aberdeen Ltd

# CONTENTS

Preface     v
David Sellar

The Geology and Landscape of Moray     1
Cornelius Gillen

Man in Moray: 5000 Years of History     25
Ian Keillar

The Moray Aerial Survey:     47
Discovering the Prehistoric and proto-Historic Landscape
Barri Jones, Ian Keillar and Keith Maude

The Picts in Moray     75
Ian A G Shepherd

Further Thoughts on Sueno's Stone     91
Anthony Jackson

Sueno's Stone and its Interpreters     97
David Sellar

The Historical MacBeth     117
Edward J Cowan

The Wolf of Badenoch     143
Alexander Grant

The Great Hall and Roof of Darnaway Castle, Moray     163
Geoffrey Stell and Michael Baillie

The Culbin Sands: A Mystery Unravelled     187
Sinclair Ross

The Historic Architecture of Moray     205
Ronald G Cant

The Pattern of Moray Building:     225
An Introduction to Traditional Building Materials and Practices
Elizabeth Beaton

Names in the Landscape of the Moray Firth     253
W F H Nicolaisen

List of Abbreviations     263

## CONTRIBUTORS

MICHAEL BAILLIE is Professor of Palaeocology at the Queens University, Belfast.

ELIZABETH BEATON lives in Hopeman. She was formerly an Assistant Inspector of Historic Buildings.

RONALD CANT was formerly Reader in Scottish History at the University of St. Andrews. He is a former President of the Society of Antiquaries of Scotland.

EDWARD COWAN is Professor of History at the University of Guelph, Ontario. He is a former President of the Scottish Society for Northern Studies.

CORNELIUS GILLEN is Deputy Director of the Centre for Continuing Education at the University of Edinburgh.

ALEXANDER GRANT is a Senior Lecturer in the Department of History at the University of Lancaster.

ANTHONY JACKSON is a Senior Lecturer in the Department of Social Anthropology at the University of Edinburgh.

BARRI JONES is Professor of Archaeology at the University of Manchester.

IAN KEILLAR lives in Elgin. He is a retired chartered engineer and a former President of the Moray Society.

KEITH MAUDE is an Instructor in the Department of Archaeology at the University of Manchester.

BILL NICOLAISEN was until recently Professor of English and Folklore at the University of New York at Binghampton.

SINCLAIR ROSS lives in Forres. He is a meteorologist (retired) and geologist and a former Chairman of the Moray Field Club.

DAVID SELLAR is a Senior Lecturer in the Department of Scots Law at the University of Edinburgh. He is a former President of the Scottish Society for Northern Studies.

IAN SHEPHERD is Archaeologist for Grampian Region.

GEOFFREY STELL is Head of Architecture, Royal Commission on the Ancient and Historical Monuments of Scotland.

# PREFACE

*Moray: Province and People*, like the earlier volumes in this series noted on the back cover, stems from an Annual Conference of the Scottish Society for Northern Studies: the Moray Conference held at the Ramnee Hotel, Forres in April 1987. The title of the volume partly reflects also that of its immediate predecessor, *Galloway: Land and Lordship*, and Lachlan Shaw's celebrated *History of the Province of Moray*, first published in 1775. The bounds of Moray have varied widely over the years and according to context: Dark Age Province, Medieval Earldom, Diocese, Sheriffdom, County and District have all borne the same unadorned designation but have differed in area. The editor imposed no three-line whip, but most contributors have concentrated on the modern District of Moray, which includes the historic heart of Moray in all its guises.

In keeping with the traditions of the Society the contributions range over a number of disciplines. There are papers on geology, archaeology, architecture, dendrochronology and place-name studies; but the bulk of the writing is historical, and includes particular studies of two of the most celebrated figures in the history of Moray — MacBeth and the "Wolf of Badenoch". The Scandinavian element surfaces in a number of contributions, as befits the objects of the Society, even if the association of Sueno's Stone with a king or warrior of that name has to be rejected.

As editor I should like to thank all the contributors for their co-operation and patience, and particularly — if this does not seem invidious — those who did not speak at the Conference but who later agreed to contribute to the volume: Barri Jones who was prevented from attending the Conference by a road accident; Ted Cowan and Sandy Grant who agreed to write on MacBeth and the Wolf respectively; and Geoff Stell and Mike Baillie who volunteered on Darnaway. My thanks are due also to Lisa White, Sheila MacMillan and Elaine Yuill for much assistance with typing and word processing, to Ian Keillar, to my wife Sue, and to BPCC-AUP. All of them made my task a great deal easier.

Finally the Society is indebted to Historic Scotland, to the Royal Commission on the Ancient and Historical Monuments of Scotland, and to the National Maritime Museum at Greenwich for permission to reproduce the illustrations detailed in the text.

David Sellar
Edinburgh 1992

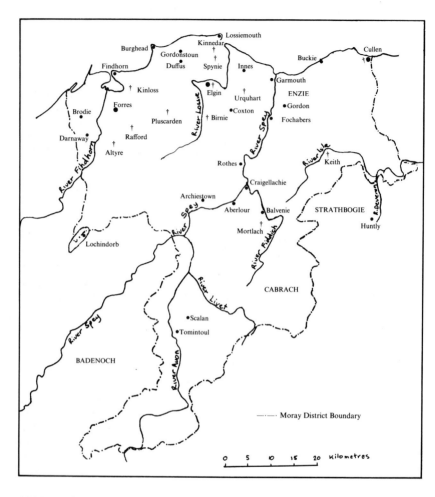

*MORAY showing principal places mentioned in text. (See also appendix to Keillar "Men in Moray".)*

# THE GEOLOGY AND LANDSCAPE OF MORAY
## Cornelius Gillen

## SOLID GEOLOGY

### Introduction

The geology of Moray consists of an ancient basement of metamorphic rocks, the Moine Schist and Dalradian Schist, intruded by a series of granitic igneous rocks belonging to the Caledonian episode of mountain building, then unconformably overlain by Old Red Sandstone sediments of the Devonian Period. Younger sediments, Permo-Triassic and Jurassic, are found along the coast, with Cretaceous rocks found only as ice-carried boulders.

The main structure-forming event to affect the area was the Caledonian Orogeny, around 500 million years ago, which caused folding and metamorphism of the older rocks. Molten granite magma was forced into these folded basement rocks and contributed to the elevation of the area as part of the Grampian mountains — a component of the Caledonian fold mountain chain which stretches from northern Norway through Shetland, then on via Scotland to Ireland and Wales. The last event in the Caledonian Orogeny was the formation of a fault system that includes the Great Glen Fault which runs parallel to the coastline of Cromarty and continues seaward into the Moray Firth.

### Moine rocks

In Moray, the oldest rocks are referred to as the Moine Schists, which form the high ground in the south and west of the district. This group of crystalline rocks forming the basement is made of quartzite, schist and gneiss. Originally the rocks were laid down as sandy, pebbly or gritty sediments with thin muds and shales, probably in shallow water, carried down by rivers and deposited in a shallow sea. High pressure and temperature effects during folding converted these sediments into metamorphic rocks — quartzite and mica schist.

The Moine rocks of the area lying to the south-east of the Great Glen Fault are divided into two major units, an older Central Highland Division and a younger Grampian Division, the junction between the two being a zone of intense shearing known as the Grampian Slide (Fig.1.1). The Central Highland Division is found between Inverness, Forres and Aviemore. Mostly the rocks are coarse-grained quartz-rich gneisses, interbanded with belts of quartzite and mica schist. Schists forming the Streens of Findhorn were previously considered to be Dalradian but are now regarded as Moinian. The gneisses suffered high-pressure, high-temperature metamorphism and were involved in a long complex history of folding and partial melting. The Grampian Slide which separates the older

1

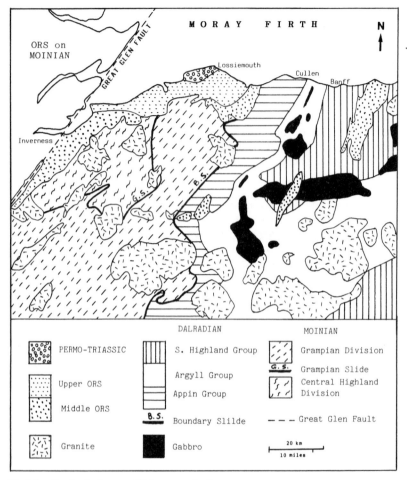

Fig.1.1   Geological map of Moray and adjacent areas.

rocks from the overlying younger Grampian Division stretches from south of Forres to Lochindorb, Grantown and Aviemore. Rocks of the Grampian Division are mostly quartz-rich metamorphosed sediments, originally sandstone with subordinate shale and limey mudstone, deposited in shallow-water marine conditions. They are finer-grained, less metamorphosed and less deformed than the rocks of the older Central Highland Division and contain fairly common sedimentary structures.

Complexities in the fold history and metamorphism of the Moine rocks make it difficult to unravel their geological history, although some radio-

2

| Groups | Subgroups | Formations | Rock types |
| --- | --- | --- | --- |
| Southern highland (600 m.y.) | | Macduff Slates<br>Boyndie Bay group<br>U. Whitehills group | slate, greywacke<br>schist, greywacke<br>schist, grit |
| Argyll (650 m.y.) | Tayvallich<br>Crinan<br>Easdale<br><br>Islay | L. Whitehills group<br>Boyne Limestone<br>Cowhythe Gneiss<br>Portsoy group<br><br>Durnhill Quartzite | calc flags, schist, grit<br>limestone, mica schist<br>biotite gneiss<br>schist, limestone, quartzite<br>quartzite, mica schist |
| Appin (> 700 m.y.) | Blair Atholl<br><br>Ballachulish<br><br>Lochaber | Sandend group<br>Garron Point group<br>Crathie Point group<br>Findlater Flags<br>West Sands group<br>Cullen Quartzite | limestone, mica schist<br>schist<br>calc-biotite flags<br>micaceous flags<br>garnet-mica schist<br>quartzite |

Grampian Division of the Moines (> 750 m.y.)

— — — — — — — — Grampian  Slide — — — — — — — —

Central Highland Division of the Moines (1000 m.y.)

*Fig.1.2   Dalradian stratigraphy of the Moray-Buchan area.*

metric dates are available.[1] The age of the deformation and metamorphism of the Central Highland Division is around 1000 million years, implying that the original sediments must be somewhat older than this. Pegmatites in the Grampian Slide zone yield an age of 780-730 m.y. (million years). The younger Grampian Division shows no evidence of any events at 1000 m.y. and would therefore appear to have been deposited in the interval 1000-750 m.y. Near Tomintoul the Grampian Division passes up into the base of the younger Dalradian rocks without a break.[2] Central Highland Division rocks were affected by the Grenville mountain-building event (or orogeny) at around 1000 m.y. ago.

**Dalradian rocks**
Dalradian rocks account for the most extensive outcrops in the district. Technically they are referred to as the Dalradian Supergroup, which is divided into three Groups and a number of Formations (Fig.1.2). The

3

rocks, which form part of the Caledonian mountain chain, were laid down in shallow seas around 700-600 million years ago and deformed in the period 530-440 m.y. ago. Igneous activity in the orogenic belt is marked by gabbro intrusions at 490 m.y. ago and granites at around 410 m.y. ago. Dalradian rocks form an enormously thick pile of sediments (at least 10 — 15 km, possibly up to 25 km thick: but this is the total thickness and does not imply that this amount of sediment was ever deposited at one particular place), the oldest found around Cullen, then progressively younger rocks eastwards from Portsoy to Banff and Fraserburgh. Most, if not all, the Dalradian rocks were deposited in Precambrian times. Sedimentation evolved as a progression from shallow water marine sands, deposited in a stable slowly subsiding shelf, to deep water muds, deposited by turbulent submarine mud flows set off by earthquake shocks in an area that was by now unstable and sinking rapidly. Faulting was taking place while sediments were being laid down, the result being a series of adjacent fault-bounded basins, each with its own separate thick pile of sediments.

**The Grampian or early Caledonian Orogeny**

The Grampian Orogeny is a term used to describe a related sequence of events that affected Dalradian and Moinian rocks during the period 550-475 million years ago. Original sediments were folded, flattened, stretched, sheared, heated and metamorphosed to produce schist, gneiss, quartzite and marble. Later they were intruded by granites and affected by over-thrusting and faulting, then uplifted to form the long, narrow, slightly sinuous Caledonian mountain chain. Relatively high-grade metamorphic rocks are found on the coast from Portsoy eastwards. It has been suggested that the intrusion of large bodies of gabbro, such as the Portsoy, Huntly, Cabrach, and Insch masses during the peak of folding brought in sufficient extra heat to produce these unusual high-grade rocks. These gabbros are around 500 million years old and were forced into the rocks during the third fold episode (out of four). Shortly afterwards, the gabbro bodies were sheared and disrupted; there is ample evidence for this around Portsoy (Fig.1.3).[3]

Grampian region is well-known for its abundant granites, many of which lie in or on the boundaries of Moray (Fig.1.4). The granites are Silurian to Devonian in age (404-415 m.y. old) and were intruded into the Caledonian mountains after the main folding and metamorphism of the Dalradian rocks. Two groups of granites are recognised, an older suite that includes Moy, Ardclach, Grantown and Ben Rinnes, and a younger group that includes Findhorn (Tomatin), Monadhliath, Cairngorm and Glen Gairn.

Modern views on the origin of the Caledonian mountain chain, developed in the last few years, are based on the recognition of the importance of large faults with a left-handed slip movement, such as the Great

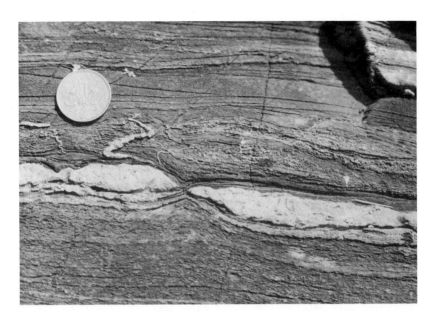

*Fig.1.3  Deformation structures in the Dalradian. (a) Pull-apart structure (bou-*
*dinage): white marble stretched in weaker impure limestone, Sandend;*
*(b) fold in impure limestone, Portsoy.*

5

*Fig.1.4    Cairngorm granite plateau; Moinian in foreground.*

Glen Fault and Highland Boundary Fault. Between these major faults lie segments of continental crust termed 'terranes' which may have formed in quite distant locations and were brought together by slipping along the faults during the early Devonian around 410 m.y. ago.[4]

Between the Great Glen Fault (GGF) and the Highland Boundary Fault lies the Grampian terrane consisting of Dalradian rocks which were compressed during the Grampian Orogeny (500 m.y. ago), then uplifted between 460 and 410 m.y. ago. Prior to 500 m.y. ago, the Northern Highlands terrane was probably remote from the Grampian terrane. The two blocks were then brought together at 460-410 m.y. ago, and any older units that originally lay between the two terranes were over-ridden. There is evidence of several unassigned units along the length of the Great Glen. The boundary between the two terranes must lie partly along the Fault (Fig.1.7).

**Old Red Sandstone**
Old Red Sandstone rocks were deposited as thick continental sediments at the end of the Caledonian Orogeny. Rapid uplift of the mountain chain was matched by equally rapid river erosion. The sediments were spread out in river valleys at the foot of the young high mountains and some merged into lake deposits of the inland Orcadian basin which encompassed Shetland, Orkney, Caithness and the Moray Firth. When these rocks were

6

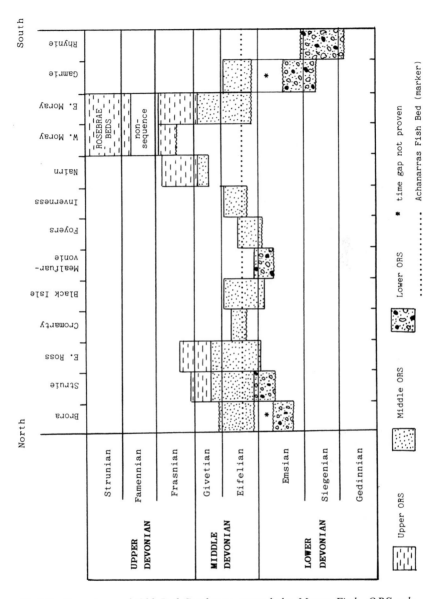

*Fig.1.5 Devonian and Old Red Sandstone around the Moray Firth. ORS subdivisions do not coincide with Devonian time divisions. Based on Rogers et al. 1989.*

7

forming 360-400 m.y. ago, Scotland lay in the centre of a large continent consisting of Britain, Scandinavia and North America. The latitude of the Orcadian basin then was around 20° south of the equator and the climate was semi-arid.

The sediments were deposited in alluvial fans, rivers and lakes, unconformably on top of an eroded landscape of Moine and Dalradian rocks surrounding the Orcadian basin. Alluvial fans built out from high uplands to the NW and S, producing thick, coarse conglomerate sequences. Crossbedded sandstones were produced by rivers flowing across the alluvial plains.

Lower Old Red Sandstone (ORS) sediments occur in a number of isolated outliers at Aberdeen, Tomintoul, Rhynie, Cabrach and Turriff (Fig.1.7). The Rhynie outcrop is famous for its fossil chert, a silicified peat deposit containing perfectly preserved primitive land plants and the earliest known insects. Deposition in this area was mainly in alluvial fans or temporary lakes. Coarse breccias and conglomerates occur at the base of the Lower ORS, containing pebbles and boulders of Dalradian rocks.

The Middle Old Red Sandstone crops out extensively between Rothes and Buckie, and as small outliers SW of Elgin. The Middle ORS of the Orcadian Basin varies from being mainly cyclic lake deposits in Caithness, to mainly river sediments south of the Moray Firth. Fossil fish beds occur at Gamrie and Fochabers (the Tynet Burn), which probably represent an interruption of river sedimentation by an unusually large extension of the Orcadian lake.[5]

A considerable thickness of Upper ORS overlies the Middle ORS around Elgin and Rothes. The sequence consists of grey and red cross-bedded sandstone with thin conglomerate, subordinate mudstone and several fish beds (Fig.1.5). These sediments are the deposits of northward flowing braided streams and meandering rivers which drained into a basin to the north of the Moray Firth. In the west of the region, the highest unit, the Rosebrae Beds, oversteps older formations and rests directly on Grampian Group Moine rocks. The top of the Rosebrae Beds could possibly be as young as lowermost Carboniferous (i.e. around 355 m.y. old).

The term 'Old Red Sandstone' is used in the sense of a description of rock types, rather than rock ages. In fact, the ORS was deposited mostly during the Devonian period, but Lower, Middle and Upper ORS do not correspond to the divisions of Lower, Middle and Upper Devonian time. An important rock unit used to date rocks is the Achanarras Fish Bed. The fish bed at Tynet Burn near Fochabers belongs to this same marker horizon and has yielded many examples of fossil fish in the past (Fig.1.6).

**Great Glen Fault**
Although Moray is rather far to the east of the Great Glen, the Fault has had such a profound effect on the shaping of the Moray Firth that a few

# a Coccosteus

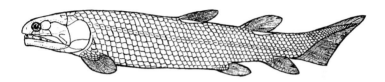

# b Osteolepis

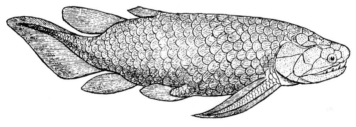

# c Holoptychius

# d Bothriolepis

*Fig.1.6    Fossil fish reconstructions; Old Red Sandstone of the Moray Firth basin.
Scale bar = 50 mm.*

words on the origin and history of the Fault will not appear out of place here. The GGF can be traced offshore from Mull through the Great Glen and north towards Shetland, where the Walls Boundary Fault is probably a splay off the GGF. The GGF has controlled the shape of the Black Isle and Tarbat Ness peninsula coastlines. Much controversy has surrounded the magnitude, age and direction of movements on the GGF.[6] The fault initiated as a late-Caledonian vertical structure, with around 80 km (50 miles) left-handed slip taking place before the start of Lower ORS deposition. Post-ORS lateral movements were right-handed in sense and 25-29 km (15-17 miles) in direction (Fig.1.7). During the Mesozoic, the GGF

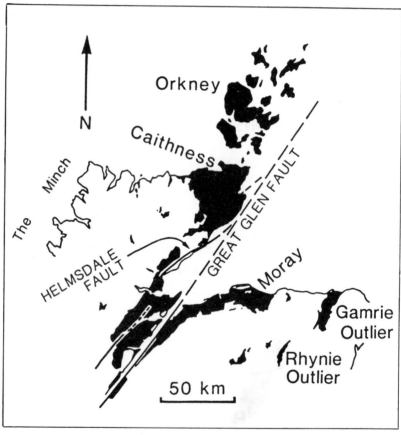

*Fig.1.7    Original configuration of ORS rocks in the Orcadian basin, i.e. movements on GGF restored. After Rogers et al. 1989.*

became reactivated as a vertical fault with downthrow to the SE. Fault movements during sedimentation allowed great thicknesses of sand and shale to be deposited in the Moray Firth basin.

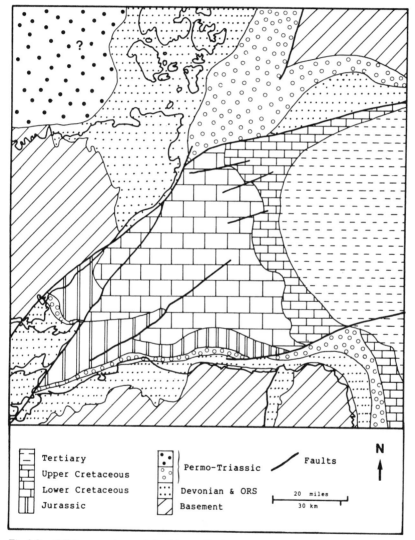

*Fig.1.8   Offshore geology of the Moray Firth.*

11

## Permian and Mesozoic Rocks

Narrow outcrops of Permian, Triassic and Jurassic rocks occur along the Moray Firth shores, from Burghead and Hopeman to Elgin and Lossiemouth. Much greater thicknesses are found in the Moray Firth Basin and northern North Sea (Fig.1.8) and are the source of the oil and gas deposits.

Permo-Triassic ('New Red Sandstone') sediments are unconformable on or faulted against Old Red Sandstone, and like the latter they consist of red beds where the colouration is due to iron oxide (haematite) in the cement around quartz sand grains. The red beds are mainly continental in origin and contain few fossils, apart from the famous reptile skeletons and footprints near Elgin and Hopeman (Fig.1.9). The oldest formation onshore is the Hopeman Sandstone, consisting of dune-bedded desert sandstones containing wind-faceted pebbles. It is unconformable on the ORS, but the two rocks look so similar that they were mistaken at first until reptile finds proved a late Permian or Triassic age. The overlying Burghead Beds are unfossiliferous Middle Triassic yellow, cross-bedded river deposits (Fig.1.10). Above lies the third unit of the New Red Sandstone, the Late Triassic Lossiemouth Sandstone, Sago Pudding Stone and Cherty Rock. The aeolian (wind-blown) Lossiemouth Sandstone contains a reptilian fauna.[7] Fossils from Moray are well displayed in the Elgin museum.

Older rocks are found offshore: the Early Permian Rotliegendes, consisting of 500 m (1800 ft) of fluvial and aeolian sandstones, mudstones and evaporites, and the overlying Late Permian Zechstein Group — 1500 m (4900 ft) of marine carbonates and evaporites. Oil has been found in these Permian rocks, principally in the Zechstein carbonates. The Permo-Triassic sandstones offshore are 300-500 m (1000-1800 ft) thick SE of the Great Glen Fault. They are unconformable on the ORS and are themselves unconformably overlain by Jurassic rocks. A very narrow outcrop of Lower Jurassic is found at Lossiemouth.[8] Much thicker Triassic deposits are found farther out into the North Sea in the Northern Viking Graben and Central North Sea (Fig.1.8), where the sequence is over 1000m (3300 ft) thick.

Upper Jurassic Kimmeridgian black bituminous organic shales and mudstones are widely distributed in the North Sea and are generally thought to be the source rock of the oil. Similar rocks occur onshore in Sutherland, between Brora and Helmsdale. Most of the oil and gas deposits have been found in fault-bounded basin structures called grabens (German *Grabe* = 'grave'). Reservoir rocks are sandstones of Jurassic to Tertiary age, or Zechstein (Upper Permian) carbonates.

Solid outcrops of Cretaceous rocks are absent from North-east Scotland, but fairly large ice-carried erratics brought inland from the North Sea floor are found near Fraserburgh. Upper Cretaceous rocks occur everywhere in

12

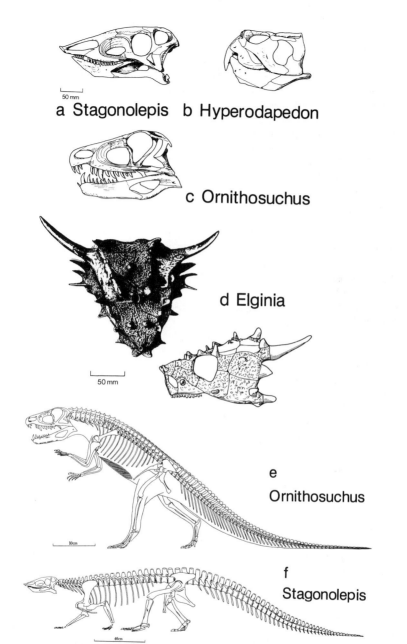

a Stagonolepis   b Hyperodapedon

c Ornithosuchus

d Elginia

50 mm

e
Ornithosuchus

f
Stagonolepis

*Fig.1.9   The Elgin reptiles. (a)–(d) reconstructed skulls, (e)–(f) reconstructed skeletons. After Benton 1977 and Benton & Walker 1985.*

13

*Fig.1.10   River channel in cross-bedded Burghead Beds, Burghead.*

the North Sea (Fig.1.8), including 1400 m (4600 ft) of chalk in the Central Graben, gradually giving way to shales in the northern Viking Graben.[9]

During the Early Permian (about 275 m.y. ago), the Moray Firth was at about 15° north of the equator at a time of widespread desert conditions throughout Europe. The area around the Moray Firth was a low-lying basin containing sand dune fields and wadi deposits of intermittent torrential rivers, surrounded by the arid uplands of the Grampian mountains. In the Late Permian, the edge of the Zechstein Sea was close to the present shoreline of the Moray Firth. Great thicknesses of halite (salt from evaporating sea water) accumulated in parts of the basin.

In the Early Triassic the lowlands around the Moray Firth were being filled with evaporites and sands from the uplands, while the North Sea was occupied by shallow lakes. In Late Triassic to Early Jurassic times a shallow tropical sea transgressed into the Moray Firth area.[10] By the end of the Triassic, relief was greatly subdued and erosion and deposition had almost ceased. Rejuvenation in the Jurassic led to the deposition of deltaic and estuarine sediments in the Moray Firth. Major flooding by the sea took place in the Upper Jurassic and again in the Upper Cretaceous, the latter representing an important world-wide rise of sea level.[11]

14

## Structure of the Moray Firth and Northern North Sea

The northern North Sea is dominated by graben structures, indicating stretching of the basin, with subsiding fault blocks rotating along curved faults, steep at the surface and shallowing at depth. Slip on these faults occurred in distinct episodes, during the Triassic, Late Jurassic and Early Cretaceous, with sedimentation continuing to fill the basins. The Inner Moray Firth basin contains over 3000 m (10,000 ft) of Jurassic and Lower Cretaceous sediments in the vicinity of the Great Glen Fault.[12]

# LANDSCAPE DEVELOPMENT

## Tertiary erosion

During Tertiary times, 65-2 million years ago, the North Sea was again a major sedimentary basin which received over 3000 m (10,000 ft) of sands, shales, mudstones and volcanic ash in the most rapidly subsiding part. In the early Tertiary, some 65-50 million years ago, the Hebridean volcanic

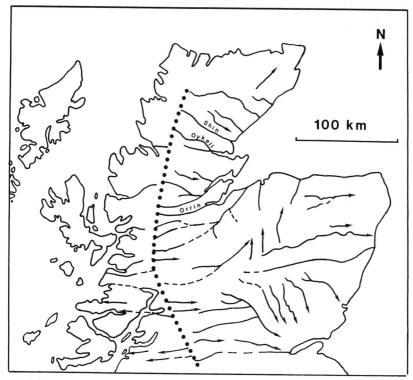

*Fig.1.11    Original drainage pattern and watershed of northern Scotland, established in Tertiary times, 50 m.y. ago.*

*Fig.1.12    Granite tors on Ben Avon.*

province was being formed, with the intrusion of central complexes in Skye, Rum, Ardnamurchan, Mull and Arran. The west coast was uplifted by over 1500 m (4900 ft) and an easterly-dipping slope was established over northern Scotland. It was at this time that the main river pattern became established and great volumes of rock were stripped off the Highlands by east-flowing streams and deposited in the North Sea basin (Fig.1.11). During the Tertiary, the climate was warm and humid, with weathering effects penetrating deep beneath the land surface. Granite tors are a remnant of this weathering (Fig.1.12).

**Quaternary Glaciation**
Climatic conditions in northern Europe deteriorated rapidly at the end of the Tertiary, plunging Scotland into a glacial epoch about two million years ago, at the start of the Pleistocene. The great ice age was characterised by numerous fluctuations from glacial to mild climatic episodes, with the last ice disappearing around 12,000 years ago. Sugden notes that North Sea glacial sediments indicate the presence of an ice sheet 700,000 years ago, but that evidence of earlier glaciers has now been destroyed.[13] The ice age consisted of the cyclic build-up and wastage of glaciers every 100,000 years, separated by warmer interglacials lasting 10,000 years. The

16

centre of the ice sheet was near Rannoch Moor and it was 1800 m (nearly 6,000 ft) high over the Cairngorms. Ice moved down Tertiary river valleys, such as the Spey, taking ice into the Moray Firth. The blue-grey drift, though, indicates onshore movement of ice from the Moray Firth area. The ice sheet melted comparatively rapidly, with most of Scotland completely free of ice only 5,000 years after the glacial maximum. Consequently, vast volumes of meltwater carried great loads of sediment which had been trapped in the ice and contributed to erosional and depositional features that helped shape the landscape. Scratch marks (or glacial striae) are caused by pebbles embedded in the ice sheet causing grinding, polishing and scratching. Examples can be found in Quarry Wood, Elgin.

The Cairngorms and the Mounth were areas of extensive upland glacial erosion, as witnessed by corries, U-shaped valleys, smooth, rounded granite tops and glacial troughs, e.g. Loch Avon (Fig.1.4). Glacial deposits in the highland areas are represented by moraines and in lowland areas by water-laid deposits such as river terraces, lake deposits and sands and gravels of eskers and kames deposited from streams flowing beneath and around the edges of the ice sheet. Tills predominate around the east, deposited by ice moving SE from the Moray Firth.

In the Moray Firth, glacial drift up to 70 m (230 ft) occurs in five elongate E-W basins, parallel to the coast between Lossiemouth and Fraserburgh. The inland drift consists of till (boulders set in a matrix of sand or clay) and meltwater sands, especially in the wide Spey valley. Along the Moray coast there is the blue-grey drift, containing rock derived from the sea bed. The drift contains glacial tills, meltwater and lake deposits. Ice-margin features, such as ridges and mounds known as eskers and kames, are quite common east of Elgin. Terrace features are found in the Spey, Findhorn and Avon (Fig.1.13). The lower Spey may have been dammed by ice, so that a lake formed which was rapidly filled by fine sediments. Once the ice began to melt and retreat, the water level in the lake dropped and the river cut a series of terraces into the lake deposits.[14]

### River system

The drainage of Moray is adequately covered by Sinclair Ross in *The Moray Book*.[15] In general we may say that the river system is controlled by the underlying geological structure and that most of the rivers occupy wide valleys relative to their streams.

This is an indication that the river system is very old, dating back to the Tertiary erosion event (Fig.1.11). Some general principles may be illustrated by reference to the Spey, Moray's largest river. The Spey rises in the southwest and its initial course is controlled by the NE-striking Ericht-Laidon fault which runs parallel to and is associated with the Great Glen Fault. Most of the tributaries of the Spey drain the extensive mountain country to the south of the river, consisting of granites intruded

17

*Fig.1.13   Terrace features in the River Avon at Tomintoul.*

into Moine rocks. Thus, large volumes of granite, gneiss and schist are transported, especially during sudden snowmelts or floods. Sediment has accumulated over a long time interval in the broad strath areas and wide rock basins; these alternate with narrow sections where rock gorges and rock bars have caused restrictions. In its wide floodplain, the middle Spey flows along a gentle gradient and the area is characterised by broad alluvial plains, marsh and open lochs. Downstream of the middle stretch, the Spey flows down a moderately steep bedrock channel in a NNE direction through the Pass of Sourden, near Rothes. On emerging on to the coastal plain, the river retains a moderate gradient. It cuts down 10 m (30 ft) into glacial outwash deposits and forms the most extensive braided river system in Britain. The Spey carries great quantities of coarse sediment into the river mouth and contributes to the growth of coastal spits in Spey Bay and to the accumulation of deltaic deposits just offshore.

**Formation of the coast**
The evolution of the coastline of Moray is controlled by the underlying geology and owes much to the interplay of glaciation, deglaciation and changes in sea level. The outer coast of the Moray Firth, extending east-wards from the Spey is dominated by rocky headlands and cliffs alternating with small bays and coves reflecting the changes in rock types of the

Dalradian succession. The schists and flags are almost vertical and strike at right angles to the coast. Variations in hardness and resistance to erosion are reflected in a series of promontories and bays or coves. Beaches are sheltered and thus quite stable.

During the ice age, the enormous weight of the ice sheet depressed the land surface. Once the ice began to melt, the weight was removed relatively rapidly and the land began to rise in a rebound fashion. Periodic uplift caused a relative fall in sea level, with the level of each pulse of uplift being reflected in a sequence of raised shorelines. In the early post-glacial period, sea level rose worldwide as a result of the melting of the Arctic ice sheets. Around 6,500 years ago, this rise was at a maximum and caused flooding around the Moray Firth. Coastal peat and woodlands were drowned and a narrow post-glacial coastal plain formed.[16] Sea level has remained essentially constant for the last 3,000 years.[17]

Evidence for these former sea levels can be seen in raised beaches backed by cliffs along much of the outer Moray Firth coast. Caves, arches and stacks now sit well back from the previous waterline. The middle coastline[17] stretches from Ardersier to the Spey and is dominated by sand and shingle forelands and raised beaches. The outline of the coast here is fairly smooth and there is considerable sediment drift westwards parallel to the shore. Rivers such as the Spey and Findhorn are and have been important in helping to shape the coastline. Both rivers contribute substantial amounts of sediment and their channels have migrated westwards. There are long sections of coast with rapidly extending spits, bars and dunes.[18] The Culbin area is well known for its dune system, built on the shingle bars and ridges of an old storm beach, and now protected by afforestation.

The Loch of Spynie was once an arm of the sea, resulting from flooding of the coastal area in post-glacial times. Ships were once able to navigate the Lossie as far as Spynie. The loch seems to have been cut off from the sea during the period 1380-1450 AD by sediment deposition by the Lossie. The loch grew in area behind its dam; a canal was dug in 1810 but final draining did not occur until 1880.

## Soils

Arguably the most important soil in the district is that of the Laich of Moray. The Moray Firth lowlands contain yellow and pale red Old Red Sandstone and some light yellow New Red Sandstone (Permo-Triassic) with a drift cover of reddish brown sandy loam. Dominant soils are podzols derived from acid parents — schist, quartzite and granite — with a coarse texture and free drainage. Fluvioglacial, raised beach and alluvial soils are very rich in sands, which are liable to wind erosion.

*Fig.1.14   Reconstructed crushing mill and old spoil heaps at the Lecht iron and manganese mine.*

## ECONOMIC GEOLOGY

Middle Dalradian rocks around the Lecht area contain strata-bound deposits of iron and manganese.[19] Iron ore was first mined in 1730 and transported to Nethybridge for smelting, using charcoal derived from the Speyside forests. The venture was unprofitable and the mine closed in 1737, but re-opened in 1841, this time for its manganese. At one time, 65 workers were employed and there were fairly extensive workings including adits, an 85-foot deep shaft and 60-foot deep pits.[20] The crushing mill has been reconstructed (Fig.1.14). The ore was crushed then hand-picked and taken to Portgordon before being shipped to Newcastle for use in bleaches. Cheaper Russian imports caused a price collapse and the mine closed in 1846. Reconnaissance work by the Geological Survey led to the conclusion that the area has around a quarter of a million tonnes of 7% manganese oxide.[21] The Middle Dalradian has the potential for base metal exploration in the future.

Some other potentially useful minerals have been reported.[22] These include fluorite in the Hopeman Sandstone and baryte which cements some of the sandstone at Covesea and is found along joint surfaces at Lossiemouth. The Stotfield Cherty Rock has galena, hematite, fluorite, baryte, calcite and quartz mineralization associated with it. Galena (lead sulphide) was once worked at Stotfield around 1880, but attempts proved unsuccessful.

Building stones in the district include the New Red Sandstone and Old Red Sandstone. The Hopeman Sandstone (NRS) was particularly prized for its colour and toughness. Locally, Moine and Dalradian schist have been used for building materials, for roadstone, paving and, formerly, roofing slates. Glacial sands and gravels are another important source of construction materials.

Limestone occurs in the Dalradian, and quarries once worked at Tomintoul, Keith and Dufftown. Impure limey 'cornstones' occur in the Lower ORS near Elgin, and these were once exploited as local sources of agricultural lime, together with Triassic cherty limestone at Inverugie. Large blocks of Jurassic rock, carried in by the ice, were exploited to destruction.

| Period | Age (m.y.) | Major geological events |
|---|---|---|
| Recent | 0.01 | Uplift; raised beaches; modern rivers; coastal landforms |
| Quaternary | 1–2 | Ice Age: erosion in uplands, sands, gravels and drift deposited in valleys |
| Tertiary | 60–65 | Deep erosion; rivers established; deposition in North Sea |
| Cretaceous | 144 | Warm tropical sea in area of North Sea; subdued relief on land |
| Jurassic | 213 | Shallow tropical sea, fine sediments laid down in North Sea grabens; oil and gas source rocks |
| Triassic | 248 | New Red Sandstone desert deposits, rivers, salt evaporites; reptiles |
| Permian | 286 | |
| Carboniferous | 360 | No sediments: area above sea level |
| Devonian | 408 | Old Red Sandstone deposition in lakes and fans on slopes of young, high Caledonian mountains; fish in lakes. Great Glen Fault. Granites |
| Silurian | 438 | Folding, metamorphism, Grampian Orogeny; |
| Ordovician | 505 | intrusion of gabbro, thrusting, uplift |
| Cambrian | 590 | (Top of Dalradian could be Cambrian in age) |
| Vendian | 670 | Dalradian sedimentation in fault-bounded basins, rapid subsidence, crustal stretching |
| Riphean | | Grampian Division Moine deposited |
| (Precambrian) | 1000 | Central Highland Division Moine deposited; then deformed in Grenville Orogeny |

*Fig.1.15* Geological History of Moray

There are fairly extensive deposits of brick clay of marine origin in the Spynie basin, also at Cullen and Craigellachie. Peat is found in higher areas of the district, but it is no longer an important fuel, although it does still have its use in the whisky distilling industry.

The North Sea oil and gas deposits are an asset of considerable importance and are likely to last beyond the end of the century. Deposits are found in association with graben-type structures in the Jurassic Kimmeridge Clay. Oil occurs in traps beneath shales of Jurassic to Tertiary age, while gas is usually restricted to the Lower Tertiary. Reservoir rocks are usually Jurassic sandstones, like the Hopeman Sandstone. Fig.1.15 summarises the geological development of Moray.

**Notes**

1. *An Excursion Guide to the Moine Geology of the Scottish Highlands* edd. I Allison, F May and R A Strachan (Edinburgh 1988); *Later Protozoic Stratigraphy of the Northern Atlantic Regions* ed. J A Winchester (Glasgow 1987).

2. A L Harris and M R W Johnson 'Moine' in *Geology of Scotland* ed. G Y Craig (3rd ed. Edinburgh 1991) 87-124; M R W Johnson 'Dalradian' in the same, 125-60; A L Harris 'The growth and structure of Scotland' in *Geology of Scotland* 1-24; C Gillen 'Excursions to Portknockie, Cullen and Sandend; Portsoy; Huntly, Elgin and Lossiemouth' in *Excursion Guide to the Geology of the Aberdeen Area* edd. N H Trewin, B C Kneller and C Gillen (Edinburgh 1987).

3. Gillen 'Excursions'.

4. D H W Hutton 'Strike-slip terranes and a model for the evolution of the British and Irish Caledonides' *Geol.Mag.* 124(5) (1987) pp.405-25.

5. Gillen 'Excursions'.

6. J S Smith 'The last glacial epoch around the Moray Firth' in *The Moray Firth Area Geological Studies* ed. G Gill (Inverness Field Club 1977).

7. J D Peacock, N G Berridge, A L Harris and F May, *The Geology of the Elgin District*, Memoirs of the Geological Survey of Scotland, Explanation of One-inch Geological Sheet 95 (HMSO, Edinburgh 1968); J P B Lovell 'Permian and Triassic' in *Geology of Scotland* 421-38; Gillen 'Excursions'.

8. *Geology of the Elgin District*.

9. *Introduction to the Petroleum Geology of the North Sea* ed. K W Glennie (3rd ed. Oxford 1990).

10. Lovell 'Permian and Triassic'.

11. A Hallam 'Jurassic, Cretaceous and Tertiary sediments' in *Geology of Scotland* 439-54.

12. J A Chesher and D Lawson 'The Geology of the Moray Firth' *Rep.Inst.Geol. Sci.* no. 83/5 (1983).

13. D Sugden 'The Landscape' in *The Moray Book* ed. D Omand (Edinburgh 1976) 48-68.

14. Sinclair Ross 'The Physical Background' in *The Moray Book* 3-27; *Geology of the Elgin District*.

15. Ross 'Physical Background'.

16. Smith 'Last glacial epoch'.

17. J S Smith 'The coastal topography of the Moray Firth' *Proc.Royal Soc.Edin.* 91B pp.1-12 (1986).
18. Ibid.; Ross 'Physical Background'.
19. C G Smith, M J Gallagher, J S Coats and M E Parker 'Detection and general characteristics of strata-bound mineralization in the Dalradian of Scotland' *Trans.Inst.Min.Metall.* B 93 pp.B125-33 (1984).
20. K Nicholson 'The geology and history of the Lecht iron-manganese mine, Tomintoul, Banffshire' *Museums Information Sheet* no.8 (1986), Elgin, Moray District Council.
21. Smith *et al* 'Strata-bound mineralization'.
22. I O Morrison 'Geology of Moray' *Museums Information Sheet* no.3 (1983), Elgin, Moray District Coucil; Ross 'Physical Background'; *Geology of the Elgin District.*

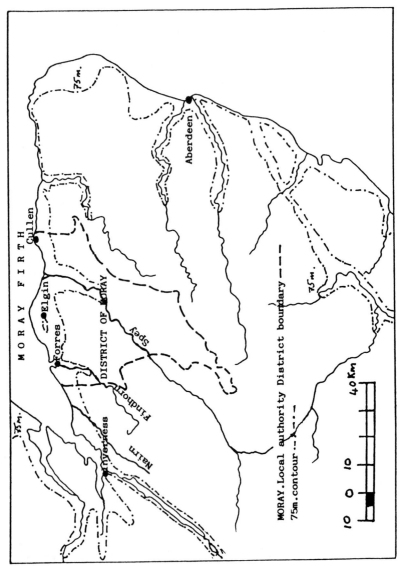

Fig.2.1  Moray.

# MAN IN MORAY
## 5,000 years of history
### Ian Keillar

**Synopsis**
The extent of Moray is defined and the physical conditions briefly described. Traces of Mesolithic man have been found in the Culbin, and later Neolithic peoples found Moray an attractive place to settle. As metal working became established, trades routes followed and Moray flourished. As the climate deteriorated, so, apparently, did the political situation and defensive sites became necessary. The Romans came and went and the Picts rose and fell. The Vikings did not linger on these shores and MacBeth never met any witches near Forres. The Kings of Scots divided and ruled until they themselves set a pattern, which still continues, that if you want to get on you must go south to London. In distant Moray, brave men like Montrose and foolish men like Prince Charles Edward, fought for their rightful king. The Stuarts, however, ill rewarded their followers. Road makers and bridge builders half tamed the rivers, and the railways completed the process. With wars came boom years for the farmers, but even feather beds wear out and Moray is once more in apparent decline. However, all declines are relative and the old adage still has relevance: 'Speak weel o the Hielans but live in the Laich.'

**Physical**
The name Moray is now applied to a local authority administrative District extending from west of Forres and the Findhorn to Cullen and stretching down in an irregular triangle into the highlands of the Cairngorms (Fig.2.1). In Medieval times, Moray reached as far as Lochalsh on the west coast and there has always been some difficulty in defining the boundaries of the province. Professor Barrow suggests that since river valleys tend to possess an historic unity, then a narrower but more acceptable definition of Moray would be the lands of Strathnairn, Strathdearn and Strathspey.[1] This is the Moray of this article.

Moray consists of two main different topographical regions. The major part is highland, once heavily forested but now mainly moorland. Due to extensive soil degradation it is now capable of supporting only a few people, but in the gentler climate of 3,000 years ago, pastoralists lived the year round up to the 600m contour and until recent times transhumance to the summer sheiling was a feature of highland livestock management. The Laigh of Moray, that is land below 75m above datum, is, by comparison with the inland highlands, a land flowing with milk and honey (Fig.2.2). Long term average rainfall is less than 800mm, with sheltered parts reaching as low as 650mm.[2] However, these averages hide wide annual variations. The summer of 1985 was exceptionally wet; some months having twice the usual amount of rain.

The influence of the mass of water in the Moray Firth is quite considerable. By August the water temperature can reach +13°C and although this falls to around +4°C in February the moderating effect is to delay the onset of winter and mitigate its harshness when it eventually arrives.[3] There are about 1,300 hours of annual sunshine and, as Ross points out, 'seasonally the Moray coast has more sunshine in the winter months of November to March, than does London, but is reversed in the summer period in spite of there being some two hours more daylight in the north at midsummer.'[4] With a low rainfall and reasonable amounts of sunshine, lowland Moray, with its predominantly light sandy soils, is ideally suited for grain growing, despite the fact that it lies further north than Moscow.

From the Spey to the Nairn there is a coastal band of sedimentary rocks of various ages, while the higher inland is underlain with metamorphic schists. The drainage is substantially north-east in direction. The main river is the Spey which is turbulent and fast flowing, rising far south in the Monadliath mountains and nourished on its way to the sea by streams like the Feshie and the Avon (pronounced A'an) which are fed by the long

*Fig.2.2   Elgin with the rich Laigh of Moray stretching down to the sea.*

26

lasting snows of the Cairngorms. The Findhorn, which enters the sea near Forres, and the Nairn also rise in the Monadliaths and, like the Spey, are liable to produce flash floods.

The longshore drift from east to west is continually pushing the mouths of the Spey and Findhorn westward. Long sandy or gravel spits build up and these are eventually punched through by the river or have to be cut by bulldozers. 5,000 years ago sea level was some five metres higher than at present, and falling. About 2,000 years ago, sea level was possibly about the same as present but there was a salt water channel running from about Burghead to Lossiemouth. According to Peacock, 'the harbour area of Burghead was once an island and is now connected by a 10m storm beach to the mainland at Clarkly Hill.'[5] The Findhorn entered the sea to the west of its present course while the Spey probably emptied into an estuary, partially enclosed by a long spit of gravel, reaching out from the eastern bank of the river.

Earlier, during successive ice ages, Moray was encased in ice. With the final melting the lowlands were left covered with fluvio-glacial outwash sands and gravels. The light soils produced on the low ridges and drumlins proved very attractive to early farmers and remain attractive to their descendants to this day. 'The contrast between the intensively farmed coastal plain and the forest and moorland of the greater part of the uplands bears witness to the difference in productivity of the soils, resulting from the combined effect of those inter-related factors; parent material, relief and climate.'[6]

**Early Peoples**

Lacaille found no trace of Palaeolithic man in Scotland,[7] although the insufficiently investigated caves at Allt nan Uamh near Inchnadamph in Sutherland, may have revealed some evidence. Now, alas, the boots of countless pot-holers have destroyed what little remained of possible ice-age man.

About 5,000 years BC, hunter gatherers, conveniently labelled Mesolithic, hunted and gathered food in the area west of Forres known as the Culbin. The living sites of the early Culbin inhabitants have not been extensively studied, but by analogy with similar sites elsewhere in Britain and Europe there is evidence that the Mesolithic peoples hunted red deer, wild boar, and aurochs, while fish and plant material were also a significant part of their diet.[8] These hunter-gatherers were early destroyers of the environment, for evidence from Yorkshire shows that the North York moors were once forested and that the process of deforestation was initiated by hunting communities long before agriculture was introduced into Britain.[9]

Agriculture was introduced by the Neolithic or new stone age people. The ancestry of their animals and grain lay in the Middle East, probably in that once fertile land lying between the Tigris and Euphrates, but by what route and wanderings and how many millenia passed before small groups jumped ashore in Britain, archaeology remains silent. Case postulates that the boats used could carry as many as eight or nine people, along with three to four cattle or up to twenty five sheep and goats.[10] There is no reason to suppose that the Neolithic invaders exterminated the Mesolithic inhabitants and Kinnes argues that there was an 'incorporation of existing, formally Mesolithic communities.'[11] Whatever happened, the available carbon 14 dates show that Neolithic culture was well established throughout Scotland by the last quarter of the fourth millenium BC.

The Neolithic farmers used polished stone axes and well fired round based pottery. Efforts have been made to associate this pottery with standard models from Grimston-Lyles Hill (Yorkshire) and Ballymarlagh (Ireland) but Kinnes rightly points out 'A determination to find external origins for each new idea has severely restricted the possibilities for processual understanding ... For example, the quantity and contextual integrity of early pottery in north-east Scotland exceeds those in Yorkshire, yet constant resort is made to this perceived fount for explanation.'[12] The site at Boghead (Fochabers) has produced some fine pottery associated with a radiocarbon date of 3,000 BC while the now lost site of Roseisle, near Burghead, must have been of a similar age. Scattered early Neolithic pottery, unassociated with any site has also been discovered at Culbin and Urquhart near Elgin.

Stone circles and cairns are associated with the later Neolithic, and the great chambered tombs at Clava in the valley of the Nairn have analogues, though much more dilapidated, on the banks of the Avon just before it joins the Spey at Ballindalloch. However, as the Neolithic farmers herded their cattle and sowed their wheat and barley and raised great monuments to their dead, a development elsewhere was to revolutionise their society. That development was the ability to smelt and alloy metals.

**Early Metal in Moray**
Modern society is so used to metal tools that it is difficult to imagine life without iron and steel, copper and zinc. Yet within living memory, tribes in New Guinea existed without any knowledge of metal, and until 150 years ago the Maoris of New Zealand led a complex social life and produced intricate wood work and other consumer goods with only stone, wood, bone, feather and vegetable fibre as the source of their materials and tools.

Metal is believed to have been first smelted in the Middle East, and Cyprus is traditionally and etymologically associated with copper. In its elemental state, copper is too soft to be useful, so from an early age it has been alloyed with other metals in order to increase its hardness and durability. The first alloy appears to have been with lead, followed by tin and then, much later, with zinc. Today, copper is commonly alloyed with nickel to produce the common 'silver' coins rattling valuelessly in our pockets. Moray has no copper deposits, but *galena* (lead ore) is found near Lossiemouth and if the theory of cup and ring markings being associated with metallic ores is accepted,[13] then the finely marked rocks at Inverugie fit neatly into the pattern.

Early metal use is associated with the beaker people; an allegedly round headed (ba heided) race, still believed to be identifiable today in north-east Scotland. They are called the beaker people because they buried their crouched dead in a kist made of stone slabs and placed alongside the deceased a beaker presumably containing a drink which hopefully reached parts that other drinks could not. Many of the beakers found around the shores of the Moray Firth are of the type known as the British-North Rhine group (N/NR)[14] and it is thus reasonable to assume that the people who introduced the beakers to Moray crossed the North Sea by boat.

Circular ditched enclosures or henges are associated with the beaker people and there is a fine henge in Quarry Wood, some three kilometres north-west of Elgin. Shepherd casts doubts on the acceptability of this henge,[15] but a flat axe mould was discovered there in 1956. This would appear to link the site to the known axe cult of Scandinavia and, in conjunction with the non-defensive nature of the site (it is not on the highest ground and remote from water) would indicate that its use must have been mainly ceremonial.

The number of bronze flat axes found in Moray indicates that in the days of early metal working Moray must have enjoyed a period of prosperity. A thousand years later, perhaps as a result of climatic deterioration, the wealth of Moray as judged by the material remains had decreased. With the deterioration of the climate came a marked deterioration in the political situation as iron supplanted bronze as the preferred metal for tool making.

Iron, which requires a much higher temperature than copper to smelt, was first worked in Asia Minor in the second millenium BC and the technology reached Britain about 700 BC. The chronology is imperfectly understood and there is no certainty that the metal was originally introduced by new people. However, about the time that iron was being worked in Britain, it is believed that Celtic peoples came into Moray, and the hill forts and defended homesteads are associated with this period. It is not clear whether the forts were designed to shelter the existing inhabitants, or provide a refuge for the new. Perhaps they were ostentatious follies, built by chiefs to impress the tribe as well as the neighbours. No doubt in the hurly burly of these unsettled times the forts served many purposes. Some are unfinished. It was once fashionable to blame the arrival of the Romans for this lack of application, but perhaps it could be put down to the indolence of the builders.

Some of the forts are vitrified and for over a hundred years argument has raged as to whether the burning was deliberately initiated by the builders as a means of strengthening the structure, or by an enemy intent upon slighting the fortification.[16] Without in any way disparaging the excellent experimental work carried out by latter distinguished investigators, the words of James Macdonald, written a hundred years ago are worthy of quotation: 'From these observations I infer that the vitrification is not of design, and formed no part of the original purpose in construction. If it was the intention to bind the material together, even on the surface, except to a very limited extent it thoroughly failed. The action of the fire has split up the unfused stone, and these have in course of time fallen down, undermining the fused masses, which have slipped from their original position, and now appear here and there on the sides of the ramparts ... It seems to me hard to believe that they began to vitrify, and were unable or unwilling to continue the work, unless we can imagine that all the builders of vitrified forts throughout Scotland tried the same experiment and failed.'[17] Macdonald was writing about Tap o Noth, but, as his own words make clear, his observations are applicable to all vitrified forts.

## Picts and Romans

Recent aerial archaeological surveys have revealed in Moray small square ditched enclosures without corners, which, although not yet excavated, are thought to be burial sites dated to around 100 AD. There are enclosures near Pitairlie and in a field to the west of Forres and also to the southwest of Nairn. Pitairlie, despite its attractively Pictish sounding name, is not of ancient origin, but a modern introduced name, dating back about a hundred years. The earliest literary reference to the Picts is in 297 AD, contemporary with Roman activity in Britain.[18] Who the Picts were and what language they spoke have excessively exercised the minds of scholars over many years.[19] A simple view, not at variance with the facts, is that the Picts were the Iron Age people who were living in Moray and most of Scotland at the time and that they spoke a P-Celtic language akin to Welsh. However, there are suggestions that the Picts spoke two languages.[20]

The Picts were accomplished workers in metal and carvers in stone. The boar's head in bronze, part of a war trumpet found at Deskford, testifies to their talents with metal, while the many carved stones bear witness to their masonic skills. Pictish stones are divided into three classes. Class I stones, traditionally considered the oldest, consist of boulders carved with incised abstract symbols or animals. The famous bulls of Burghead are fine examples of this genre. Class I stones probably pre-date the introduction of Christianity to Moray while Class II and Class III stones, with their crosses carved in relief on dressed blocks, testify to the widespread adoption of Christianity.

Two hundred years before the name Pict appeared in Roman literature, the people of Moray must have seen the Roman fleet sail along the coast in the Autumn of 84 AD while others may have died in the battle of Mons Graupius or, sullenly, post battle, surrendered their grain and livestock to the requisitioning quartermasters of the Roman army. Thirty years ago, aerial photography revealed two Roman marching camps near Keith[21] while, in the last few years, what appear to be two Roman fort sites have been discovered west of the Spey. There is the documented site at Thomshill[22] (Fig.2.3) near Birnie and the remains of a site at Easter Galcantray near Croy. Jones[23] and Keillar[24] argue that the latter is indubitably Roman. Four seasons of excavation have revealed a site which has the morphology of a Roman auxiliary fort, but has yielded disappointingly few artifacts. The C14 date of 100 AD is however very encouraging.

While the Picts may have lost the occasional battle with the Romans they did win the war and Moray was neither colonised nor made a client state of Rome. Pictish civilisation succumbed to attack, not always military, from the Scots, a Northern Irish tribe of shinty hooligans, swarming across to Dalriada (Argyll) and from there all over Pictland. The Scots may well have allied themselves with the Norse so that Moray was squeezed between the Norse advancing from the north and the Scots sweeping up

*Fig.2.3   Possible Roman fort site at Thomshill near Elgin, adjacent to two distilleries.*

from the south. Sueno's Stone at Forres may represent a Scottish victory over the Picts with a pictorial representation of what happened to the vanquished and a none too subtle warning of what will happen to any other Pict who dares revolt against his new master. By about 844 AD, Kenneth MacAlpine was ruler of both Picts and Scots and the Pictish language or languages went into a swift decline. The language of the court tends to become that of the people and all that is left of the Picts are their incomparable carved stones, a little fine metalwork and a few place names containing elements such as Pit, Aber and Carden.

**Christianity**
Popular mythology has it that Saint Columba single-handedly converted Scotland to Christ. Columba was of a prominent Irish (Scottish) family and 'we are the greatest' has always been the cry of the victors. Columba, that hot headed temporal and spiritual prince, crossed the North Channel and landed in Iona, circa 563 AD. He died in 597 AD having, according to his biographer,[25] converted all the Picts and Scots and, in his spare moments, written 300 books.

Yet 150 years before Columba was born, St. Ninian of Whithorn carried the Cross north into Pictland, and while Simpson may be a bit too opti-

*Fig.2.4   Burghead with remains of Dark Age fort behind modern harbour.*

32

mistic in his attribution of so many sites to Ninian,[26] yet Ninian and other missionaries must have been working in Alba (Scotland) before civilisation, such as it was, collapsed all over Britain in the wake of the Roman withdrawal. When it was reasonably safe for missionaries to return, one who evangelised in Moray was St Brendan of Clonfert. Born in Kerry about 484 AD he travelled to the Faroe islands and allegedly voyaged safely to and from what is now known as North America.[27] He landed in Iona some twenty years before Columba. Brendan is associated with Aberbrandely,[28] while the foundation of Birnie may also be attributed to the same far travelled saint.[29] St Moluag of Bangor, who based himself on Lismore, founded the church at Mortlach and died at Rosemarkie in 592 AD. A hundred years later, St Maelrubha, also from Bangor, established his Scottish base at Applecross (*Aporcrosan*) and is associated with Christian Celtic foundations at Keith, Fordyce, Forres and Rafford. St. Maelrubha died in 722 AD. Other early missionaries associated with Moray are Morgan and, possibly, Bridget. However, there are many saints with the name of Bridget, so it may be that Lhanbryde is named after a latter Medieval saint.

Celtic Christianity survived until the Scots had the misfortune to lose their queen, Ingibjorg, wife of Malcolm III, nicknamed Canmore or Bighead. For his second wife he chose the English refugee, Margaret; a strong willed dynastically determined woman, whose baneful dislike of most things Scottish released a vial of poison of such virulence that its effects continue to this day. The democratic and somewhat disorganised Celtic religion was suppressed by the centralised and dogmatic Roman Catholic church. However, Margaret cannot be blamed for introducing the rule of Rome. As early as 710 AD, Nechtan, king of the Picts, accepted Roman Catholicism and he expelled the Celtic clergy from his lands, but it was only during the reigns of Margaret's numerous progeny that the Roman Church became firmly established.

By 1080 AD there were Roman bishops in Scotland[30] while the first recorded Bishop of Moray sat at Birnie from 1107 to 1115. Simon de Toeny, the fourth bishop (1171-89), lies buried at Birnie. From Birnie the bishops appear to have moved their chair to Kinneddar from where they moved to Spynie in the early 13th century. About 1220 AD Bishop Brice Douglas petitioned the Pope to translate the Cathedral of Moray from Spynie to Elgin and in July 1224 the impressive service of dedication was performed by Bishop Gilbert of Caithness and the Church of the Holy Trinity '*juxta Elgyn*' was transformed into the Cathedral church of the diocese of Moray.

The sons and descendants of Margaret granted large areas of land to the church. David I, that 'sair sanct for the croon', founded the Benedictine Priory of Urquhart in 1136 AD and the Cistercian Abbey of Kinloss in 1150. Alexander II sent to France for monks from Val des Choux in

Burgundy and granted them land for a priory at Pluscarden. He also brought Franciscans or Grey Friars to Elgin and introduced Dominicans or Black Friars to the haughland just to the north of the royal castle.

## Divide and Rule

Controlling Moray with its easy access to and from the Highlands and its remoteness from central Scotland was difficult for the crown. Emulating the new feudal system, introduced by William the Bastard, alias Conquerer, south of the border, the King of Scots gave large tracts of land to foreign barons. Whatever their nominal feudal duties the barons' main function was to keep the natives under control. However, if barons were allowed to amalgamate their holdings either through marriage or conquest, they could become too powerful and could present a threat to the crown. To minimise this threat the canny Scots kings gave land to the Church, so that the ecclesiastical holdings formed buffers between the barons. In the early Middle Ages, no baron would dream of annexing Church lands. It was to be a different story four hundred years later.

Just in case the local temporal and spiritual magnates plotted together, the king established castles in the royal burghs. The constables of these castles reported directly to the crown so that the king had an independent source of information and a garrison of soldiers who were not answerable to a local baron for their pay and rations. Royal castles were established at Cullen, Elgin, Forres, Auldearn, Nairn and Inverness, while there were early baronial fortifications at Fochabers, Innes, Duffus and Rait, with many more being built as the centuries progressed.

Burghs grew up where the needs of marketing coincided with convenient means of communication.[31] Elgin, Forres and Nairn had access to the sea and a hinterland which could supply salmon, grain and wool. Since buying and selling was the prime reason for the establishment of the burgh then the important place was the market, usually positioned in the middle of the town. This happenstance was not due to any clever town planning but because population naturally aggregated round the market. Early burghs received royal charters detailing their rights and responsibilities. Rights usually included the privilege of raising revenue by means of customs duties or tolls and so the gates or ports where merchandise came in and left were important features in the history of any burgh. There was sometimes a palisade or fail (turf) dyke surrounding the burgh.[32] This was not so much for defence as a delimiting boundary to mark out the territory within which the rights and privileges of the burghers were exercised. It was also useful for keeping out strangers in time of pestilence.

Little is known of the life of the burgher or peasant during the Middle Ages, although as Duncan felicitously points out 'the church was ever solicitous lest the peasant imperil his soul through failure to pay teind, and that to the right kirk.'[33] Peasants were not allowed to grind their own grain but were thirled to a particular mill. In Moray many of the mills were owned by the church and were valuable assets, prominent in many charters.[34] Arable land was probably assessed by the davach, a Celtic measure of indeterminate size and related in some way to the amount of grain that could be held in a large tub or vat.[35]

When Alexander III became King of Scots at the age of eight in 1249, both Scotland and Moray were at peace. The dynastic struggles of earlier years when the Men of Moray fought to restore the descendants of Malcolm III by his first wife, Ingibjorg, had ended in 1230 when an infant MacWilliam had her brains dashed out against the market cross of Forfar.[36] The victory of the Scots over the Norse at the battle of Largs in 1263 further consolidated the nation, and unpublished archaeological evidence shows that at this time Elgin was trading with the continent and that there was stained glass in the windows of the cathedral.[37]

**Times of Trouble**

This increasing prosperity died with Alexander III in 1286. His son had predeceased him and his daughter, married to Eric II of Norway was also dead, leaving Eric's daughter, Margaret, as heir to the throne of Scotland. Into this scene slithered the ambitious expansionist Edward I of England. Like so many English he disguised imperialism as bringing 'law and order' to the somewhat unruly inhabitants of the lands on his borders. Wales was conquered and then held down by garrisons quartered in the latest high technology castles. Dispossessed Welshmen, handy with the long-bow, were recruited into the English army and sent to fight in France. Having dealt with Wales, Edward now turned his attention to Scotland.

The death of Margaret in 1290 gave Edward his opportunity. The naive Scots invited their powerful neighbour to adjudicate amongst the claimants to the vacant Scottish throne. There was no shortage of applicants. Thirteen applied and John Balliol had the strongest claim to the crown and, quite properly, Edward awarded him the prize, but, quite illegally, Balliol had to swear fealty to Edward as the feudal superior of Scotland.[38] This and other happenings were not popular in Scotland and by 1296 matters were drifting from bad to worse. Edward moved north, sacked Berwick with a cruelty which was extreme even by medieval standards. He caught up with Balliol near Montrose and ceremoniously stripped him of all his regalia and, metaphorically, put the crown on his own head. On 26th July 1296, Edward I entered Elgin by the east port and was welcomed by the town band. He took up residence in the castle on Lady Hill while his army of 35,000 lay encamped on the plain to the south, devouring the stock and crops of the terrified locals.[39]

Next day the burgesses of Elgin swore an oath of fealty to Edward referring to him as 'our Lord, the King of England'.[40] Fortunately, the clergy were made of sterner stuff and some years later Bishop David of

Moray preached 'that it was no less meritorious to rise in arms to support the Bruce, than to engage in a crusade against the Saracens.'[41] Edward left Elgin on Sunday 29th to return south via Rothes, Balvenie and the Mounth. He stopped at Scone long enough to ransack the abbey archives and steal what he and his entourage believed was the Stone of Destiny. Behind him in Elgin he left Reginald de Chen of Duffus in charge of the English garrison at Elgin castle.

During the winter of 1296/97 the Scots smouldered and by the summer of 1297 the revolt burst into flames. In the south, William Wallace led the patriots, while in Moray, Andrew Murray regained the castles of Elgin and Forres which he then demolished. His men also destroyed de Chen's castle and church at Duffus. By late summer the English had been cleared out of the north and in September Wallace and Murray joined forces to oppose an English army at Stirling. The outcome of the battle was a great tactical victory for the Scots but a sore strategical setback. Andrew Murray was fatally wounded and although he lingered for some time, his death was a severe blow to Scotland and to Moray. By 1303, Edward, now old and ailing, felt that he had to return to Scotland to grind its people into the dust once more. Making peace with France he transferred his army north and again entered Elgin at the head of a great force. He moved on from Elgin to Kinloss, moving south later in the year to spend the winter at Dunfermline.

With the betrayal of Wallace in 1305 and his disgraceful and illegal trial, followed by his savage mutilation and death, Edward must have thought that he had imposed a final solution on the vexed Scottish question. But even before Wallace's final agony at Smithfield, Robert Bruce, grandson of one of the 1292 contenders to the throne, had started plotting against the occupying English. In 1306 Bruce was crowned at Scone by Isabel Countess of Buchan. Bruce and the Countess were both to pay dearly for what Edward construed as treason. In that same year, Nigel Bruce, brother of Robert, was hanged along with many others, after trials in which they were not allowed to speak in their defence. The Countess of Buchan was kept in a cage in Berwick castle and no Scotsman or Scotswoman was allowed to speak to her. It was to be four years before her confinement was made less rigorous. Fortunately, Bruce evaded capture and in 1307 he was in Moray, attacking the English and their collaborators where they were weakest. He destroyed the castles of Inverness and Nairn and on Christmas day at Slioch near Huntly he committed his tiny force of seven hundred to an indecisive battle with John Comyn, Earl of Buchan. Next year Bruce attacked the castles of Balvenie, Tarradale, Skelbo and Elgin. Then with his rear more or less secure in Moray he moved south to his ultimate victory over the Engish at Bannockburn on 24th June 1314.

Despite Bruce's great victory, the English would not leave the Scots in peace. Bickering and warfare continued. Cultural ties with England were loosened and links with France and the Continent strengthened. In 1313 Bishop David of Moray proposed that four poor scholars from his diocese be sent to the university of Paris and in 1325 he provided an endowment to make the scheme possible. By 1336 there were so many Scots at the university of Orleans that they constituted a separate 'nation' or student association.[42]

Edward I (hammerer of the Scots) died in 1307 and his son, also named Edward, met an untimely and very unpleasant end at the hands of his nearest, but not exactly dearest. It was left to Edward I's grandson, another Edward, to continue hammering the Scots during the intervals of mutual hammering with France in what was to drag on into the Hundred Year's War. Edward III tried to settle the Scottish problem before turning his attention to France, and in 1336 he dashed into Moray to lift a siege of his supporters in the castle of Lochindorb. He then descended into the Laich of Moray and burnt Forres, Kinloss, Elgin and Aberdeen before returning south to prepare for France, leaving garrisons behind him. The uncaptured leader of the resistance fighters in Moray, Sir Andrew Murray, posthumous son of Wallace's friend, gradually cleared the English from their strongholds in the north, as his father had done before him.

With all this warfare, civil and external, sweeping the land it is not surprising that the most popular residence for a major laird was a tower house. This type of building was still being built in the first half of the 17th century, although gunpowder had made it useless against a well-armed foe. As the years went past the plan of the tower became more elaborate. A fine example of a late simple tower is at Coxton, while Burgie was once a fine example of a Z-plan but only one of its towers now stands. Blairfindy and Easter Elchies, both conveniently near distilleries, are good examples of L-plan towers. The peasants in their turf hovels were expendable and town burghers were usually quick enough to swear allegiance to the most recently arrived military force and pay any reasonable ransom in order to avoid pillage and rape. In this they were not always successful, for many armies relied on loot in lieu of pay.

**The Reformation and After**
As the years of what we call the Middle Ages passed the attitude of the barons to the Church changed from that of benefaction to exploitation. As early as 1390, the Earl of Buchan, alias the Wolf of Badenoch, fourth son of King Robert II, somewhat incensed by the Pope and Bishop of Moray disapproving of his extra-marital liaison with a lady by the name of Mariette, swooped down and burnt Forres.[43] The Church was not sufficiently intimidated, so a month later, his henchmen returned and burnt Elgin including the church of St. Giles, eighteen manses of the canons and the cathedral church of Moray "with all the books, charters and other valuable things of the country therein kept."[44]

As the barons gradually appreciated that the reformation of the Catholic Church could well result in good pickings for themselves, so their enthusiasm for the doctrines of Luther increased. In this they were but following the example set by James V who in 1531 obtained a Papal bull allowing him to tax church lands. These taxes soon reached such a level that the only way they could be paid was for the land to be let or feued to laymen. Once the practice was established of alienating church lands the prelates were not slow to appreciate how they could improve their own pension prospects by the judicious disposal of church lands. Patrick Hepburn, the last Roman Catholic Bishop of Moray alienated to his numerous relatives much of the church lands in his care.[45] When the storm of the Reformation burst upon Moray, the commercially astute Bishop shut himself inside his palace at Spynie, charged with powder and shot the two brass cannon covering the main gate, and continued with his dissolute life.

With the Reformation, while the mob was diverted into destruction, the lairds attended to the more profitable business of securing the land once owned by the Church. Many a Moray estate started off as stolen property; but time sanctifies theft. For almost two hundred years after 1560, many Moray lairds sitting on reset goods, were apprehensive that prelates might be introduced;[46] prelates who would need the produce from many acres to keep them in the style to which they felt entitled. When Charles I wished to introduce prelacy, the Moray lairds, almost to a man, became Covenanters. Never were men so simultaneously devoted to the 'True Faith' and to their own interests. God and Mammon reconciled.

The barons had also no wish to see their power in Parliament diluted by the admission of religious magnates and in 1637 they protested about the 'price and avarice of the prelates seeking to overrule the haill kingdom.'[47] When a National Covenant, protesting at what was happening, was tabled on 28th February 1638 at Greyfriars in Edinburgh, one of the first to sign was James Graham, Earl of Montrose. War between Charles and his revolting Scottish subjects broke out in 1639. James Graham was a leader of the Covenant but within a year he was disillusioned. Tolerant and pragmatic and by no means a fanatic he was particularly disturbed by the actions of the Earl of Argyll with his policy of private aggrandisement. By 1644 Montrose was on the side of the King and with two companions made his way into the Highlands to rendezvous with Alasdair MacDonald whose Irish fighters were to ensure victory for Montrose in many battles. Montrose knew, as had generals before him, that he had to secure Moray before he could gain Scotland. On September 1st 1644 he gained his first victory at Tippermuir near Perth, but instead of heading south to Edinburgh he turned north to Aberdeen. Incensed by the murder of a drummer boy under a flag of truce, Montrose allowed his men to sack the city. He was victorious at a skirmish at Fyvie and then in the depths of winter he led his men over the mountains to attack Argyll at Inverlochy on 2nd February 1645. Argyll escaped ignominiously in his galley while better Campbells died fighting. Montrose diverted to Dundee and narrowly escaped from disaster. In May he returned north to defeat another Army of the Covenant at Auldearn. On 2nd July he won a victory at Alford and with Moray secured he then turned south to his final and greatest victory at Kilsyth on 15th August. All Scotland was now nominally under the control of Montrose acting on behalf of Charles I.

The subsequent defeat of Montrose, the massacre of his troops' women and children 'the better the day the better the deed', Montrose's refusal to take reprisals on the prisoners he held, his adventures in Gothenburg and his subsequent return to Scotland and betrayal at the hands of MacLeod of Assynt is not part of the story of Moray. But Moray was to see this great leader once more when, on his way to execution, mounted on a sheltie with his feet tied round the belly of the beast, he was led through the towns while the populace were encouraged to pelt him with rubbish. At Keith, the fanatical Mr. William Kinninmonth, preached a special sermon on the iniquities of the wretched prisoner in his congregation. 'Rail on', said the condemned man as the minister continued with his spiteful oration.[48]

Within a month of Montrose's judicial murder in Edinburgh, watched over in secret by a gloating Argyll, King Charles II landed at Spey Mouth on 23rd June 1650. He disembarked from a Dutch frigate commanded by Cornelis Maartenzoon Tromp, son of the famous admiral who carried a broom at his masthead as a sign of his ability to sweep the English from the sea.[49] There is a story that to avoid Charles getting his feet wet the local ferryman presented his back and shouted 'Loup on yer Majesty: I've cairried mony a heavier wecht.'

Charles disappeared south to defeat and further exile while Scotland suffered invasion by Cromwell, whose troops were quartered in the cathedral at Elgin and whose vandalistic bullet holes can still be seen in the fabric. During this time the stones of Kinloss Abbey were taken to Inverness to be used in the making of Cromwell's citadel. The reformed kirk was mightily concerned with sexual morality and later with witchcraft.[50] In Auldearn in 1662 some forty persons from the village or therabouts were accused of being witches and many were strangled and burnt. A year later, Brodie of Brodie noted with satisfaction that 'Isobel Elder and Isabel Simson were burnt at Forres: died obstinat.'[51]

During the final years of the 17th century, famine stalked the land. In upland Banff people died in their hundreds and others struggled to the coast to eat buckies and seaweed. In Moray there was barely enough food for the locals and nothing to spare for the starving beggars who had struggled from as far away as south of the Mounth. What little free capital was available was not spent on improving conditions at home but was invested in the disastrous Darien adventure. As the 18th century dawned,

Moray was poor but viable; but Scotland was ruined. The aristocracy and merchants sought their salvation in a union with the Auld Enemy. England was willing to help. With Scotland under control and with her rear secure, England could now confidently engage in world wide piracy and colonisation.[52]

Some Scots were not too happy about this new order, though, for once, Moray was on the side of the establishment. In 1715, 1719 and in 1745 the Highlanders drew their broadswords in the defence of the indefensible. In 1745, the handsome but not overtly intelligent Charles Edward Stuart, Bonnie Prince Charlie of myth, landed in Scotland in an effort to gain the throne of Britain for his father. After initial success he retreated through Moray and spent most of March 1746 in bed in Thunderton House in Elgin. Detractors say that he was prostrate with the pox; modern apologists say that it was all due to lack of vitamin C. Charles fell back with his army to Inverness and, always well fed himself, he neglected to ensure that his soldiers had adequate rations. With an excess of incompetence he lined up his starving irregulars against men well fed on bread, beer and cheese who were also supplied with plenty of cannon which they knew how to use. What happened on Drumossie Moor on the 16th of April 1746 was not a battle. It was a massacre and the massacring continued, on and off, for a long time afterwards.

**The Recent Years**
The old ways died along with the Highlanders on that chill April day. The people of Moray were either delighted, or appeared delighted, with the result. The town council of Elgin sent an obsequious message to the king on 19th May 1746[53] while the parish ministers enthusiastically compiled lists of persons concerned in the rebellion, or even those just disaffected. Lists of Episcopalians and Roman Catholics were also drawn up.[54] A minor Moray landowner, a staunch Presbyterian, who had moved to Perthshire, came out for the Prince: William Harrold died in one of the stinking hulks used as prison ships while his wife and children were brutally evicted from their comfortable home. One of the daughers, Anne, came to an aunt in Elgin and became the mother of Isaac Forsyth, the founder of the Moray Farmer Club and the Elgin Museum.

The lairds' power of pit and gallows was abolished in 1747 and so Sir Robert Gordon and his kind could no longer 'incarcerate (Margaret Collie) without any warrant, for taking the head of a ling out of a midden or dunghill, which the woman thought was good for curing the gout.'[55] As peaceful times brought prosperity there was need for better communications to help increase trade and expand markets. Bridges were built over the lower Spey at Fochabers in 1804 and at Craigellachie in 1814. The Findhorn was spanned in 1800 and a network of turnpikes replaced the old pack tracks and inadequate military roads. To accommodate the rising population lairds laid out new towns in the hopeful belief, not always realised, that their tenants would lead active and useful lives in spinning and weaving. Tomintoul, proposed in 1750 but not actually built until 1775, was described in 1793 as 'inhabited by 37 families, without a single manufacture.... All of them sell whisky, and all of them drink it.'[56] Books were written about local history and problems.[57] Parish ministers, with varying degrees of enthusiasm, sent in their answers to John Sinclair's questionnaire.[58] Societies were formed, museums opened and railways encouraged by the merchant classes, though not always by the aristocracy.

Peace, prosperity and progress were not necessarily the smooth process which memory and myth perpetuate. In 1820 a general election was held. The voters were few in number and expected to be bribed, in some cases quite lavishly.[59] The Earl of Fife was handing out dresses, shawls, bonnets and one pound notes on behalf of his brother, while in Strathspey the chiefs of Grant supported a Mr Farquharson. As the Grants could not outbid the Duffs (Fife), Lady Ann Grant sent to Strathspey for a contingent of Highlanders to come to Elgin. Great was the alarm of the burgesses when some 700 Highlanders assembled in front of Grant Lodge. As one writer delicately put it 'if the Highlanders ... got drink ... a battle would certainly ensure'.[60] Food was provided but no drink and the Highlanders were persuaded to go home. After much legal argument, Mr Farquharson was declared the winner. In 1827 the first Moray newspaper, 'The Elgin Courier' was published. This failed but 'The Courant' started up and was able to carry the news about the Moray meal riots. In 1846 the potato crop substantially failed and the price of meal rose beyond the means of even the working poor. However, grain was still being exported from Burghead, Findhorn and Lossiemouth so the lower orders, their natural subservience overcome by their empty bellies, tried to prevent the ships from loading.[61] The Moray bourgeoisie were terrified, troops were summoned from Edinburgh and the ringleaders, mainly women, were arrested and savagely dealt with, to the exultation of the press and the relief of those who did not know what it was to go hungry.

Whisky had been distilled for years in Strathspey and adjacent glens, but in 1824 an act came into force which lowered the price of a distilling licence and savagely increased the penalty for unlicensed distillation. Many poor people were unaware of the new act and the Justices in Moray were moved to write to the Controller of Customs quoting the most pathetic cases and pleading to be allowed to set a lower penalty than the statutory £20.[62] The legalised distilleries prospered and despite some recent setbacks, the distillation of fine malt whisky is still a major industry in Moray. Despite recent health education, the drinking of fine malt whisky is also a well established industry in Moray.

As mechanisation reduced the need for labour on the farms there was emigration from the land to the cities of the south and to the colonies.

Some of the emigrants who left Moray in the early years of this century returned within a few years wearing bush hats or carrying Ross rifles; only to disappear, never to return, into the mud of Flanders. The Second War introduced far more material and social changes than the First. Although fewer died, more were involved. Every few miles along the Moray littoral there was an airfield. In the hills there were Canadians, like their fathers before them, cutting down the trees which had been too young to die for freedom in the previous struggle. In the summer of 1940 there was a great fear of invasion and defences were erected on the shore and far inland. Home Guards poured candle wax into their shotgun cartridges and those lucky enough to have a P17 rifle, counted and recounted their five rounds, painfully aware that their machine gun needed a different size of ammunition. As the war progressed and prisoners helped out on the land, fraternisation, officially illegal, like most things illegal in wartime, flourished undercover.

Changes came even more rapidly after the war. Bus services increased and killed the railways, but it was not long before the car killed the bus. Opportunities for manual labour decreased while the provision of administrative work increased. As workers left the land, rural communities declined, schools closed, kirks amalgamated, young people left, the old remained and the graveyards became overgrown. But the incomparable land remains. The forests sweep down to the fields and the fields to the sea and beyond the sea the mountains of Sutherland arise blue and remote. 'Speak weel o the Hielans, but live in the Laich.

**Select Bibliography**
L Shaw *History of the Province of Moray* (Edinburgh 1775)
H B Mackintosh *Elgin, Past and Present* (Elgin 1914)
R Douglas *The Annals of Forres* (Elgin 1934)
*The Moray Book* ed. D Omand (Edinburgh 1976)
*The Grampian Book* ed. D Omand (Golspie 1987)
S Wood and B C Kneller *History in the Grampian Landscape* (Aberdeen 1982)
M Seton *Forres and Area* (Elgin 1982)
M Seton *Moray, Past and Present* (Elgin 1982)
M Seton *Laich o Moray* (Elgin 1985)
I A G Shepherd *Scotland's Heritage: Grampian* (Edinburgh 1986)
C McKean *The District of Moray* (Edinburgh 1987)
*Geology of the Aberdeen Area* edd. N H Trewin et al (Edinburgh 1987)

**Notes**
1. G W S Barrow 'Badenoch and Strathspey' 8 *Northern Scotland* (1988) 1.
2. Sinclair Ross 'The Physical Background' in *The Moray Book* ed. D Omand (Edinburgh 1976) 30.
3. Ibid., 32.
4. Ibid., 38.
5. J D Peacock, *The Geology of the Elgin District* (Edinburgh 1968) 112.

6. R Grant in *The Counties of Moray & Nairn* ed. H Hamilton (Glasgow 1965) 33.
7. A D Lacaille, *The Stone Age in Scotland* (Oxford 1954).
8. *The Early Postglacial Settlement of Northern Europe* ed. P Mellars (London 1978).
9. J G Evans, *The Environment of Early Man in the British Isles* (London 1975).
10. H J Case 'Neolithic Explanations' *Antiquity* 43 (1969) 176-186.
11. I Kinnes, 'The Neolithic of Scotland as seen from outside' *PSAS* 115 (1988) 19.
12. Ibid., 21.
13. R W B Morris, *The Prehistoric Rock Art of Argyll* (Poole 1977) 15, and *The Prehistoric Rock Art of Galloway and Man* (Poole 1979) 16.
14. *British Prehistory* edd. J V S Megaw and D D A Simpson (Leicester 1979) 181.
15. I A G Shepherd 'The Early Peoples' in *The Grampian Book* ed. D Omand (Golspie 1987) 127.
16. See, for example, V G Childe and W Thorneycroft 'Vitrified Forts' *PSAS* 72 (1937) 44-55; J Engström 'Ett murexperiment på Gotland' *Tor* 19 (1983) 53-75; and I Ralston 'Vitrified Wall Experiment at East Tullos' *PSAS* 116 (1986) 17-39.
17. J Macdonald, *Place names in Strathbogie* (Aberdeen 1891) 37.
18. Eumenius in A Holder, *Alt-Celtisher Sprachschatz* (Leipzig 1904) ii, 993.
19. See *The Problem of the Picts* ed. F T Wainright (Edinburgh 1955); I Henderson, *The Picts* (London 1967); and I Ralston and J Inglis, *Foul Hordes* (Aberdeen 1984).
20. W F H Nicolaisen, *Scottish Place Names* (London 1976) 150.
21. J K St Joseph *Journal of Roman Studies* xli (1951) 65; and xlviii (1958) 93.
22. C Gordon 'Parish of Birnie' *NSA* 86; C Daniels 'A Roman Castra at the Foths?' *Pop.Arch.* 17 no.3 (1986) 10.
23. B Jones 'Roman Military Site at Cawdor' *Pop. Arch.* 17 no.3 (1986) 13.
24. I Keillar 'In Fines Borestorum' *Pop. Arch.* 17 no.3 (1986) 2.
25. *Adomnan's Life of Columba* edd. A O and M Anderson (Edinburgh 1961).
26. W D Simpson, *The Celtic Church in Scotland* (Aberdeen 1935).
27. G J Marcus, *The Conquest of the North Atlantic* (Woodbridge 1980) 17.
28. E Beveridge, *The 'Abers' and 'Invers' of Scotland* (Edinburgh 1923) 4.
29. G A F Knight, *Early Christianizing of Scotland* (London 1933) i, 391.
30. C Plummer, *Two Saxon Chronicles* (Oxford 1892) i, 289.
31. G W S Barrow, *Kingship and Unity* (London 1981) 88.
32. L Mackintosh, *Elgin Past and Present* (Elgin 1891) 103.
33. A A M Duncan, *Scotland: The Making of the Kingdom* (Edinburgh 1975) 326.
34. *Moray Registrum* 27.
35. A A M Duncan, *The Making of the Kingdom* 317.
36. Ibid., 546.
37. Pers. comm. from Mr William J Lindsay.
38. E L G Stones and G G Simpson *Edward and the Throne of Scotland* (Oxford 1978) ii, 2 47.
39. Mackintosh, *Elgin Past and Present* 167.
40. *Ragman Rolls* 1291-6 (Bannatyne Club 1834).

41. Mackintosh, *Elgin Past and Present* 55.
42. *Miscellany II* (Scottish History Society 1904) 51.
43. *Moray Registrum* 353.
44. Ibid., 381. For the career of 'The Wolf of Badenoch' see Alexander Grant in this volume.
45. Ibid., 391ff.
46. T C Smout, *A History of the Scottish People 1560-1830* (London 1969) 66.
47. J Spalding, *History of the Troubles* (Edinburgh 1828) i, 47.
48. J F S Gordon, *The Book of Keith* (Glasgow 1880) 31.
49. G Anderson, *Kingston-on-Spey* (Edinbugh 1957) 5.
50. W Crammond, *Records of Elgin* (Aberdeen 1903) ii, 282, 293ff.
51. A Brodie, *The Diary of Alexander Brodie* (Aberdeen 1863) 296.
52. I Henderson, *Scotland: Kirk and People* (London 1969) 13.
53. W Crammond, *Records of Elgin* ii, 456.
54. E D Dunbar, *Social Life in Former Days* (Edinburgh 1865-6) i, 376.
55. Ibid., ii, 145.
56. *Stat.Acct.* xii, 440.
57. Eg. L Shaw, *History of the Province of Moray* (Edinburgh 1775); J Grant and W Leslie, *Survey of the Province of Moray* (Aberdeen 1798); and W Leslie, *General View of the Agriculture in Nairn & Moray* (London 1813).
58. *Stat.Acct.*
59. R Young, *Annals of the Parish & Burgh of Elgin* (Elgin 1879) 261.
60. Ibid., 263.
61. I Keillar 'The Moray Meal Riots of 1847' *Moray Field Club Bulletin* no.14 (1986) 15.
62. P Duff, Letter to Controller of Customs, 1825 (Moray Record Office).

**Appendix**

### Places within Moray mentioned in the text

(OS number refers to the Ordnance Survey map number in the 1/50,000 series)
*Physical*

| | |
|---|---|
| MORAY | OS 1/50,000 Nos 27 & 28 Now a District of Grampian Region. |
| FORRES | OS No 27 NJ040590 Royal burgh with royal castle site. |
| FINDHORN | OS No 27 North flowing turbulent river. Village at mouth. |
| STRATHNAIRN | OS No 27 Broad, reasonably fertile valley. |
| STRATHDEARN | OS No 27 The Strath of the Findhorn river. Narrow in places. |
| STRATHSPEY | OS No 28 Long and usually broad strath of the river Spey. |
| FESHIE | OS No 35 Tributary of the Spey. Joins Spey near Kincraig. |
| AVON | OS No 28 Tributary of the Spey. Joins Spey at Ballindalloch. |

| MONADHLIATHS | OS No 35 Hills to the north of Kingussie. |
| BURGHEAD | OS No 28 NJ109692 Promontory with fort and enigmatic well. |
| LOSSIEMOUTH | OS No 28 NJ 235705 Fishing port, 8km north of Elgin. |

*Early Peoples*

| CULBIN | OS No 27 Forested coastal area to west of river Findhorn. |
| BOGHEAD | OS No 28 NJ 359592 In forest land, north of A98. |
| ROSEISLE | OS No 28 NJ149651 Easterton. Site now lost. |
| URQUHART | OS No 28 NJ 285626 Village, 8km east of Elgin. |
| BALLINDALLOCH | OS No 28 NJ165359 Easter Lagmore, dilapidated cairn. |

*Early Metal in Moray*

| QUARRY WOOD | OS No 28 NJ185630 Henge, 3km west of Elgin. |
| ELGIN | OS No 28 NJ215626 Royal burgh with royal castle site. |
| TAP O NOTH | OS No 37 NJ484293 Magnificent vitrified fort. |

*Picts and Romans*

| PITAIRLIE | OS No 28 NJ256654 Farm, 4km north east of Elgin. |
| DESKFORD | OS No 29 NJ505615 Village, 6km south of Cullen. |
| KEITH | OS No 28 NJ430507 Roman camps are 5km east on the A95. |
| THOMSHILL | OS No 28 NJ210574 5km due south of Elgin. |
| BIRNIE | OS No 28 NJ207587 Cathedral site, 3km south of Elgin. |
| EASTER GALCANTRAY | OS No 27 NH 811483 Site on south east bank of river Nairn. |
| CROY | OS No 27 NH796496 Village, 15km south west of Nairn. |
| SUENO'S STONE | OS No 27 NJ046595 Stone on eastern outskirts of Forres. |

*Christianity*

| ABERBRANDELY | OS No 28 NJ190418 Old (prior to 1550) name for Knockando. |
| KNOCKANDO | OS No 28 NJ186428 Scattered community to north of Spey. |
| MORTLACH | OS No 28 NJ324392 Now part of Dufftown. |
| ELGIN CATHEDRAL | OS No 28 NJ221630 At east end of Elgin. |
| FORDYCE | OS No 29 NJ556637 Village, 5km south east of Cullen. |
| RAFFORD | OS No 27 NJ060567 Village, 5km south east of Forres. |

45

| | |
|---|---|
| LHANBRYDE | OS No 28 NJ273612 Village, 7km east of Elgin on A96 road. |
| KINNEDDAR | OS No 28 NJ222695 Kirkyard with cross. |
| SPYNIE | OS No 28 NJ231659 & NJ228654 Palace and graveyard. |
| URQUHART | OS No 28 NJ295629 Site of Benedictine priory. |
| KINLOSS | OS No 27 NJ065615 Cistercian Abbey, now very ruinous. |
| PLUSCARDEN | OS No 28 NJ142576 Valliscaulian priory, now Benedictine Abbey. |

*Divide and Rule*

| | |
|---|---|
| CULLEN | OS No 29 NJ515670 Royal burgh on coast. |
| AULDEARN | OS No 27 NH917556 Site of castle and 1645 Montrose victory. |
| FOCHABERS | OS No 28 NJ345588 Planned village on A96, 13km east of Elgin. |
| INNES | OS No 28 NJ283651 Motte, somewhat inaccessible. |
| DUFFUS | OS No 28 NJ189672 Magnificent motte and bailey castle. |
| RAIT | OS No 27 NH893525 Unique 13th century hall house. |

*Times of Trouble*

| | |
|---|---|
| LADY HILL | OS No 28 NJ212628 Castle Hill, towards west end of Elgin. |
| ROTHES | OS No 28 NJ278495 Castle town some 15km south of Elgin. |
| BALVENIE | OS No 28 NJ326408 Great castle at Dufftown. |
| SLIOCH | OS No 29 NJ554390 Battle site, 2km south east from Huntly. |
| COXTON | OS No 28 NJ261607 Anachronistic stone tower from the 1640's. |
| BURGIE | OS No 27 NJ093593 Castle ruin, 6km east of Forres. |
| BLAIRFINDY | OS No 36 NJ199286 Castle, near Glenlivet Distillery. |
| EASTER ELCHIES | OS No 28 NJ280444 Restored tower house at Macallan. |

*The Reformation and After*

| | |
|---|---|
| SPEY MOUTH | OS No 28 NJ342647 Alleged site of Charles II's landing. |

*The Recent Years*

| | |
|---|---|
| CRAIGELLACHIE | OS No 28 NJ345588 On A96, east of Elgin. |
| TOMINTOUL | OS No 36 NJ166190 In Strathavon on A939. |

# THE MORAY AERIAL SURVEY
## Discovering the Prehistoric and proto-Historic Landscape

### Barri Jones, Ian Keillar and Keith Maude

Moray was of significance in the history of Scotland because it was an area capable of supporting a sizeable population sufficiently remote from the Scottish lowlands to form an alternative and independent power base. In historical times the crescent along the coast from Aberdeen to Inverness was to witness a series of major battles in the Roman, late Pictish, medieval and Hanoverian periods. Scotland, in historic times, could not be considered conquered until at least the Laigh of Moray had been subdued. Thus Edward I in 1303 only considered his task done when, after a period of vengeful butchery at Elgin, followed by a less bloodthirsty stay at Kinloss Abbey, he despatched a squadron of cavalry to Tain on the southern edge of the Dornoch Firth. It has generally been assumed that there may have been a considerable population based in Moray in earlier periods but the evidence for this is sketchy and only hinted at in, for example, the Pictish period where the number of previously attested settlement sites is minimal in contrast to a number of stones.[1] Likewise, in the prehistoric period, although a few major sites are known such as North Kessock, Craig Phadraig and Burghead (the latter two certainly being in use in the Pictish period)[2] there is an almost complete absence of the evidence that one would expect in the middle and lower ends of the settlement hierarchy. There is, furthermore, a geologically related imbalance in the record of survival for a variety of reasons. Stone-built cairns, for instance, long exemplified by the well-known Clava type and the Garbeg cemetery at Drumnadrochit, do survive in considerable numbers on the higher ground. Are we to assume that the known distribution is in any way a comprehensive view of the distribution of such burial patterns? The answer from the aerial survey described in this chapter must be firmly negative. The existence of known graves of this type simply reflects the survival of stone-built megaliths on higher ground. This pattern of imbalance also pervades our knowledge of settlement sites. These have been typified by the class of monument known to archaeologists as a *dun* (*doon, doone*), such as Barevan in Strathnairn, surviving on hilltops generally above the 600ft contour, often with their ramparts affected by vitrification.[3]

Yet a glance at the geological and climatic patterns prevailing in Moray shows that, even allowing for the very substantial coastal area which must be written off as neither habitable nor cultivable by ancient man, there remain substantial areas of good quality land ripe for exploitation in the middle and later prehistoric periods. This article, incorporating the results of aerial survey initiated from fieldwork in the early '80s, triggered by the 1984 drought, and pursued annually until 1989, shows the growth in

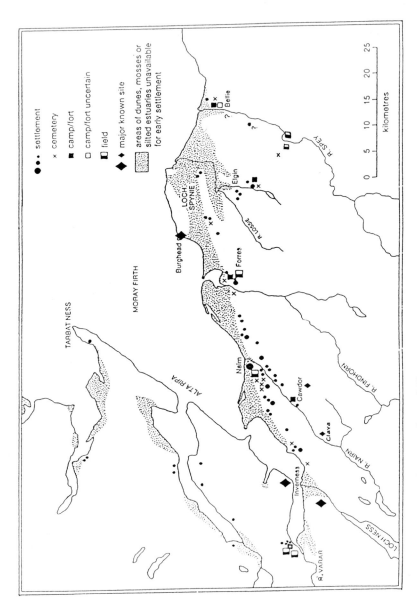

Fig.3.1 *Moray Aerial Survey: General Map.*

understanding of the ancient landscape prompted by systematic reconnaissance at annual climatic optima. This emphasis on long-term preliminary fieldwork, then on locally selected criteria for photo-reconnaissance (whether of climate, crop or even light conditions) is one we would emphasise in the centralising tendencies of current air photographic practice in the United Kingdom. The authors are deeply indebted to the local finance that made the Moray Aerial Survey viable and the individuals whose interest and support made the work possible. To all who granted access to land, or excavation or helped in other ways, the authors express their gratitude.

## The Land

The Laigh of Moray below 75 metres enjoys a dry mild climate with an average rainfall of less than 800mm (31 inches). Sheltered parts of the area reach as low as 650mm (25 inches). The number of fine days is particularly noticeable and accounts for the presence of major aerodromes in the area. In this respect, although there can be considerable variation particularly in the summer (especially July) weather patterns, the climate provides a relatively favourable area for examination. The influence of the sea and the Moray Firth is also considerable, and by August the water temperature sometimes reaches + 13 degrees centigrade falling to around + 4 degrees centigrade by February. These temperatures tend to moderate the onset of winter and mitigate its harshness except in periods of high wind, the 'blows' which are attested to have caused considerable topsoil erosion in the last century. As well as relatively low rainfall and reasonable amounts of sunshine the Laigh of Moray also enjoys predominantly light and sandy soil suited for cereal production, a characteristic from which it appears to have benefited throughout its history. It is important to realise, however, that the bands of fertile land are limited by a number of factors. The area between the metamorphic schists of the Monadhliath mountains and the coast is drained in a north-east direction by great rivers such as the Spey, the Findhorn and the Nairn; all three rivers, fed by the Cairngorms or the Monadhliaths, are liable to produce flash floods. As part of the resultant silt disposition the longshore drift from east to west is continually pushing the mouths of the Spey and Findhorn westwards. Long sand or gravel spits built up and these were eventually punched through by the river itself or, in the case of the Spey, cut through in modern times by bulldozers.[4]

About 2000 years ago, the sea-level was about the same as at present but there may have been an open channel running from approximately Burghead to Lossiemouth. The detached mass of the harbour area of Burghead peninsula may arguably once have formed an island but is now connected by a 10m storm beach to the mainland at Clarkly Hill. The Findhorn probably entered the sea to the west of its present course, while the Spey probably emptied into an estuary partially enclosed by a long spit of gravel reaching out from the eastern bank of the river. This means that in any reconstruction of the landscape towards the end of the pre-historic period we must make considerable allowance for a substantial variation in land morphology created by areas that were either seasonal marsh or liable to suffer from flooding.

Thus in detail (as shown in Fig.3.1) the coastal area at the mouth of the Spey was unsuitable for settlement north of Bellie where a slight ridge used by both Roman and Hanoverian armies offers a potential crossing point of the Spey. One of the greatest problems of interpretation, however, occurs further west where effectively there were major differences in the ancient landform from today. The Lossie (presumably, but not certainly, the *Loxa* cited by Ptolemy) is a smaller river whose capacity to flood can be seriously underestimated today. The river clearly changed its channel extensively north and south of Elgin. It is on the north-east side of the town, however, that some idea of the variations may best be appreciated. The progressive changes in the mouth of the Lossie in the area of Lossie-mouth are documented at least in the early modern period. Originally, however, at the time when Duffus Castle acted as a port, Loch Spynie (now reduced to a marginal area of shallow water to the east) formed an inland harbour in the 12th and 13th centuries. There may be a suggestion that inland navigation was possible between Spynie and Burghead to explain the apparent passage of the Viking fleet in this direction, in the eighth century, or later.[5]

The evident changes further west around Findhorn Bay are relatively clear today, including not only the extensive accretion of land in the lee of Culbin Sands but also changes in the pattern of the mouth of Findhorn proper. The out-turned bow of land between Findhorn and Nairn is also geologically and morphologically recent. The outflow of Strathnairn on the other hand appears to be relatively fixed by the presence south-west of Nairn of an elongated ridge which has played a significant part in the history of the area. It was along this route that we may expect Roman land-based penetration of the inner Moray Firth to have passed, as did the Hanoverian army in April 1746 on its way from Nairn to the battlefield of Culloden. The ridge, hereafter termed the Croy ridge, confines the course of the Nairn within a relatively restricted channel as far as Cawdor, whereafter a broader flood-plain leads down to Nairn and a relatively constricted exit to the sea. On the north side the Croy ridge also marks the northern limit of habitable land. Until the construction of the railway in the late 19th century the intervening area, now occupied in part by Inverness airport at Dalcross, was largely marsh, terminating to the north in the foreshore west of Ardersier. The former mossland, broken by occasional drumlins, extends in a narrowing belt all the way south-west towards Balloch on the edge of modern Inverness.

It is nowadays perhaps at times difficult to understand the significance of these former land configurations, particularly in view of the way in which land reclaimed in the last century today comprises some of the best agricultural land in Moray. In considering the ancient situation, however, these areas indicated in general terms in Fig.3.1 should be dismissed from our archaeological assessment of potential for ancient settlement. Perhaps man could, however, cultivate the light soils produced by sequences of fluvio-glacial outwash on the low ridges and drumlins between the Monadhliaths and the littoral. These areas were, in fact, highly attractive to the prehistoric farmer just as they remain today.

**Distribution**

The principal results of the Moray Aerial Survey are here described in an order that is inevitably controlled by the zones where evidence has been recovered. This means, in particular, that the lower end of Strathnairn takes pride of place in terms of the recovery of information. Accordingly, to give an idea of the breadth of the evidence, Strathnairn appears first in the topographical units described. To help in the assimilation of the crop-mark phenomena it has been divided into a number of zones (Fig.3.2): namely *Nairn*, including the major site immediately south-west of the town (Figs.3.3, 4; Pl.II); *Strathnairn North* which covers the major discoveries

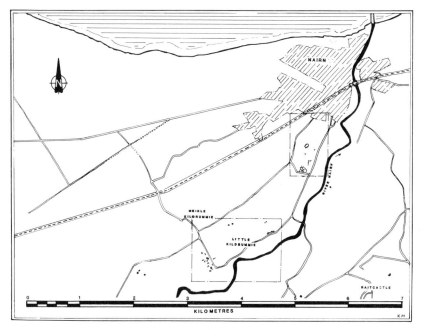

*Fig.3.2  Nairn and Lower Strathnairn: location map.*

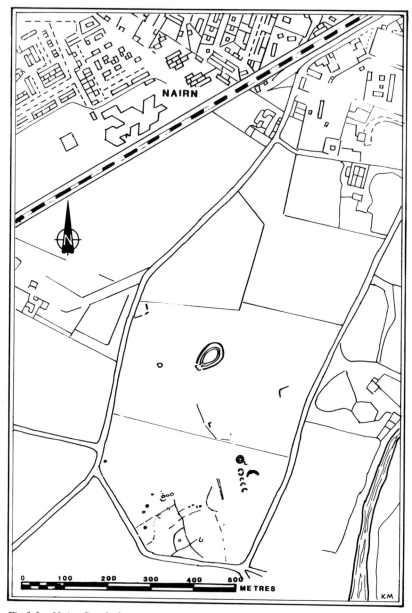

NAIRN

0   100   200   300   400   500
METRES

KM

Fig.3.3   Nairn South: location map of crop marks. Note the presence of souterrains
and land divisions (bottom).

52

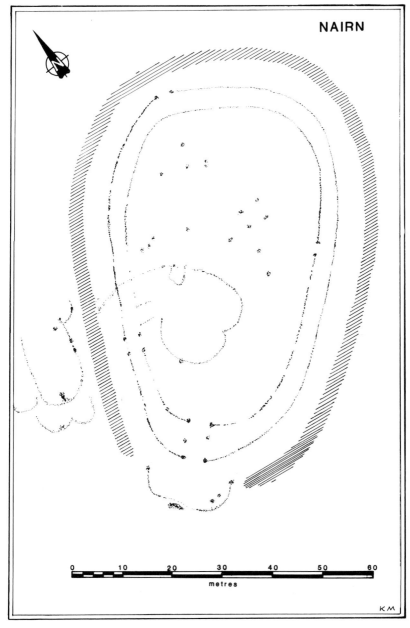

NAIRN

0    10    20    30    40    50    60
metres

KM

*Fig.3.4    Nairn South: detailed transcript of the principal settlement (cf. Pl.II).*

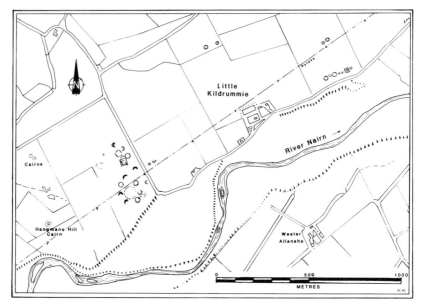

*Fig.3.5    Kinchyle and Kildrummie: general location map. Note the square barrows*
*visible amidst the linear cemetery at Little Kildrummie (Pl.V) and also*
*(centre left) at the Kinchyle cemetery (cf. Pl. VI).*

in the area of Kildrummie (Fig.3.5); *Strathnairn South* covering the south
side of the Strath in the area between Brackla and Geddes, where much
new information has been forthcoming; and finally *Flemington* on the
north side of the Croy ridge where in an area unaffected by modern
woodland a group of monuments has been identified around Loch Flemington and further to the north along the Ardersier road (Fig.3.6). Each
of these areas is presented with its own appropriate map. In the Laigh of
Moray a number of selected areas are then presented as dictated by the
air photographic evidence. Several zones, notably that south of Burghead
along the edge of the former mainland, have not proved amenable to air
photographic reconnaissance for a variety of reasons, and the areas under
discussion should not be treated as necessarily the only zones of prehistoric
settlement. They are simply those zones where a combination of the subsoil
and the pattern of cereal rotation between '84 and '89 has allowed the
recovery of substantial material. Some of the evidence incorporated here
derives by kind permission from the work of Ian Shepherd of Grampan
Regional Council and Dr Ian Ralston, who advised on a number of
points. The areas concerned comprise Forres where, despite the substantial
changes in the lower course of the Findhorn, very important evidence has

54

survived of prehistoric and Roman date (Fig.3.7) west of the modern town (Pl.Ia,b); and Elgin South, the area lying between Manbean and Birnie on the south side of the modern town, an area again substantially affected by changes in the course of the Lossie which probably explains the presence of several prehistoric and one Roman site well to the south of the present main east-west communications axis.

The inner Moray Firth was also sampled at a number of points. One of the most fertile is undoubtedly the littoral immediately east of Inverness towards Smithton and Balloch where, for instance, a major site is now known at Allanfearn. The distribution of ancient settlement in this area may be compared with that in a similar geomorphological setting along the north-western corner of the Beauly Firth near Muir of Ord. It will be apparent by this stage that areas of archaeological productivity are to some extent predictable in the area. In terms of the coast these are often defined by the land configuration at the head or side of a loch. Much more needs to be understood in geomorphological terms about the extent of the sea lochs at the end of the prehistoric period than at present, for instance, Haggart has conducted a survey of the alluviation patterns at the head of

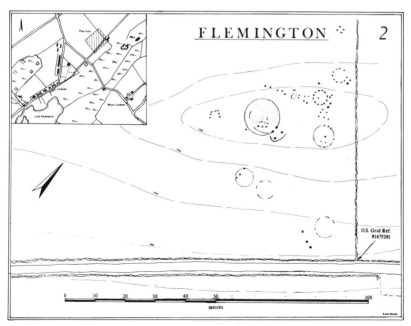

Fig.3.6    Flemington 2: detailed transcription of the settlement north-east of Loch Flemington. Note the elaborate entrance to the principal enclosure and the apparent rows of pits.

55

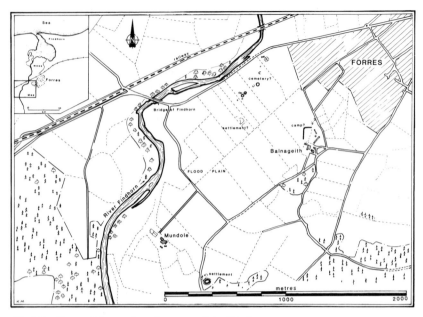

*Fig.3.7   Forres West: a location map of the Findhorn area.*

the Beauly Firth, north and south of Kirkhill, where clearly the Firth extended much further inland in comparison with the present morphology.[6] Likewise, the head waters of the Cromarty Firth, which has clearly infilled considerably within the historic period, call for greater archaeological investigation.

Nonetheless, our understanding of the sites which may have formed the framework of settlement in the period remains largely to seek. The Black Isle, well-known today for its rich farming land, has singularly failed to produce traces of ancient settlement. The Moray Aerial Survey was deliberately extended into this area in the hope of identifying at least some zones where subsoil conditions would promote the development of cropmark phenomena. In the event, as already stated, the results proved relatively uninformative in terms of additional evidence. Nonetheless, in view of the fact that evidence was sought in apparently environmentally favourable areas across four separate seasons, it should henceforth probably be assumed that cropmarks will remain very limited in the Cromarty and Dornoch zones. Whether this represents a true picture of later pre-historic settlement density remains doubtful. It is puzzling that the lee side of the Black Isle, particularly the very sheltered Udale embayment, has consistently failed to provide diagnostic information; this despite Class 2 and Class 3 soils that should theoretically have encouraged ancient exploration and the extensive modern cereal regimes that would facilitate cropmark recognition. There is at the moment no explanation of the general hiatus either there or across the sheltered Cromarty Firth. Between Alness and Invergordon the raised shelf of land, here termed Rosskeen, is well drained (as opposed to the equivalent littoral north-east of Invergordon); it has produced a number of cropmarks but as yet none diagnostic of any extensive settlement. Accordingly the evidence from Cromarty and Dornoch is limited to two sample areas, that around Rosskeen and a further example (hereafter designated Fearn) towards the head of the Dornoch Firth some 5 km. south-east of Bonar Bridge. On the north side of this point the promontory created by Dun Creich provides a wedge of arable land on which cropmarks have been observed, while on the opposite side the alluvial fan of the eastern Fearn Burn has also produced evidence alongside the modern railway line that may represent the original monastery site of that name. Elsewhere, towards Tain, limitations on flying imposed by the R.A.F. practice ranges coincide with areas of dune formation where recovery of information is most unlikely. There remains, however, one particularly intriguing site at Portmahomack, observed in 1984 and later, which must have major historical connotations whatever its date. A large enclosure, partly incorporating the southern side of the present village and evidently protected by a ditch and palisade, clearly relates to the church and anchorage on the south side of the modern fishing port. A radio-carbon date from recent excavations is awaited.

A major battle with the Norse and generally assumed to have taken place at sea is known to have been fought near Tarbat Ness, but the battle may in fact have been on land. It remains more probable, however, that proximity to the church is more significant. Fine eighth century carvings have been found at the latter and the likelihood of an associated *scriptorium* should be considered, set within a lay enclosure similar to that identified from the air alongside the early church at Ninkirk, Cumbria, or Ruthwell, Dumfries.

**Interpretations**
Overall there remains considerable room for conjecture regarding the precise interpretations of the cropmarks. The evidence may be divided into several broad categories. First and foremost there are a broad range of circular or ovoid sites associated with penannular ditches or darker markings partially reflecting a circular nucleus (Fig.3.8). Second, the evidence clearly assignable to funerary use is often outstanding in quality but is not as yet wholly susceptible to chronological differentiation. Lastly, the evidence of farming in the form of field divisions is rare, being limited effectively to the extensive Nairn, Forres and Tarradale complexes. If contemporaneity can be assumed, it is possible that the souterrains in the Nairn complex may be associated with field systems.

Undoubtedly the main problem surrounds the circular or oval settlements.[7] These have been regarded as either settlement foci or, when the evidence comprises a single circle of apparently large post-pits, a form of megalithic structure (Pl.IV). Some advance may probably be made in defining this group of material. Although not all such sites exhibit traces of an umbra or 'aureole' (see below), those that do may almost certainly be regarded as settlements rather than burial sites. The cropmark phenomenon involved takes the form of darkened cereal (or even grass) growth relating directly to a penannular ditch or occurring independently within it (Fig.3.8). There are therefore some sites that exhibit a quarter- or half-moon shaped intensification in the tonal range of the crop, and this darker intensification can be further demarcated by the presence of a pennanular ditch. Alternatively the outer penannular features may contain in a central nucleus either the shape of a quarter- or half-moon umbra or a circular disposition of post-holes apparently reflecting the interior of a hut.

Two points arise from this, one the nomenclature to be used, the other the interpretation to be applied. The term 'aureole' suggested by Maxwell[8] is understandable but not perhaps the best applicable with its anatomical or pictorial connotations. In particular the term does not carry with it the implication of the chemical origin from which the marks derive. It can be suggested more positively that the umbra represents a phosphate and nitrate build-up in the subsurface soil from animal and human refuse. This phenomenon thus relates to settlement rather than burial sites. Obviously, however, within this context there is room for variation. Some sites may be animal compounds or enclosures, while others appear to reflect through the visible presence of post-holes the underlying presence of large huts implied by Tacitus' perhaps realistic reference in the aftermath of the battle of Mons Graupius to 'burning roofs' (fumantia tecta, Agricola 38.2). While Cassius Dio (76.12) on the other hand mentions the use of (hide?) tents amongst the Maeatae and Caledonii, he also emphasises the large extended family groups which might reflect the apparent size of the hut and compound configurations. In this context, therefore, priority should be given to a fieldwork programme to identify the placement of middens and comparable areas through analysis of the phosphate content of the interior. Likewise areas may have been set aside as latrines or standing areas for stock. Again these may be detectable from phosphate survey. The very detailed picture emerging from Flemington 2 would make an admirable starting point (Fig.3.6).

The presence of extensive cemeteries is evident in a number of places. Agglomerations of square barrows and ring ditches evidently forming barrows are particularly known at Forres (Figs.3.7, Pl.Ia,b) and at two places, Kinchyle and Little Kildrummie, in the evidence from lower Strathnairn (Pl.V, VI). The evidence for the mixture of burial styles involving ring ditches and square barrows is best shown at Little Kildrummie,

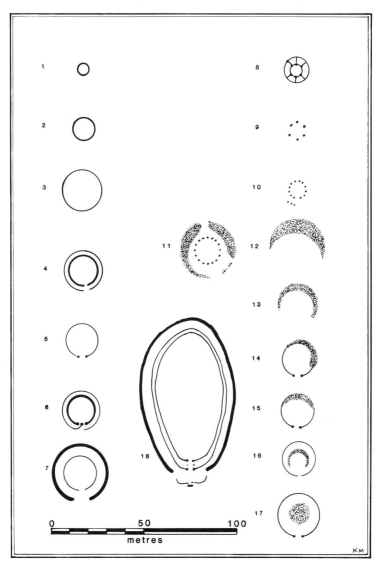

*Fig.3.8* *Morphology: comparative sizes of circular and oval crop mark sites. (1)*
*West and East Kildrummie; (2) Forres and Kildrummie; (3) Balloch; (4)*
*Forres; (5) Balloch; (6) Forres; (7) Brackla; (8) Nairn; (9) Lochside;*
*(10) Loch Flemington; (11) Lochside; (12) Nairn; (13) Forres and West*
*Kildrummie; (14) Kildrummie and Kinchyle; (15) Kildrummie and Kin-*
*chyle; (16) Gollanfield; (17) Loch Flemington; Kildrummie and Gol-*
*lanfield; (18) Nairn.*

59

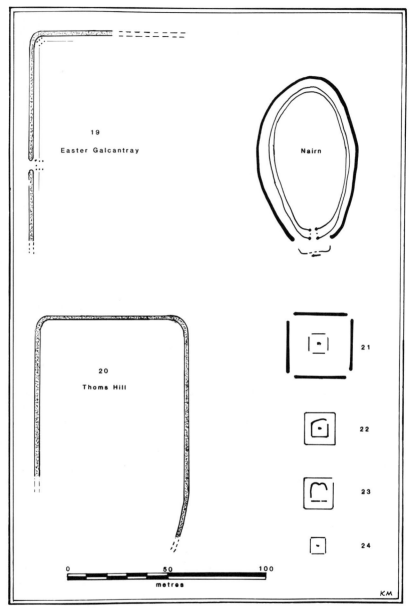

Fig.3.9   Morphology: comparative sizes of rectilinear sites, square barrows, etc.
(19) Easter Galcantray, Cawdor; (20) Thomshill; (21) Forres; (22) West
Kildrummie; (23) East Kildrummie; (24) Forres.

60

whereas further west at Kinchyle the evident cemetery area lies adjacent to a settlement on the south side. Little can be said of the ring ditch features because of lack of excavation. The same applies to the square barrows but there are some variations of internal arrangement and a major variation in size. The best preserved examples from Kinchyle and Little Kildrummie (Fig.3.9 nos. 22 and 23) occupy roughly the same area within the external ditch. The Little Kildrummie example shows the central burial clearly, whereas the Kinchyle example does not. They are, however, very closely comparable in size. Morphologically the Kinchyle example lacks a corner but is nonetheless distinct from the kind of square barrow evident at Forres. In these cases there is again a mixture of ring ditches and square barrows but as the examples show (Fig.3.9 nos. 21 and 24) the boundary ditch is not continuous and all four corners are incomplete. This has led to doubts as to the contemporaneity of this form with the type previously mentioned. Pictish burials showing discontinuous stone banks take a closely comparable form.[9] There remains, however, the problem of size. For the largest of the funerary enclosures at Forres is on a scale far greater than any of the other examples, an aspect that may therefore relate to its chronology rather than status; but this remains entirely conjectural for the moment.

Elements of land divisions are few and far between. How this relates to the prehistoric economy remains open to debate. For the record, however, there is evidence of what may be field divisions associated with the settlement previously discussed north of Balnageith at Forres. The prime example, however, remains lower Strathnairn (Fig.3.3). There the main site at Nairn South does not appear to have directly associated field systems but evidence of this kind does exist some half kilometre to the south-west close to the modern road to Cawdor. An area of ditched enclosures is evident in which there is also evidence of pits. The area as a whole also contains a number of souterrains to judge from the air photographic evidence.[10] While there may be a broad contemporaneity between all these features, any hope of a detailed chronology remains dependent on excavation. To date only the presumed settlement site at Brackla (Pl.VII) has been sampled yielding material suggesting a late 2nd-early 3rd century date.

**Historical Synthesis**
What conclusions can be gleaned from the evidence arguably from the historical period? We can see that in distributional terms it is now possible to define population centres for tribal septs centred at the western end of the Beauly Firth, on the shelf of land adjoining the inner Moray Firth, around Balloch west of Inverness, above all where the lower reaches of Strathnairn provide rich agricultural soils between Nairn and Cawdor and a major site is now known (Fig.3.4, Pl.II), then less clearly at Auldearn and at the débouchement of the Findhorn. Moving eastwards the rather

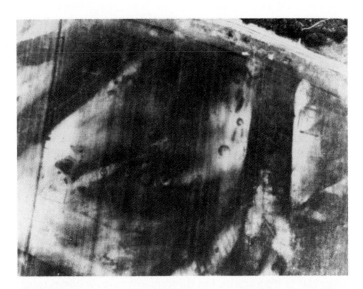

*Pl.Ia,b*   *Settlement a, b—Forres: the major agglomeration of cropmark evidence*
*visible on the flood plain of the Findhorn (Fig.3.7). The upper picture*
*(courtesy of Dr. I. Shepherd, Aberdeen Archaeological Services) shows*
*(top) the exceptionally large burial enclosure, various penannular and*
*circular marks associated with a settlement in the centre and a ditched*
*enclosure at the bottom. The lower picture shows the three circular settle-*
*ments visible in the centre of the upper photograph in an oblique view*
*(1986).*

62

*Pl.II   Settlement—Nairn (Figs. 3.3 & 3.4): The horseshoe shape of the major
settlement located south-west of the town (1986). Inside the major ditch note
the two thin lines that may represent palisades and also the faint traces of a
horn-work at the entrance.*

dispersed pattern of settlement south of Elgin, allowing for a reconstruction of the ancient morphology, appears to have its principal centre
in the area of Birnie and Thomshill. Further east in the Deveron Valley
settlement nucleii can be predicted and have been located at one to one
and a half kilometre intervals on spur sites along the valley. Into this
picture we have, of course, to add the presence of Burghead which, while
shown by radio carbon dating to belong to the fourth century AD, is
presumed for our purposes to have earlier antecedents.[11]

Against this background it is possible to move to a fuller and firmer
picture of the tribal territories involved as known through Ptolemy and
the Ravenna Cosmography. It is also salutary to remember just how much
material is contained in the Ravenna Cosmography naming sites that
remain at present unlocated. It is, however, the coordinates that give
Ptolemy's Geography its unique importance, as all scholars have recognised. Unless one adopts a position that his coordinates are textually
incorrect, then one has to follow their implications. These indicate that

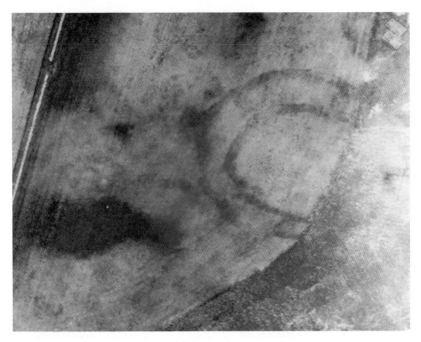

*Pl.III   Settlement—Rait Castle: The ditch of a bivallate site occupying the scarp of a terrace in Lower Strathnairn (1984).*

*alta ripa* is to be equated with the Ord or, more likely, on the relative northings, the line of cliffs either side of the Sutors broken by the mouth of the sheltered Cromarty Firth. Varar is preserved in the name of the Farrar flowing into the Beauly Firth. Like Rivet and Smith therefore it seems ineluctable to place the' site of *Pinnata Castra* along the Moray coast. We are less concerned here with locating it than with the other information that can coalesce with it. Thus the land of the Vacomagi lay west of the promontory of the Taezali, namely Kinnaird Head, and therefore some of the sites named by Ptolemy, notably Tameia, are given coordinates that place them in the Moray littoral. It would be unprecedented in Ptolemy's set of coordinates to find the name for a marching camp listed. His '*poleis*' clearly must be seen as more substantive locations, whether these are native sites or, as Rivet and Smith argue, Roman forts.[12]

The presence of camps[13] or even forts, thus implied by Ptolemy along the Moray littoral reflects, of course, the climactic historical event of the Flavian advance, the battle of Mons Graupius at which the Caledonian confederacy was defeated.[14] The search for the actual battlefield has tended

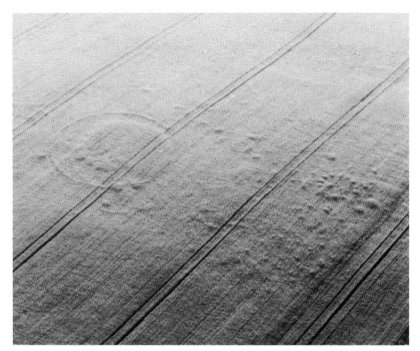

*Pl.IV  Settlement—Flemington: The exceptional precision of cropmarks in barley reveals the layout of a large circular site with prominent gate posts at its entrance (centre), the marks of a circular post setting (right) and numerous pits on this ridge top site (1989) (see Fig.3.6).*

to obscure the subsequent events attested by Tacitus in his biography (*Agricola* 38).

Here one might argue by analogy from two comparable invasions, namely that of Edward I in 1303 and the Hanoverian march in 1746. From this it is apparent that any would-be conqueror of north-east Scotland like Agricola must have followed a coastal line of march and it is interesting that in both cases the coast was reached near Banff[15] whereafter the line of march was almost entirely controlled by the major physical barriers such as the Spey and the Findhorn. If there is indeed a Roman site at Bellie on the Spey near Fochabers, then it lies within a matter of a few hundred metres from the Hanoverian crossing point. The general lesson one might draw from these arguments by analogy is that on commonsense grounds the present terminal point of agreed site locations in the Pass of Grange near Keith cannot be the end of the Roman line, whatever problems of date may be posed by the two very differing sites known at

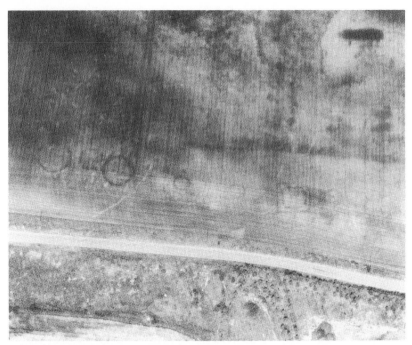

*Pl.V Cemeteries—Nairn West, Little Kildrummie: A near vertical view of the linear cemetery at Little Kildrummie (Fig.3.5). Note at least two square mortuary enclosures amongst the ring ditches (1986).*

Auchinhove and Muiryfold.[16] As a further extension of this line of argument one could adduce the map of first century finds from the area. This includes two finds of Domitianic *asses* of AD 86, namely the familiar pay issues known at Inchtuthil, Strageath, Cardean, Stracathro, Camelon, and other sites. These come from Forres, where two such coins may be involved, and from Fortrose, still an anchorage on the north side of the Moray Firth to be sought under stormy conditions.[17]

It will be clear enough from the preceding section that local topography is the controlling factor; likewise that there are great fluctuations in local geomorphology. Both factors require detailed understanding to explain site location and survival. Thus to summarise, east of the Spey podsolisation and surface erosion through aeolian action are major problems affecting the recognition and survival of archaeological features. On the fluvio-glacial gravels west of the Spey major flood sequences (eg. on the lower Findhorn at Forres) and the erosion or deposition caused by sandstorms (the 'blows') have the same effect in archaeological terms. Nonetheless amidst the tens of curvilinear crop mark sites described on the

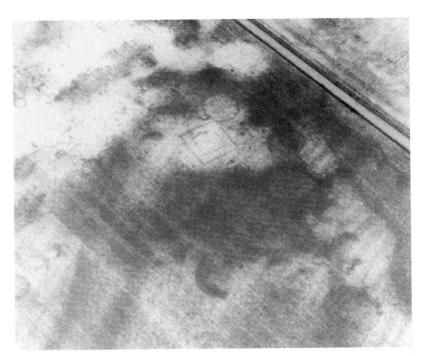

*P.VI   Cemeteries—Nairn West, Kinchyle: The presumed mortuary enclosure and ring ditch at Kinchyle showing remarkably in a crop of peas (1986). Note also the traces of other penannular and circular features probably forming an extensive settlement (Fig.3.5).*

previous pages a very small but obvious number exhibit the morphology of Roman military sites, the location of which is best explicable in terms of the influence of any westward invasion along the Laigh of Moray. Thus a rectilinear site at Boyndie west of Banff controlling the coastal corridor to the west and access to the sea morphologically resembles a small camp or fort at the point where both subsequent Edwardian and Hanoverian invaders sought to gain the coast from the Deveron valley. At the Spey crossing, if the overbuilt site at Bellie is indeed Roman as is generally supposed,[18] detailed reconstruction of its shape from the archive of the Gordon Estate and Luftwaffe air photographs demonstrates that with a size of less than six acres it is unlikely to have formed a temporary camp comparable with evidence from the far larger examples in the nearby Pass of Grange.

This is not the place to expatiate on the evidence from Bellie but west of the Spey we enter for Romanists uncharted ground [19] where detailed

*Pl.VII   Settlement—Brackla: The crisply preserved remains of a presumed settle-
ment with traces of an internal palisade (1984). Note the fainter remains
of a similar feature (bottom).*

knowledge of geomorphological change within the proto-historical period
is a pre-condition. Thus the rectilinear site at Thomshill south of Elgin
(Figs.3.1, 2.3), investigated by C M Daniels of the University of Newcastle
upon Tyne, is only comprehensible in the light of the vastly greater size of
Loch Spynie and its effect on the lower Lossie system at the time together
with the discovery of a substantial native settlement nearby at Hillhead
(Pl.VIII). On the site itself the V-shaped ditches with cleaning slot are
classics of their kind but also show that to one side at least two metres of
soil has been eroded through aeolian action. Small wonder then that, like
Boyndie, no internal features survive, only the ditch circuit.[20]

The next logical position of strategic significance must have been the
Findhorn crossing on the south side of Findhorn Bay west of Forres
(Fig.3.7). After repeated search, exceptional soil moisture deficit in early
July 1989 produced the north-western corner of a site morphologically
resembling a Roman fort or camp (Pl.IX). The discovery was indeed
fortunate because most of the site proved to have been levelled by the
massive 1829 flood. At the surviving corner, however, not only has the
ditch been recovered but also the post-holes of a six-posted timber tower
suggesting that the site was more than purely temporary.

*Pl.VIII    Part of the extensive settlement at Hillhead, Birnie, south of Elgin. The site of Thomshill lies 1 km. to the south-east.*

Some seventeen miles further west at the edge of the main settlement concentration in Strathnairn and close to the land corridor of the Croy ridge lies the site of East Galcantray, Cawdor, astride a flat shelf slightly raised above the valley floor (Pl.X). Again the site has suffered very extensively from erosion, this time the loss of over fifty per cent of the interior, also in the 1829 flood, as attested by eye-witness accounts. In five seasons of excavation the surviving interior has yielded evidence of a V-shaped ditch with a single recut, a box rampart with the south gate and southern-western corner tower, associated road and rectilinear timber buildings suggestive of barracks. The Carbon 14 date recovered from the demolition of these timber buildings falls into the bracket 1880 +/− 20 B.P.; 80-130 cal A.D. (GrN-14643) and, despite the lack of readily diagnostic finds, when taken with the structural evidence now available makes it very difficult to argue against identification as a briefly held (three years at most) single period fort; from the literary sources we know that the only possible historical context within the dating bracket lies in the mid-to-late eighties A.D. and the campaigns of Agricola or his unknown successor

*Pl.IX    Forres: The distinctive curved corner of a Roman camp located and test
excavated on the edge of the floodplain of the Findhorn at Balnageith (1989).
One of the flood channels of the infamous 1829 storm accounts for the darker
colour of the lower picture (Fig.3.7).*

prior to the abandonment of the northernmost territorial holdings in
Britain by the Emperor Domitian.[21]

Amidst the generality of settlement sites from the later prehistoric to
Pictish periods these five sites — three of which were discovered and one
rediscovered from the air — form a distinct group to which that at Tarradale at the head of the Beauly Firth may be added. They compare either
morphologically or through excavated evidence with Roman military sites
elsewhere, and by their locations logically spaced along the Laigh lend
weight to Tacitus' claim that following Domitian's policy the whole of
Britain had been overrun but almost immediately abandoned; the brevity
of occupation, exactly paralleled at Forres and Cawdor, explains the lack
of artefacts recovered.

Another even smaller group is arguably of early medieval date and
religious by association. These comprise two polygonal enclosures that
find no parallels in the morphology of the prehistoric settlement evidence.

*Pl.X   Easter Galcantray, Cawdor: Photographed in 1984, this oblique view shows the site on a central ridge massively eroded by the River Nairn in the 1829 floods. The single ditch forming the southern side is broken by an entrance excavated in 1986 and less than half the western side has survived erosion. Excavation continues.*

Both occur alongside sites of known religious significance. The enclosure at Portmahomack mentioned at the end of the descriptive section appears to form a lay enclosure attached to the churchyard with its evidence of eighth century carving suggesting the additional possibility of a *scriptorium* nearby.[22] The second, shown in Pl.XI, is a distinct polygonal enclosure alongside the oval enclosure of the church at Birnie south of Elgin. Birnie was the original early medieval seat of the Bishopric of Moray prior to its removal first to Spynie then to Elgin. The associated enclosure at Birnie can best be interpreted as the circuit of the early lay enclosure. As such it finds parallels with the church and lay enclosure from Ninkirk near Brougham in Cumbria, as does the layout discovered at Portmahomack at Ruthwell across the Solway in Dumfries.

Altogether nearly eighty previously unknown sites have been located in Moray from the air whether through the contribution of the Moray Aerial

*Pl.XI  Medieval—Birnie: The small historic church at Birnie was the original seat of the Bishops of Moray. The remains of the old church are visible amid the trees, while to the left are cropmarks showing the former existence of a secular enclosure (1984).*

Survey described here or by other researchers such as Ian Shepherd for the Grampian Regional Council or Gordon Maxwell for the Royal Commission on the Ancient and Historical Monuments of Scotland. Whatever the source, corporately the new information has begun to reveal the buried location of the majority of sites originally occupying the more fertile lowlands of the Laigh, to counteract the prevailing academic picture derived from a minority of sites owing their upstanding survival to location on higher ground and consequently construction in stone. Moreover, within the broad corpus of new material we can now attempt to identify the differing morphology that may, with carefully selective excavation, help us to distinguish between prehistoric, Roman military, Pictish and early Christian sites.

**Notes**

1. L Alcock 'A Survey of Pictish Settlement Archaeology' in *The Picts: A new look at old problems* ed. A Small (Dundee, 1987) 7; I A G Shepherd 'Pictish Settlement Problems in N.E. Scotland' in *Settlement in North Britain, 1000 BC - AD 1000* edd. J C Chapman and H C Mytum (*British Archaeological Reports [BAR]* no.118, 1983) 327; T Watkins 'Where were the Picts?: an essay in settlement archaeology' in Small, *The Picts* 63. See also Shepherd in this volume.

2. A Small 'The Hillforts of the Inverness Area' in *The Hub of the Highlands* ed. L Maclean (Inverness, 1975) 65; D C W Sanderson, F Placido and J O Tate 'Scottish Vitrified Forts: The Results from Six Study Sites' *Nuclear Tracks Radiation Meas.*, 14, 1/2 (1988) 307.

3. I Ralston 'Portknockie: promontory forts and Pictish settlement in the North-East' in Small, *The Picts* 15; Sanderson *et al* 'Scottish Vitrified Forts'.

4. Sinclair Ross 'The Physical Background' in *The Moray Book* ed. D Omand (1976) 16. Cf. also B A Bagnold, *The Physics of Blown Sand and Desert Dunes* (1954), and Gillen and Ross in this volume.

5. R Young, *The Parish of Spynie* (Elgin 1871) 5; J D Peacock *et al*, *The Geology of the Elgin District* (HMSO, 1968).

6. B A Haggart, *Flandrian Sea Level Changes in the Moray Firth* (Unpublished PhD thesis, University of Durham, 1982).

7. G S Maxwell 'Recent Aerial Survey in Scotland' in *The Impact of Aerial Reconnaissance in Archaeology* (CBA Res. Report 49, 1983) 27; and 'Settlement in Southern Pictland: A New Overview' in Small, *The Picts* 32.

8. Maxwell 'Recent Aerial Survey' 33.

9. J B Stevenson 'Garbeg and Whitebridge: Two Square-Barrow Cemeteries in Inverness-shire'; L M M Wedderburn and D M Grime 'The Cairn Cemetery at Garbeg, Drumnadrochit'; and J Close-Brooks 'Pictish and Other Burials'; all in Small, *The Picts* at 145, 151 and 87 respectively.

10. F T Wainwright 'Souterrains in Scotland' *Antiquity* 22 (1953) 82.

11. I Ralston, K Sabine and W Watt 'Later prehistoric settlements in the North East: A Preliminary Assessment' in Chapman and Mytum *Settlement in North Britain* 149; I Ralston 'Portknockie: promontory forts and Pictish Settlement' 15. For Burghead, see Shepherd in this volume.

12. G D B Jones and D J Mattingley, *An Atlas of Roman Britain* (1990) 20.

13. G S Maxwell 'The Evidence of the Temporary Camps' in *Agricola's Campaigns in Scotland* (*Scottish Archaeological Forum* 12, 1981) ed. J Kenworthy, 25. This includes a bibliography of relevant J K St. Joseph articles.

14. J K St. Joseph 'The Camp at Durno and Mons Grampius' *Britannia* 9 (1978) 271-88; see also Maxwell 'The Evidence of the Temporary Camps'.

15. *Atlas of Roman Britain* 76.

16. Maxwell 'Evidence of the Temporary Camps' 25.

17. *Atlas of Roman Britain* 201.

18. O G S Crawford, *Topography of Roman Scotland* 122.

19. I Keillar 'In Fines Borestorum'; C M Daniels 'A Roman Castra at the Foths'; and G D B Jones 'A Roman Military Site at Cawdor?'; all in *Popular Archaeology* for April 1986 at 2, 10 and 13 respectively.

20. C M Daniels, forthcoming.

21. *Atlas of Roman Britain* 102.
22. And see John Higgitt 'The Pictish Latin inscription at Tarbat in Ross-shire' *PSAS* 112 (1982) 300; also Isabel Henderson, *The Art and Function of Rosemarkie's Pictish Monuments* (Groam House Museum Trust, Inverness 1990).

# THE PICTS IN MORAY
## Ian A G Shepherd

The Men of Moray, those difficult, pugnacious people who remained remote from central Scottish authority until as late as the second half of the 12th century, were possibly first depicted on one of the stones from Kinneddar now in Elgin Museum (Fig.4.1).[1] This shows both cavalry and foot soldiers, suggesting, as do other later Pictish carvings, the stratification of society into a warrior elite,[2] perhaps equating to knights, squires and freemen (plus a bonded class). The 26 carved stones from Kinneddar also serve to remind us both of the richness of the evidence for the Picts that is to be found in Moray and of its complexity. Such evidence should not, however, be used to build a picture of the Picts as mysterious or unknown: of the four peoples of early historic Scotland, divided by language rather than culture,[3] as much is now known of the Picts as of the Angles, Scots or Britons put together. We can also appreciate what Leslie Alcock has called the 'potential for balkanization'[4] that was caused by the existence of different kindreds within these four peoples, to which process the Men of Moray must have been potent contributors.

A geographical definition of Pictish Moray must look beyond the current western boundaries of the modern district or those of the old county, although the River Spey would seem to be a sensible eastern frontier with Buchan and Mar. The 12th-century *de Situ Albanie* names Moray and Ross as the vast territories of Fidach, one of the seven eponymous sons of Cruithne;[5] we must envisage Moray stretching west beyond the head of the Great Glen to Druim Alban, the ridge of the Moine.[6] Indeed, its influence once reached to Loch Alsh on the west coast,[7] but for the purposes of this article, we will concentrate on the area defined by the present district, with particular reference to the rocky coastal ridge between Burghead and Lossiemouth.

The antecedents of Pictish society in Moray can be found in the later prehistoric forts and settlements in the area and in such Celtic place-names as *Loxa*, which is generally taken to denote the River Lossie on Ptolemy's map.[8] The late Iron Age artefact evidence is also relevant; for example the fine metalwork from the Culbin Sands, including horse trappings and heavy bronze armlets,[9] indicate a Celtic society in which can be seen the origin of the Pictish fondness for patronage of elaborate crafts such as metalwork. 'The lord as giver of rings', the Anglo-Saxon epithet, applied equally to the warrior aristocracy of Pictish Moray. On the cross slab in Elgin Cathedral is a rare scene of hawking, depicting a grouse, two dogs, and a horseman with a hawk: an activity that combined the sport of potentates with training for military service.[10] Smyth provides a succinct summary of current thought on the origins and nature of Pictish society:

*Fig.4.1  Kinnedar. Carving of
men and horses.*

'an indigenous servile population ruled by a warrior Celtic aristocracy
whose origins may have lain in different parts of the wider Celtic
world, but whose essential cultural unity was sufficiently self-evident
to draw from Tacitus the comment that the northern Britons were
basically no different from their cousins in the south and further afield
in Gaul'.[11]

The surviving evidence for the Picts in Moray consists of thirteen symbol
stones, plus the six surviving bull stones from Burghead, three cross slabs
as well as some late carvings such as Sueno's stone and the Kinneddar
group.[12] In addition there are several forts, some better associated with
the Picts than others,[13] some probable burial sites revealed by aerial photography and, towards the end of our period, two important ecclesiastical
foci, Kinneddar and Birnie. That is to say, the evidence is concentrated in
the Laich, although certain important groups of evidence are also to be
found along the Spey, for example the group of four symbol stones at St
Peter's, Inveravon.[14] In addition, place-names such as the well-known *pit*
(*pett*, a piece [of land]) and *cardden* (copse) and *pres* (thicket) seem to be
of genuine Pictish origin.[15] Fraser has recently suggested that the surviving
names may indicate 'a form of settlement that existed in a heavily forested
landscape'.[16] All this evidence is combined in Fig.4.2.

76

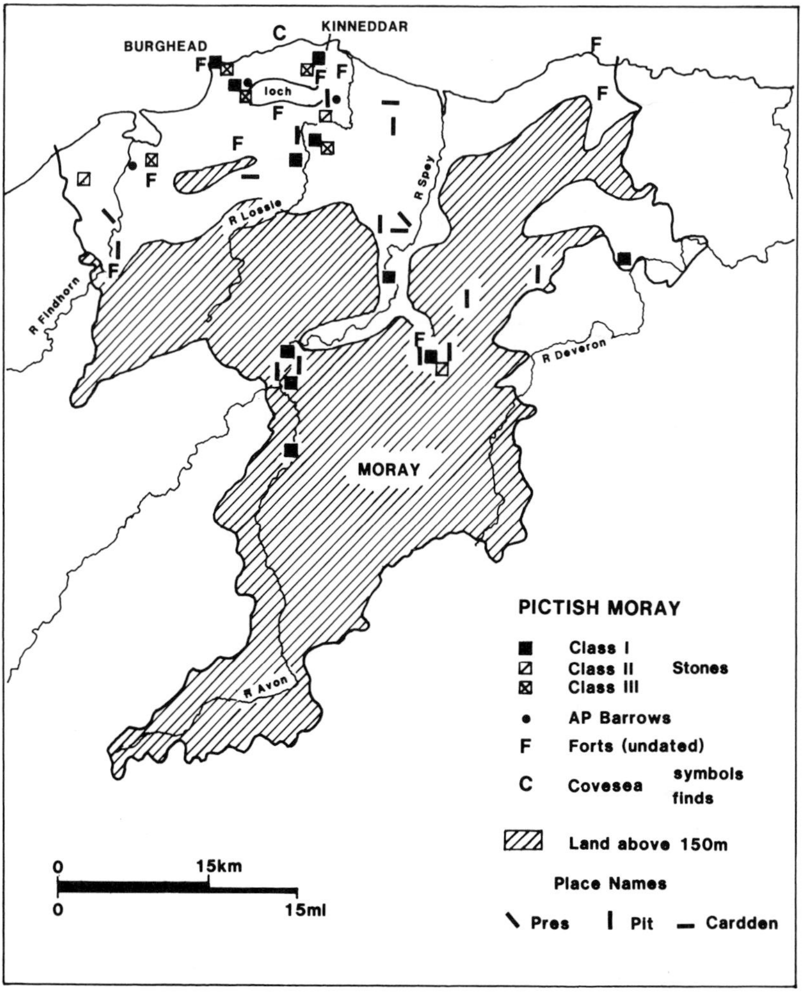

KINNEDDAR
BURGHEAD
C
F
loch
R Spey
R Lossie
R Findhorn
R Deveron
R Avon
MORAY
PICTISH MORAY
Class I
Class II
Class III
Stones
AP Barrows
Forts (undated)
Covesea
symbols finds
Land above 150m
Place Names
Pres
Pit
Cardden
0
15km
0
15ml


*Fig.4.2 Pictish Moray.*

The most important area is the sandstone coastal ridge running between Burghead and Lossiemouth which shelters a number of sites of almost unique character in Pictish times. They include Burghead, the largest (by a factor of three) fortified site in early historic Scotland; the Sculptor's Cave, Covesea, a cave site of apparently ritual significance, and Kinneddar, imperfectly understood in all its aspects but which presents evidence of having been a place of manufacture of early Christian crosses long before its role as one of the pre-13th century seats of the bishops of Moray.[17] The Burghead-Covesea ridge would have been an island, literally because of the extent the Loch of Spynie,[18] and figuratively owing to the agglomeration of Pictish power which such sites represented. These three sites will be examined in more detail.

The fort of Burghead bestrode a headland thrust into the Moray Firth (see Fig.2.4). Three hectares were enclosed by three cross ramparts of considerable size: the Doorie Hill, on which the culmination of the annual fire festival known as the Clavie takes place, itself of considerable antiquity,[19] represents the last remnants of the innermost line. Inside lay a citadel, separated from a lower ward by a cross rampart, and the famous well, a subterranean vaulted chamber, 4.9 m square and 3.7 m high, containing a rockcut basin.[20]

The subject of much debate, the 'Roman' or more properly 'Baillies' [in the bailey of the fort?] well should be seen in the context of other elaborate water sources in places of later prehistoric power. For example finely constructed wells or chambers are found beneath northern brochs such as Warebeth (Stromness Cemetery),[21] Knowe of Burrian, Harray (the find-spot, significantly of the fine Class 1 eagle stone),[22] Midhowe in Rousay,[23] — all Orkney — Crosskirk, Caithness,[24] and indeed at the important Pictish settlement on the Brough of Birsay, also in Orkney.[25] Such structures should not be viewed as merely utilitarian: water shrines were of considerable importance to the Celtic peoples,[26] while it has recently been suggested that the Burghead well itself may have been used as a drowning pool.[27]

The dating of Burghead relies on a range of radiocarbon dates from rampart timbers which indicate occupation between the fifth and seventh centuries AD, although the possibility of earlier (and later) habitation cannot be ruled out.[28] In particular, one third-century date and the configuration of three cross ramparts, unique among Pictish promontory forts, suggest that a pre-Roman Iron Age fort remains a possibility to be confirmed by further excavation.[29] Certainly, a stone head discovered in Burghead of possible Celtic origin which was recently reported to Inverness Museum would support such a possibility.[30]

The identification of the *munitio* of King Brude (mentioned by Adomnan) is still uncertain; it is generally held to have been in the vicinity of the Great Glen, not far to the south of the Beauly Firth,[31] probably at Craig Phadraig or Urquhart.[32] Yet the sheer size of Burghead when compared with the relatively tiny areas enclosed at both sites[33] (or at Castle Hill, Inverness, another candidate[34]) leads to speculation that Burghead could have been in the top grade of Pictish royal sites, equivalent to a *civitas*.[35] This is particularly so if its various rare or unique features are considered.

These include the hierarchy of space which its upper and lower wards display, although the division of space has not been developed as far (because of a less suitable topography?), as at that other possible *civitas*-equivalent in Pictland, Dundurn in Perthshire.[36] Other unique features include the use of nails or augered-in spikes,[37] to fasten the rampart timbers, the famous series of bull stones[38] apparently mounted high in the wall as a frieze[39] and the Anglo-Saxon blast-horn mount[40] whose military connotations are entirely appropriate to a royal site.

The fragments of an early Christian corner-post shrine, dating from the late seventh or early eighth century[41] found in the modern cemetery within the area of the fort and now in the Burghead Library are also significant to this discussion as they are an unusual discovery in a Pictish fort, but one that might be interpreted as a survival from the 'impact phase' of conversion at a royal centre. The Burghead shrine is represented by the roughly square corner-post with two grooves and a zone of crude relief interlace on an outer face[42] and a low relief hunting scene.[43] It is assumed that the shrine must have stood against a wall in a church or chapel, presumably of monastic origin[44] which prompts the questions: was there indeed an early monastic foundation at Burghead; if so, where precisely was it situated; and whose relics did the shrine house?

The precise end of Burghead is as intriguing as its putative beginning. The burnt rampart core indicates a conflagration, presumably terminal. Certainly Small could detect no signs of gradual decay of the wall, and so he surmised a swift end.[45] Undoubtedly burning was a favoured method of attack in the early historic period,[46] but whether this fire did indeed lead to the abandonment of the fort is unclear as there is evidence of repairing of the rampart and the latest Carbon 14 date calibrates to between 855 and 1040, i.e. most probably into the 10th century. That is to say, it is conceivable that Burghead, like Green Castle, Portknockie, 25 miles further east, which has a very late wall,[47] could have inhibited Norse expansion into Moray.

The absence of extensive evidence of Norse occupation in Grampian may be due to such strong coastal defences and entrenched Pictish presence, although responsibility for the final conflagration should probably rest with the Vikings.[48] The existence of a Pictish navy is also relevant to such speculation, given the reference in the Annals of Ulster to the Orkneys being 'destroyed by Brude' in AD 681.[49] It is certainly possible that the forts of the north coast such as Burghead or Green Castle, Portknockie were 'home ports', overlooking galleys readied for war.[50]

Three miles to the east of Burghead, in a cliff of sandstone, is the Sculptor's Cave, Covesea, so named from the symbols carved at the entrance.[51] The precise function that this deep coastal cave performed in Pictish times is still far from clear in spite of two campaigns of excavation.[52] Covesea had seen a long period of use during the late Bronze Age largely as a settlement site, albeit one where a surprisingly large quantity of fine metalwork was lost and/or deposited. The evidence of subsequent use indicates that the cave was not a settlement site in Pictish times. This conclusion is drawn from three types of evidence which cannot be related closely.

First, the later phases of use consisted of sterile layers of soft humic material spread in the entrance passages, which material was never consolidated by regular trampling. Second, a range of small bronze objects (fourth-century Roman bronze coins — range AD 353 to 365[53] — tweezers, and ten ring-headed pins, one of which was silver, comprising three types[54]) was deposited inside the cave (the coins concentrating around square B4[55]) perhaps in a single event sometime in the late fourth century or slightly later.[56] Third, at least fifteen Pictish symbols were carved on the walls and roof of the entrance passages.[57]

We do not understand how the Picts used such caves as this great cavern at Covesea or the Wemyss caves in Fife.[58] Henderson has suggested a role in the manufacture or dissemination of metalwork, in particular the Pictish chains, for the Fife examples.[59] No evidence of metalworking was recovered from Covesea and no such chains are known from Moray (while the Gaulcross hoard[60] was found around 30 miles to the east), but the Sculptor's Cave did produce a proto-hand pin amongst its pins and other, perhaps more tenuous links have been suggested.[61] Given the proximity of both the Sculptor's Cave and the Wemyss caves to kingly forts (Burghead and Clatchard Craig respectively[62]) it is possible that the explanation of the caves lies in the area of ceremonial related to the forts.

Certainly in the case of Covesea, the recent discovery in Aberdeen University of a manuscript report alluding to the 'two thousand' human bones which Miss Benton recovered from the cave but which were not included in the excavation report must raise the suggestion of an ossuary, but of what date cannot now be determined. Even if it were to have been of late Bronze Age or early Iron Age date, it is conceivable that its ritual importance was still potent in Pictish times, perhaps similar to the propinquity of Pictish sculpture in Aberdeenshire to prehistoric ritual sites noted by Inglis.[63] In this context the simple Latin crosses on the west wall of the west entrance (which are closely similar to ones in the Wemyss caves[64]) could be seen as a continuation or recognition of a long-established ritual use for the site, a recognition that seems to have persisted for some time, given the fine Russian cross dated to the 12th century or somewhat later by R B K Stevenson (pers. comm.) on the west wall of the east entrance. (The significance of the simple crosses to a consideration of Christianity in Moray is discussed below.)

Finally, further comment on the Sculptor's Cave, Covesea may be confined to noting a greater range of accomplishment in the carving of the symbols than is sometimes supposed for Pictish cave art. In all, the fifteen symbols[65] range from the crude and basic, such as the crescent and V-rod on the west wall of the west entrance,[66] to the stylish and orthodox, such as the triple oval and flower on the roof of the entrance (Fig.4.3).[67] An early date for the symbols found in caves was proposed some time ago.[68] The radiocarbon dating of a stone from Pool, Sanday, Orkney[69] bearing a symbol of equal simplicity to, say, one of the Covesea crescents and V-rods, to a date between the fifth and sixth centuries might seem to support the early dating of the cave symbols. However, all that the Pool date and the range of symbols at Covesea really indicate is that the development of Pictish art was a lengthy process, stretching over several centuries.[70] (Stevenson's view that the symbols found on the prestigious metalwork are the earliest and among the best, albeit starting comparatively late, in the seventh century, and that the so-called 'primitive' symbols are degenerate should also be noted.[71])

*Fig.4.3    Covesea. Triple oval and flower.*

East again along the sandstone rige, beside Lossiemouth, is Kinneddar, one of the pre-13th century seats of the Bishops of Moray.[72] The *New Statistical Account* describes a formidable medieval castle, with a central tower and hexagonal surrounding walls backed by earthen ramparts of possibly earlier date whose levelling revealed a cist cemetery:

'The great tower of Kinneddar was defended by two walls, about 50 paces from each other, each wall having its ditch in front, and, what was more uncommon, an earthen rampart, from eight to ten feet wide, and as many feet high, behind each wall. The space enclosed comprehended about two acres, the form aproaching to a hexagon .... The fortifications on the east side were guarded by a morass, and two ditches, one of 24 and, a little beyond it, another of 12 feet wide.... The labourers who filled up the ditches were astonished at the quantity of ashes and oak charcoal, and the number of broken urns and human bones they met with, in levelling these earthen ramparts, more especially under their foundations ... the present incumbent examine[d] more minutely what remained of the earthen rampart ... under the foundations he found the graves closely packed. On removing the earth, there appeared first peat or turf ashes, then within the rude stone chest, oak charcoal, and some fragments of human bones.[73]

The account goes on to describe two types of cist: those with dressed stones contained smooth ashes of oak charcoal and very little bone, those of 'rude' construction had more turf ashes, less oak charcoal and imperfectly cremated bones. What can be made of this extraordinarily tantalising account and what relevance does it have to the story of the Picts in Moray?

Today the evidence consists of a dark cropmark on an early RAF air photograph,[74] which seems to show one of the angles of the hexagonal enclosure, the foundation courses of the middle of the north wall of the graveyard which are unusually massive[75] and the collection of 25 carved fragments found in the kirkyard walls and now in Elgin Museum,[76] some of which indicate that slabs bearing angular crosses were being manufactured on site.[77] The excavations in 1939 by Gordonstoun School at Kinneddar were never published, but interesting results are now coming from geophysical survey.[78] One carved fragment is of considerable interest: the high relief carving of David the Shepherd rending the lion's jaw[79] which is comparable to one of the scenes on the St Andrews sarcophagus of the later eighth or very early ninth century.[80] With its local school of stone carving and earthen ring work built over a cist cemetery of uncertain date (although it should be remembered that the Pictish cist grave at Easterton of Roseisle probably contained a cremation) does Kinneddar represent an early monastic enclosure similar to that postulated for St. Andrews, which site also had its own school of stone carving?[81]

Kinneddar is clearly vital to a consideration of the beginnings of Christianity in Moray. In this discussion, its potential relationship with the great fort at Burghead should be borne in mind, particularly if, as is suggested above, the Burghead/Lossiemouth ridge functioned as an island of royal power with a range of inter-related sites. It has already been suggested (above p.79) that the corner-post shrine from Burghead, which dates from the late seventh or early eighth century[82] and has at any rate a respectable pagan background as merely an above ground cist,[83] could represent one of the earliest manifestations of Christianity in Moray, if not the conversion phase then certainly a time when relic cults were in full swing.[84]

For the purposes of this review the reservations that can be expressed about the evidence for the extent of seventh-century Columban Christianity in Pictland as a whole[85] are taken to apply with even greater force to Pictish Moray. The technique of corner grooving seen on the Burghead corner-post shrine was a trait of ultimately Classical Mediterranean origin which came to Pictland via Northumbria,[86] possibly through contact during the seventh century.[87] By extension, the cross slabs and relief sculpture from Kinneddar (and the putative ditched enclosure) could represent the establishment of a more concrete faith during the eighth century, one in a suitable location to be supported by royal patronage. In any event, the range of carved fragments indicate that a religious centre was in existence at Kinneddar by 934, the traditional date of St. Gerardine/Gervadus's oratory at *Kenedor*.[88]

Other indications of early Christian activity are the simple Latin crosses incised on the west wall of the west entrance at Covesea which could conceivably reflect the 'eremetic and ascetic' tradition of the Columban church,[89] although reservations about its impact in Moray have already been expressed. The establishment and subsequent development of Christianity elsewhere in Moray may also be traced in such sites as Birnie kirk with its early bell,[90] class III fragments[91] and the recently discovered adjacent cropmark enclosure;[92] the simple Class IV[93] cross stone from Botriphnie[94] (whether indicating the spread of Irish-based monasticism,[95] a Ninianic presence[96] or a connection with the techniques used to incise symbols[97] remains to be determined); the cross slabs at Elgin, Brodie and Roseisle (now at Altyre),[98] the last two bearing ogam inscriptions (probably derived from the activities of Irish churchmen);[99] the more distant cross slab of Mortlach (perhaps an early church site),[100] and the great preaching cross — 'the most awe-inspiring in northern Britain'[101] — and/or cenotaph of Sueno's Stone.

Moray can also offer some important evidence of Pictish burial sites. The cist grave with re-used symbol stone as side slab at Easterton of Roseisle[102] has been known since last century but over the last thirteen years air photography has identified three locations in the Laich where the cropmarks of square barrows, presumptively of Pictish date may be seen in suitable conditions. At Pitairlie (coincidentally, not a Pictish name but a 19th-century creation[103]), north-east of Elgin, is a line of contiguous square features, two of which have circular internal marks (Fig.4.4), while

*Fig.4.4    Pitairlie. Possible Pictish burial site.*

at Greshop, west of Forres, a small group of square barrows is in close proximity to a larger double square enclosure with gaps at the corners. This last feature has echoes of late Iron Age ritual features such as the shrine at Heathrow, Middlesex,[104] but a much closer parallel lies at the Pictish cemetery at Garbeg, Drumnadrochit,[105] almost certainly in association with a symbol stone. The third possible site is at Alves (Fig 4.2.)

Other square barrow cemeteries of presumptively Pictish date on the coastal plain of the Moray Firth include Hills of Boyndie, Banff[106] and Gollanfield, Nairn.[107] Further afield the Dairy Park, Dunrobin produced a class 1 stone over a female grave.[108] The mix of square and round forms evident in some of these sites has been interpreted as the result of uncertainty at the time of conversion.[109] In this connection the putative role of the symbol stones both as memorials and markers of territory represent two potentially powerful explanations for these stones,[110] which interpretation may be expanded by viewing them as 'ideological technology' legitimizing the 'emergence of a powerful, unified Pictish monarchy'.[111]

Finally, Sueno's Stone at the western approach to the Burghead/

Lossiemouth island, the core of Pictish Moray, provides an insight into the society of the ninth century. The battle scene on the reverse[112] with its competing armies, single combat of champions, piles of headless corpses and the formal execution of the defeated champion demonstrates the aptness of Leslie Alcock's phrase 'two ideologies which saw their birthright in genocide'[113] to describe relations between the Picts and Scots. The full reality of a society predicated on the endemic violence of historic kingship[114] is difficult to grasp. Certainly one should be cautious of '... images drawn from [literary] compositions that glorify the behaviour and values of the armed elite for whom they were composed: a kind of self-vindicating in-house propaganda. These elites could just as well be viewed as unscrupulous aristocratic groups at the head of strict social hierarchies, prepared to kill for material gain and prestige, and to exploit and appropriate as a social right'.[115]

Given that the head-hunting theme evident on Sueno's Stone has deep Celtic Iron Age roots (although Ian Keillar (pers. comm.) sees the 'broch' as Nebuchadnezzar's furnace: — and it also could be a scene similar to the Glamis cauldron with legs protruding, used by Anna Ritchie as an illustration of possible ritual drowning[116]) it is all the more remarkable that Sueno's Stone also links us with the time of conversion through the mighty twenty feet tall cross on the other face. Preaching cross, cenotaph or a minatory boundary stone remembering perhaps a battle over the Norse in Orkney? (For Sueno's Stone see also contributions in this volume by Jackson and by Sellar).

There may of course be other sites of Pictish date in Moray. The best candidate as defended settlement is the Doune of Relugas at the confluence of the Divie and the Findhorn which is a classic early historic fort site with a craggy stepped profile eminently suitable for expressing the hierarchical divisions of Pictish society.[117] Evidence of vitrification was seen in 1976[118] while the ring-headed pin from the site is another suggestive pointer.[119] It has recently been claimed that as many as 50% or so of conventional pre-Roman Iron Age forts in Scotland are in fact early historic in some phase of use or construction.[120] Sites such as Cluny Hill, Forres, or the Knock of Alves are relevant here, while to the east, Ian Ralston's meticulous excavations at the Green Castle, Portknockie have demonstrated that it was clearly an important local centre of Pictish power.[121]

Although the ultimate end of Pictish Moray lay in absorption, in a united Scotland under the descendants of the Scots of Dal Riada, the rulers of Moray in the late ninth, tenth and even early eleventh centuries maintained an element of independence. It can be suggested from tenth- and eleventh- century records that Moray was autonomous, for the ruling dynasty in Moray 'traced their descent from a different branch of the original Irish settlers of Dalriata than did the mac Alpin dynasty':[122] the Cenel Loairn rather than the Cenel Gabrain, which division may have perpetuated 'the ancient division between northern and southern Pictland'.[123] (The most famous scion of this dynasty was MacBeth, son of Finlay mormaer of Moray, whose career is considered later in this collection.)

This division may be reflected in the usage 'king of Scots' in the Norse sagas to refer to tenth-century mormaers of Moray.[124] Certainly these sources also illustrate that the absorption of the northern Picts was accelerated by Norse pressure.[125] We have already seen that the date of the wall at Green Castle, Portknockie is late enough to represent defence against the Vikings, while Burghead was also burnt. (Dunnottar was certainly destroyed between 889 and 900). The Caithness part of Moray and Ross was conquered by Sigurd the Mighty (d c 892) in a bitter struggle,[126] while it is possible that the rulers of Orkney and the king of Scots combined against the mormaer of Moray. However, the tantalising reference in *Jarls Saga* to Sigurd building a fort 'in the south of Moray', which has been identified with Burghead,[127] remains unconfirmed. On the other hand, the suggestion that territorial reorganisation, caused by Norse pressure, is indicated by the appearance of a new series of regional names — 'Moray' for earlier 'Fidach' — is believable.[128]

Thus may we envisage that the potentate at Burghead and his system of taxation or tribute may well have underlain the feudal pattern of administration, parts of which survive to this day.

## Acknowledgments

I am indebted to Leslie Alcock, David Clarke, Ian Keillar, Ian Ralston, Anna Ritchie, David Sellar and my wife Alexandra for sharing insights into various aspects of Pictish Moray with me, and to Moira Greig for drawing the map.

## Notes

1. J Stuart, *The Sculptured Stones of Scotland* (Edinburgh 1856) pl CXXIX, no.13.
2. A P Smyth, *Warlords and Holy Men* (London 1984) 46.
3. L Alcock 'An Heroic Age: war and society in northern Britain, AD 450-850' (Rhind Lectures 1988-89: a synopsis) *PSAS* 118 (1988) 327.
4. Ibid., 327.
5. M O Anderson, *Kings and Kingship in Early Scotland* (Edinburgh and London 1980) 142-3, 245.
6. I Henderson 'Pictish territorial divisions', in *An Historical Atlas of Scotland c.400 - c.1600* edd. P McNeill and R Nicholson (Conference of Scottish Medievalists, St Andrews 1976) 9.
7. B E Crawford, *Scandinavian Scotland* (Leicester 1987) 67; G W S Barrow, *Kingship and Unity, Scotland 1000-1306* (London 1981) 25-6.
8. K H Jackson 'The Pictish language' in *The Problem of the Picts* ed. F T Wainwright (Edinburgh 1955) 136-8.
9. M MacGregor, *Early Celtic Art in North Britain* (Leicester 1976) 117, 214

10. L Alcock 'The activities of potentates in Celtic Britain, AD 500-800: a positivist approach', in *Power and Politics in Early Medieval Britain and Ireland* edd. S T Driscoll and M R Neike (Edinburgh 1988) 30.

11. Smyth, *Warlords* 54.

12. J Romilly Allen and J Anderson, *The Early Christian Monuments of Scotland* (Edinburgh 1903) 118-51.

13. A Small 'Iron Age and Pictish Moray' in *The Moray Book* ed. D Omand (Edinburgh 1976) 115.

14. *Early Christian Monuments* 152-4.

15. I Fraser 'Pictish place-names — some toponymic evidence', in *The Picts: a new look at old problems* ed. A Small (Dundee 1987) 70.

16. Ibid.

17. I B Cowan and D E Easson, *Mediaeval Religious Houses: Scotland* (2nd ed. London & New York 1976) 206-7.

18. Sinclair Ross 'The Physical Background' in Omand, *Moray Book* 16.

19. A Mitchell 'Vacation notes in Cromar, Burghead and Strathspey' *PSAS* 10(1872-74) 647-63.

20. H W Young 'The ancient Bath at Burghead, with remarks on its origin as shewn by existing baths of the same shape and design' *PSAS* 24 (1889-90) 147-56.

21. B Bell and C A Dickson 'Excavations at Warebeth (Stromness Cemetery) Broch, Orkney' *PSAS* 119 (1989) 101-31.

22. RCAHMS, *Inventory of Orkney* (Edinburgh 1946) 17; I Henderson, *The Picts* (London 1967) p.37.

23. RCAHMS, *Orkney* 199.

24. H Fairhurst, *Excavations at Crosskirk Broch, Caithness* (Edinburgh 1984) 58 (*Soc.Antiq.Scot. Monogr. Ser.* no.3)

25. C L Curle, *Pictish and Norse finds from the Broch of Birsay*, 1934-7 (Edinburgh 1982) 18 (*Soc. Antiq. Scot. Monogr. Ser.* no.1.)

26. A Ross, *Pagan Celtic Britain* (London 1967); C Thomas, *Celtic Britain* (London 1986) 25.

27. A Ritchie, *Picts* (Edinburgh 1989) 15.

28. J MacDonald 'Historical notices of "the Broch" or Burghead, in Moray, with an account of its antiquities' *PSAS* 4 (1860-1) 312-69; H W Young 'Notes on the ramparts of Burghead as revealed by recent excavations' *PSAS* 26 (1890-1) 436-7; H W Young 'Notes on further excavations at Burghead' *PSAS* 27 (1892-3) 86-91; A Small 'Burghead' *Scot. Archaeol. Forum* 1 (1969) 61-8; I B M Ralston and K Edwards 'New dating and environmental evidence from Burghead Fort, Moray' *PSAS* 109 (1977-8)202-10; Ritchie, *Picts* 12-15.

29. I B M Ralston 'Portknockie: promontory forts and Pictish settlement in the North-East' in Small, *The Picts* 16; L Alcock 'A survey of Pictish settlement archaeology' *Pictish Studies* edd. J G P Friell and W G Watson (Oxford 1984) 21 (*Brit. Archaeol. Rep.* no.125.)

30. Jill Harden, pers. comm.

31. *Adomnan's Life of St. Columba* edd. A O and M O Anderson (London 1961)39, 83.

32. Smyth, *Warlords* 103.

33. A Small and M B Cottam, *Craig Phadrig* (Dundee 1972) (Univ. Dundee, Dept. Geog. Occas. Pap. no.1.); S Foster, S T Driscoll and L Alcock, *Excavations at Urquhart and Dunnottar Castles 1983 & 1984: interim reports* (Glasgow 1985) (Univ. Glasgow, Dept. Archaeol.)

34. E Alcock 'Enclosed places, AD 500 - 800' in Driscoll and Neike, *Power and Politics* 44.

35. Alcock 'Heroic Age' 329.

36. Ibid.

37. Young, 'Notes on the ramparts'; Ralston 'Portknockie' 16.

38. The other examples from Inverness and Lomond Hills Fife are castrates: Alcock 'Heroic Age' 330.

39. MacDonald 'Historical notices'.

40. J Graham-Campbell 'The 9th-century Anglo-Saxon Horn-mount from Burghead, Morayshire, Scotland' *Medieval Archaeol.* 17 (1973) 43-51.

41. A C Thomas, *The Early Christian Archaeology of North Britain* (Glasgow 1971) 152; A C Thomas, *Celtic Britain* (London 1986) 147.

42. *Early Christian Monuments* fig.141, no.11.

43. Ibid., fig.138, no.7.

44. Thomas, *Early Christian Archaeology* 157; *Celtic Britain* 147; Ritchie, *Picts* 15.

45. Small 'Burghead' 66.

46. Alcock 'Activities of potentates' 32.

47. I B M Ralston 'The Green Castle, Portknockie, and the promontory forts of North-East Scotland' *Scot. Archaeol. Forum* 10 (1980) 32; Ralston 'Portknockie'.

48. Ritchie, *Picts* 15.

49. Anderson, *Kings and Kingship* 175.

50. Ralston 'Portknockie' 22; A Ritchie 'Orkney in the Pictish Kingdom' in *The Prehistory of Orkney* ed. C Renfrew (Edinburgh 1985) 203.

51. C Gordon-Cumming, *Memories* (Edinburgh & London 1904) 56-62.

52. S Benton 'The excavation of the Sculptor's Cave, Covesea, Morayshire' *PSAS* 65 (1930 -3) 177-216; I A G Shepherd 'Pictish settlement problems in North-East Scotland' in *Settlement in North Britain 1000BC - 1000AD* edd. J Chapman and H Mytum (Oxford 1983) 333-4. (Brit. Archaeol. Rep. no.118).

53. M Sekulla, pers. comm.

54. R B K Stevenson 'The earlier metalwork of Pictland' in *To illustrate the monuments: Essays on archaeology presented to Stuart Piggott* ed. J V S Megaw (London 1976) 247.

55. Benton 'Sculptor's Cave' 212-16.

56. Shepherd 'Pictish settlement problems' 334.

57. RCAHMS, *Pictish Symbol Stones: a handlist of 1985* (Edinburgh 1985) 10: note that its reference to Shepherd 1983 should be to Shepherd 1983 as in note 52 above.

58. Anon., *Fife's early archaeological heritage: a guide* (Glenrothes 1989)58-9.

59. I Henderson 'The silver chain from Whitecleugh, Shieldholm Crawfordjohn, Lanarkshire' *Trans Dumfriesshire Galloway Nat.Hist.Antiq.Soc.* 54 (1979) 26.

60. S Youngs, *'The Work of Angels', Masterpieces of Celtic metalwork 6th - 9th centuries AD* (London 1989) 26.
61. In Shepherd 'Pictish settlement problems' 334-5.
62. J Close-Brooks 'Excavations at Clatchard Craig, Fife' *PSAS* 116 (1986) 117-184, fiche 1:B1-C14.
63. J Inglis 'Patterns in stone, patterns in population: symbol stones seen from beyond the Mounth' in Small, *The Picts*; I B M Ralston and J Inglis, *Foul Hordes: the Picts in the North-East and their background* (Aberdeen 1984) 18.
64. *Early Christian Monuments* fig.37a.
65. RCAHMS, *Pictish Symbol Stones* 10.
66. *Early Christian Monuments* fig.135c.
67. Note that the illustration of this symbol in Shepherd 'Pictish settlement problems' fig.12b is not wholly accurate.
68. A C Thomas 'The interpretation of the Pictish symbols' *Archaeol.J.* 120 (1963) 30-97.
69. Ritchie, *Picts* 20.
70. Alcock 'Heroic Age' 331; *contra* J Close-Brooks, *Pictish Stones in Dunrobin Castle Museum* (Derby 1989) 2.
71. Stevenson 'Earlier metalwork' 248.
72. H B MacKintosh, *Pilgrimages in Moray: a guide to the County* (Elgin1924) 14, 75-6.
73. *NSA* (1840-45) xiii, 151-3.
74. RAF no. F21/82/955:0027-9.
75. A Keith, *The Parishes of Drainie and Lossiemouth* (Lossiemouth 1975) 20-3.
76. If the class I stone in the Royal Museum of Scotland is added, the total number of stones from Kinneddar is 26.
77. Eg. Elgin Museum no.1960.14.
78. N Q Bogdan, pers. comm.
79. Henderson, *Picts* 153, fig.37.
80. Ritchie, *Picts* 40.
81. Alcock 'Heroic Age' 332.
82. Thomas, *Early Christian Archaeology* 152; *Celtic Britain* 147.
83. A A M Duncan, *Scotland: the Making of the Kingdom* (Edinburgh 1975) 73.
84. Thomas, *Early Christian Archaeology* 148.
85. Eg. I Henderson 'Early Christian monuments of Scotland displaying crosses but no other ornament' in Small The Picts 45; K Hughes, *Early Christianity in Pictland* (Jarrow Lecture, 1970).
86. Thomas, *Early Christian Archaeology* 156; *Celtic Britain* 147-8.
87. Ritchie, *Picts* 30.
88. MacKintosh, *Pilgrimages in Moray* 75-6.
89. Ralston and Inglis, *Foul Hordes* 19.
90. A MacDonald and L Laing 'Early ecclesiastical sites in Scotland: a field survey, Part II' *PSAS* 102 (1969-70) 140-1.
91. *Early Christian Monuments* 136-7.
92. I Keillar and B Jones, pers. comm.
93. Henderson 'Early Christian Monuments' 46.

94. W D Simpson, *The Celtic Church in Scotland* (Aberdeen 1935) fig.15.
95. Thomas, *Early Christian Archaeology* 124-5.
96. Simpson, *Celtic Church*
97. Henderson 'Early Christian Monuments' 50.
98. Romilly Allen, *Early Christian Monuments* 132-6.
99. Ritchie, Picts 66; W M Calder and K H Jackson 'An inscription from Altyre' *PSAS* 90 (1956-7) 246-50.
100. MacDonald and Laing 'Early ecclesiastical sites' 142-3.
101. Alcock 'Heroic Age' 332.
102. *Early Christian Monuments* 124-6.
103. Ian Keillar, pers. comm.
104. B Cunliffe, *Iron Age Communities in Britain* (London 1978) 320.
105. L M M Wedderburn and D Grime, *A Cairn at Garbeg, Drumnadrochit* (Inverness 1975).
106. Ralston and Inglis, *Foul Hordes* 18.
107. G Maxwell 'Settlement in southern Pictland - a new overview' in Small, *The Picts* 34, fig.3; see also P J Ashmore 'Low cairns, long cists and symbol stones' *PSAS* (1978-80) 346-55.
108. J Close-Brooks 'Excavations in the Dairy Park, Dunrobin, Sutherland, 1977' *PSAS* 110 (1978-80) 328-45; and 'Pictish and other burials' in Friell and Watson, *Pictish Studies* 87-114.
109. Alcock 'Heroic Age' 332.
110. Ritchie, *Picts* 18.
111. S Driscoll 'Power and authority in early historic Scotland: Pictish stones and other documents' *PSAS* 116 (1986) 589.
112. Reading of stone after L Southwick, *The so-called Sueno's Stone at Forres* (Elgin 1981).
113. Alcock 'Heroic Age' 333.
114. ibid. 332.
115. P Garwood 'Social transformations and relations of power in Britain in the late fourth to sixth centuries AD' *Scot. Archaeol. Rev.* 6 (1989) 94.
116. Ritchie, *Picts* 14.
117. cf. L Alcock 'Reconnaissance excavations on Early Historic fortifications and other royal sites in Scotland, 3: Dundurn' *PSAS* 119 (1989) 189-226.
118. Ralston and Inglis, *Foul Hordes'* 25.
119. T Fanning 'Some aspects of the bronze ringed pin in Scotland' in *From the Stone Age to the 'Forty-Five'* edd. A O'Connor and D V Clarke (Edinburgh 1983) 324-42.
120. Alcock 'Heroic Age' 328.
121. Ralston 'Portknockie'.
122. Ralston and Inglis, *Foul Hordes* 16-17.
123. D P Kirby 'Moray prior to c.1100' in McNeill and Nicholson, *An Historical Atlas of Scotland* 20.
124. Crawford, *Scandinavian Scotland* 64.
125. Ibid., 48-9.
126. Ibid., 64.
127. Otherwise *Orkneyinga Saga* — see Crawford, *Scandinavian Scotland* 57.
128. Ibid., 58; Ralston and Inglis, *Foul Hordes* 16-17.

# FURTHER THOUGHTS ON SUENO'S STONE

## Anthony Jackson

The magnificently carved stone on the edge of the town of Forres, known as Sueno's stone, is classified as a Class III Pictish stone. It is 20 feet tall which is 7 times the width of the top of the monument — a point of some interest when we examine the composition of the decorated panels. The stone weighs some 7 tons and was probably first erected in the mid-9th century, to judge by the style of the decorations. Despite its current weathering, it probably lay buried (and protected) for several centuries before it was re-erected in its present position in the early 18th century. I believe that the stone was then put up back-to-front since the cross on the current west-face should have been facing the sunrise or east, like most Christian monuments.

Sacred stones are always perambulated in a sunwise fashion: east-south-west-north-east. Journeying around the stone we are confronted with a whole series of messages. These images are a deliberate attempt by the sculptors to tell a story and that is what we need to discover. In this task we will note the skill with which the whole composition is dominated by the number 7. All four sides of the stone are decorated in panels: the N and S faces are divided into 3 panels each while the E and W faces contain 4 panels — a total of 14 panels.

It will be seen that the 4 panels on the east face correspond *exactly* to those on the west face. If you refer to the sketch (Fig. 5.1, see also Figs. 6.1, 2 and 6 in the following article), then, panel A is opposite the ring-cross, panel B is opposite the cross-shaft, panel C corresponds to the 5 figures under the cross, while there is an uncarved section opposite panel D. It should be noted that panel A is twice the top width, panel B is 3 times the top width while panels C and D equal the top width: the sum total of panels is 7 times the top width. However, the length of the cross (A + B) is 5 times the top width, while at the top of panels A & B are 5 triumphant men. Is this significant?

I have discussed the composition of the panels in my book: *The Symbol Stones of Scotland* (1984). Briefly, panel A has 5 standing figures facing outwards and 8 horsemen, below them, riding from left to right. Now, if my idea is correct that this was originally the western face, then these riders are moving from *south to north*! Panel B, read downwards, has 5 standing figures above two groups of 4 men fighting; next is an execution scene with 7 decapitated bodies to the left of a group of 8 figures who seem to be celebrating this occasion; below the bodies are two pairs of fighting warriors while the bottom of the panel has 6 horsemen followed by 8 warriors, moving from south to north. Panel C depicts a tent (?) beneath which are a further 7 decapitated prisoners while all around are 8 pairs of

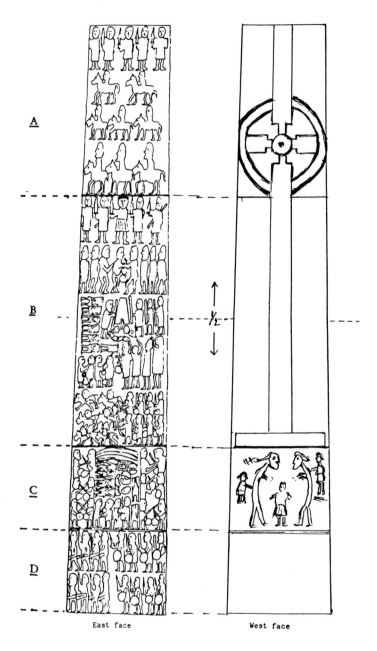

Below the figure:

East face         West face

*Fig.5.1*    *Sueno's Stone (author's sketch).*

92

fighting warriors. Panel D shows two groups of 4 warriors pursued by two other groups of 4 warriors holding spears and shields, moving from south to north.

It is clear that this stone commemorates the victory of the *southerners*, given my reading, and the corresponding defeat and execution of the *northerners*. I demonstrate in my book that if we divide the contending parties into two factions: left and right, then there is a total of 42 (7 × 6) to the left, losing side, and a total of 56 (7 × 8) for the winners. The grand total is thus 98 (= 7 × 7 × 2), including the 14 executed prisoners. As far as the living are concerned we find that the southerners outnumber the northerners by 2:1, actually 56:28. The reasons, I suggest, have to do with the composition of the two armies which are probably the Picts and the Scots.

The question arises why this stone was placed here at Forres? At that time, Forres was in the province of Moray, in the heart of the Northern Pictish Kingdom. The stone denotes a stunning defeat. It is unlikely that the Picts were commemorating their being simply vanquished by the Scots, for Kenneth MacAlpin did actually gain the Pictish crown in the mid-9th century, about the time the stone was erected in Class III Pictish style. Neither can one imagine some Christian Picts signifying a victory over the Norsemen or Scots. The skill and thought that went into this monument are tremendous for there is no parallel in the British Isles. The Norse did not erect such memorials in Scotland but the Scots did, to judge from all the Class III stones that dot the landscape, but only as claims on royal hunting demesnes. This suggestion arises because of the numerous hunting scenes with horsemen and dogs, chasing deer. Such stones are peaceful and not warlike claims.

The Pictish kingdom of Fidach, later called Moray and Ross, stretched between the river Spey to the river Oykell and the Dornoch Firth. This province was fiercely independent. Its rulers may have been based at Craig Phadraig and Cawdor in the region of Inverness. It was a centre of the Northern Picts who opposed the Christian Southern Picts, south of the Mounth. Now, Macbeth was a Mormaer (Great Steward) of Moray who seized the Scottish throne in 1040 from the descendants of Kenneth MacAlpin. Macbeth's wife, Gruoch, was first married to Gillacomgain, Mormaer of Moray, the very man who killed Macbeth's father, Findlaech, also Mormaer of Moray. This internecine feuding among generations of noble Scots for power was, perhaps, a continuation of the older confrontations between the Picts. The point is that Moray was a thorn in the side of both the Pictish and Scottish kings at Scone. This could be a clue to the position and style of Sueno's stone.

If, as I suggest, the stone is now the wrong way round then that means that the execution scenes faced west towards the power centre of Moray — something that the men of Moray could contemplate and reflect upon —

while to the east, was triumphant Christendom. The actual site is probably close to where the battle depicted took place, below the old Pictish fort of Burghead.

I suggest that this stone was erected by Kenneth MacAlpin to tell the Picts *in their own symbolic code* that they were vanquished. Why should there be two execution scenes? Why are only 7 people beheaded each time? Why are groups of 4 so prevalent?

In 839 the Norsemen defeated the men of Southern Pictland and killed the Pictish king Eoganan (Uuen, son of Oengus), the last recorded king of the Picts. This gave Kenneth the chance he was looking for and he made a bid for the kingship. Legend has it that Kenneth invited the Pictish nobles to a 'peaceful and truceful' banquet at Scone and had them murdered — this is what is represented in the lower execution scene, under a tent, I believe. At that time there were 7 kingdoms of the Picts: 7 in the south and 7 in the north, each ruled over by a 'king'. What Kenneth had done in Scone was to murder the chiefs of the 7 royal Southern lineages. The corresponding panel on the cross-side (Fig.6.6) confirms this interpretation: two large figures, with acolytes, are bending over a defaced central figure with kilt (much like the central figure in panel B). Could this not be a coronation scene of Kenneth — his rivals now dispatched? What about the two elongated figures? As they are under the cross, they must be Christians but are they archangels, saints or bishops? I would like to suggest they personify the two protective saints of the Scots: St. Columba and St. Andrew. It is interesting to note that the cult of St. Andrew appears to have emerged in the reign of Oengus II and his family (820-834). His elder brother and predecessor was named Constantine (789-820), and this was the first time that the name was used in the Scottish royal line. Interestingly enough, it was also said that St Andrew's relics came from Constantinople under the reign of the Eastern Roman emperor Constantine. I also think that a sister of that very Oengus, who ruled as king of the Scots and of the Picts married that Alpin who was the father of Kenneth MacAlpin and so provided his matrilineal claim to the Pictish throne — all this happening in a period of just a dozen years. What better symbolic coronation could there be than the joint blessing of the defender of the old Scottish Christianity (St Columba) and the new defender of the Catholic Church (St Andrew)? If this suggestion is correct, I believe the left-hand figure and his *lower* acolyte is St. Columba while the right-hand figure with his *higher* acolyte is St. Andrew, reflecting the constant predominance of the right-hand in the symbolic representations on this stone.

Let us return to panel A. We have five, very badly-weathered figures: Kenneth, flanked by his four sub-kings, above 8 riders. These are opposed, on the other side, by the ring-cross — symbolizing the triumph of the *true* Christians, at the top.

Panel B repeats the beginning of panel A: Kenneth (in kilt) flanked by his sub-kings ruling above 22 of his men and a mere 12 opponents. There are 7 executed men — the 7 rulers of the Northern Picts, defeated in battle. What is most intriguing is the 'bell', 'broch' or 'fort' which lies in the *dead centre* of the entire monument. Clearly, this is a ceremonial execution of the prisoners — their hands are tied behind their backs. We can only guess what form of ceremony this was but it is not vital to discover this for what is absolutely certain is that this beheading denotes the fruitlessness of *ever* rebelling against the powers of Kenneth. Remember that this monument is a piece of political propaganda, backed up by the sanction of the united Christian churches. The opposite side shows the 'rod' of the cross defeating unbelievers!

This star-studded case of 98 actors with all its intricate interlace patterns was not meticulously carved by the Picts for their own glorification on this stupendous monument when they were about to be defeated. It is a *definitive statement about the end of a particular era* — the end of the dominance of the Pictish lineages in the royal line of succession to the kingdom of the *Picts*. There can only be *one* man for whom this was an all-important message: Kenneth MacAlpin, the first king of *both* the Picts and the Scots. Never since his day, with the exception of the eruption of the Mormaer of Moray Macbeth, has the throne been wrested from the successors of Kenneth. Who, then, other than Kenneth, would have erected such a forbidding statement to the potentially rebellious Pictish/Scottish lieges of Moray in the 9th century? If it was not Kenneth, the erection of such a gigantic monumental stone seems an utter mystery. My suggestions might help to dispel some of the questions about this superb stone — now at last protected from natural and socially-caused destructive elements.

These suggestions are put forward simply to provoke discussion and offer some *possible* alternative solutions as to why this very special Pictish Class III stone was ever erected *at Forres*. I cannot definitively prove my case but I hope the explanation is a plausible one which also fits the general thesis I have put forward elsewhere about the Picts and their world-view.

**Bibliography**
A Jackson, *The Symbol Stones of Scotland* (Orkney Press, Stromness 1984)
A Jackson, *The Pictish Trail* (Orkney Press, Stromness 1989)
A P Smyth, *Warlords and Holy Men* (Arnold, London 1984)
L Southwick, *The so-called Sueno's Stone* (Moray District Libraries 1981)

*Fig.6.1   Sueno's Stone. West face: cross with panel below. (Crown Copyright: Historic Scotland)*

# SUENO'S STONE AND ITS INTERPRETERS

## David Sellar

Sueno's Stone is one of the most intriguing monuments in Scotland. It stands on the outskirts of Forres, by the road to Kinloss and Burghead. It is a monument which invites superlatives as well as speculation. Alexander Gordon, writing in 1726, hailed it as one of the most stately monuments of its kind in Europe.[1] More recently Joseph Anderson called it, with pardonable exaggeration, 'a unique monument, the most interesting and inexplicable of its kind in existence, either in this country or any other'.[2] The standard description of the Stone remains that of Romilly Allen in *Early Christian Monuments*.[3] He described it as 'an upright cross-slab of red sandstone, of rectangular shape, 20 feet high by 3 feet 9 inches wide by 1 foot 2 inches thick at the bottom, sculptured in relief on four sides'.[4] The obverse, or west face, is intricately interlaced, and bears a Celtic cross, set above a badly weathered panel containing various shadowy figures (Figs.6.1,6). The reverse, or east face, depicts a battle scene, intense and vivid, unique in the British Isles (Fig.6.2). Line by line, panel by panel, are portrayed warriors on foot and warriors on horseback, scenes of combat and scenes of execution. A particular feature is the abundance of decapitated bodies and severed heads. The narrow north and south sides bear vine scroll ornamentation and further interlacing, with some figures at the foot.[5] Sueno's Stone ranks as a Class III monument in the accepted typology for the early Christian and Pictish monuments of Scotland: that is, it belongs to the same tradition as the earlier Class I and Class II monuments, but does not carry any Pictish symbols.

It is generally assumed that the Stone now stands at or near the spot where it was originally erected, although it seems likely, both from its condition and from the lack of reference to it before the 18th century that it must have lain buried for many centuries.[6] Lachlan Shaw noted that early in the 18th century, 'the corn land round it being alway ploughed up, it was like to fall; But Lady Ann Campbell, late Countess of Moray, caused it to be set upright, and supported with several steps of free stone.'[7] In the process the lowest line of sculpture on the reverse side disappeared from sight, to be revealed again in 1926 when the Stone was reset in position by the Ministry of Works. More recently, worries about deterioration in the condition of the Stone and fears for its safety were increased by a nearby housing development and the opening of a by-pass in the vicinity of the Stone. Historic Scotland launched an open competition to design a protective covering. This attracted a large number of entries, and in 1991 a glass and steel canopy was placed around the Stone. Although the Stone remains *in situ* some of the sense of place has inevitably been lost.

Sueno's Stone inspires awe as well as admiration. Yet the reason for its erection remains a mystery. This paper seeks to chronicle some of the interpretations, old and new, plausible and ridiculous, which have been put forward by way of explanation. Most commentators have assumed that the Stone portrays a real event rather than a scene from scripture or mythology, or one merely copied from an earlier exemplar. Douglas Simpson wrote of the 'astonishing array of closely martialled military scenes', and thought it was 'hard to escape the conclusion that all this sculpture on the reverse of Sueno's Stone depicts an actual historical event — a victorious battle which the monument was erected to commemorate.'[8] He commented on 'the deliberate ruthlessness of the stone', comparing it to an Assyrian bas-relief.[9] Others have drawn comparisons with Trajan's triumphal Column in Rome, or with the Bayeux Tapestry.[10]

The interpretation with the longest pedigree is that associated with the traditional name of the Stone. Sueno's Stone is said to commemorate a great victory won in the early years of the eleventh century by the Scots under King Malcolm II (1005-34) over Scandinavian invaders — often referred to as 'Danes' — under their leader Sueno. A version of this interpretation was still in circulation, with official backing, at the time of the Society's Conference in Moray in 1987. 'The Monuments of Forres', a pamphlet published by Grampian Regional Council, noted that 'Many theories of [the Stone's] origin have been suggested. The one most often quoted is that it celebrated a victory over the Norsemen around the year 1008, but where was the battle fought? The Vikings were finally expelled from Burghead in 1014, that being their last stronghold on the mainland.'[11]

Little of this, I fear, is to be believed. The practice of ascribing outstanding ancient monuments — standing stones, stone circles, duns, brochs and the like — to real or imaginary events in the past, and particularly, in the case of Scotland and Ireland, to struggles against 'the Danes', the generic term used to describe all Scandinavian invaders, belongs to a well documented antiquarian tradition which passed rapidly into folk-lore. So far as Sueno's Stone is concerned the story begins with Alexander Gordon who first recorded and depicted the Stone in his pioneering *Itinerarium Septentrionale or, a Journey thro' most of the Counties of Scotland and those in the North of England* published in 1726.[12] Gordon's book is divided into two parts: part one 'Containing an Account of all the Monuments of Roman Antiquity, found and collected in that Journey'; and part two 'An Account of the Danish Invasions on Scotland, and of the Monuments erected there, on the different defeats of that People.'

In his 'Account of the Danish Invasions on Scotland' Gordon relies on those two sixteenth century purveyors of historical fiction, George Buchanan and Hector Boece. He relates Malcolm II's campaigns against the 'Danes' in some detail and describes the resulting monuments in various parts of Scotland.[13] The name of the leader of the Danes is given as Sueno, although he stays firmly in England, sending various lieutenants

Fig.6.2  Sueno's Stone. Battle scene on the east face. (Crown Copyright: Historic Scotland)

north to fight the Scots. One army under 'Olavus' [Olaf] and 'Enecus' [Angus] ravages Moray, and inflicts a severe defeat on the Scots at Kinloss, four miles from Forres. Later, however, this army is defeated by Malcolm II in a great battle at Mortlach (the modern Dufftown, over twenty miles from Forres). On Sueno's Stone Gordon comments, 'Why this Obelisk was rais'd, or how to explain the several Figures thereon, I am at a Loss, but cannot forbear thinking that it was erected by the *Scots* after the Battle of Murtloch'.[14] He suggests that the Stone commemorates not only the battle, but also the failure of the Danes to establish permanent settlements in Moray. 'The Tradition concerning this Stone,' he writes, 'favours my Conjecture, it being still call'd King *Sueno's* Stone: *Olavus* and *Enecus* the *Danish* Generals at *Murtloch*, being sent thither by *Sueno*.'[15] Gordon's assertion that the name 'King Sueno's Stone' already attached to the Stone in his time is of interest, but his ascription of its erection to events at Mortlach, so many miles away, strained even 18th century credulity.[16]

The original, unvarnished, and conceivably accurate account on which this is ultimately based is to be found, like so much else, in the pages of John of Fordun, writing towards the end of the fourteenth century.[17] Fordun chronicles the struggles of the Anglo-Saxons under Ethelred the Unready against the *Danes* under their leader 'Suenus', that is, Sweyn Forkbeard, king of Denmark and father of Canute. Later he writes that shortly after his accession (in 1005), Malcolm II defeated a *Norwegian* army and fleet, and founded a bishopric at Mortlach near the spot where he had won the victory. This is the sober foundation which underlies the later elaborate accounts which conflate Dane and Norwegian, Malcolm and Sueno, Mortlach and Forres.

Alexander Gordon's comments on the stone in the kirkyard at Aberlemno (Fig.6.3) provide another striking example of the tendency to attribute outstanding monuments to the 'Danish' wars. He gives an account, drawn from George Buchanan, of 'the first remarkable battle' fought between Scots and Danes, at Luncarty, near Perth, in the reign of Kenneth, father of Malcolm II. The outcome of the battle was in doubt and the Scots began to flee. 'That Day had certainly prov'd fatal to the *Scots*, had not Heaven interpos'd in their Behalf, and sent them a speedy and seasonable Assistance; for when the Case was desperate, and even at the last Extremity, a Man of ordinary Rank, sirnam'd *Hay*, with his two Sons, vigorous of Body and Mind, and of great Affection to their Native Country, were tilling a contiguous Field through which many of the *Scots* directed their Flight: The father snatching the Yoak from the Necks of the Oxen, and each of the Sons seizing what came next to hand, no sooner beheld the thick Companies of the fugitive Scots, but they endeavoured to stop them, first by Reproaches, then by Threatnings.'[18] According to Gordon 'the *Danish* stones of Aberlemny' were believed to commemorate a victory over the Danes, and he says of the stone in the churchyard there

*Fig.6.3    Aberlemno kirkyard stone. Battle scene on reverse. (Crown Copyright: RCAHMS)*

(Fig.6.3), 'I cannot think that there is much Improbability in conjecturing, That the two Horsemen, on the upper Part thereof, may have been designed as Emblems of part of the flying Army of the *Scots*, at this battle of *Luncharty*; and the Three Figures on Foot with the roundish weapons arresting the other Horseman may represent *Hay* and his two sons, the said roundish Weapons, may, probably, have resembled the Yoaks where-with they put a Stop to the Fugitives.'[19] In this way the fabulous origin legend of the Hays of Erroll — who are, in fact, of impeccable Norman descent, coming from La Haye-Hue in the Avranchin, and arriving in Scotland in the twelfth century[20] — was combined with stories of the 'Danish' wars to explain the stones at Aberlemno. A more credible recent interpretation of the Aberlemno kirkyard stone which also associates it with an actual event will be considered below (p.113).

*Fig.6.4a   Glamis Manse cross-slab. Obverse. (Crown Copyright: RCAHMS)*

Not all the sculptured stones of Pictland were ascribed to the Danish wars. The cross-slab by the Manse at Glamis (Fig.6.4a,b) was supposed to commemorate the murder of Malcolm II in 1034 and was called his gravestone:

'On the front is a cross; on the upper part is some wild beast, and opposite to it a centaur: beneath, in one compartment is the head of a wolf; these animals denoting the barbarity of the conspirators: in another compartment are two persons shaking hands; in their other hand is a battle-ax: perhaps these are represented in the act of confederacy. On the opposite front of the stone are represented an eel and another fish. This alludes to the fate of the murderers, who, as soon as they had committed the horrid act fled. The roads were at that time covered with snow; they lost the path, and went on to the lake of Forfar, which happened at the time to be frozen over, but not sufficiently strong to bear their weight: the ice broke, and they all perished miserably.'[21]

102

*Fig.6.4b   Glamis Manse cross-slab. Reverse. (Crown Copyright: RCAHMS)*

The Pictish stones at Meigle (Fig.6.5) were explained by reference to the Arthurian cycle of stories. 'These Stones', writes Gordon (here following Hector Boece) 'are said to be placed there as a Sepulchral Monument for Queen *Vanora*, and are, at this Day, called her Grave-Stones.'[22] 'Vanora' is the medieval Scots form of 'Guinevere'. Gordon continues, '*Buchanan* represents her as an Adultress, and the Country People have still a Tradition (whether true or false I cannot determine) that she led a very lascivious Life, and was at last devour'd in a Wood by Wild Beasts, and, indeed, many of these Stones seem to have given Colour to this Tradition, unless, perhaps, the Carvings, upon the Stones (as it sometimes happens) may have given Rise to the story.'[23] In this way the motif of Daniel in the Lions' Den, taken from the Old Testament (for this is what is represented at Meigle), came to illustrate the fate of Arthur's adulterous queen.

That no credence at all can be given to the traditional account of Sueno's Stone, elaborated by Gordon' out of Boece and Buchanan, should now be

103

Fig.6.5    *Meigle, no. 2. Daniel in the lions' den. (Crown Copyright: RCAHMS)*

clear. Yet the story of Sueno died hard. The Rev. Charles Cordiner, for example, believed that Sueno's Stone had been erected to celebrate the final liberation of Burghead, eight miles away on the coast, after a century and a half of Scandinavian occupation. The evacuation had been followed by a 'treaty of amicable alliance' concluded between Malcolm II and Canute 'or Sueno king of *Norway*'. Cordiner suggested that the panel below the cross (Fig.6.6) portrayed that reconciliation.[24] That fine historian, W F Skene, noted that the connection of the Stone 'with the name Sweno is no older than Hector Boece', but still preferred a Scandinavian explanation.[25] He suggested that the Stone commemorated the death of Sigurd the Powerful, jarl of Orkney, recorded in *Orkneyinga Saga*, after a skirmish in which he had defeated the Scottish leader Maelbrigte Tooth. Maelbrigte was killed and decapitated, and his severed head fastened to Sigurd's saddle strap; but as Sigurd rode home the protruding tooth which gave Maelbrigte his byname gashed Sigurd's leg, causing the wound from which he died. This event, if historical, must have taken place about 900 AD. Sigurd was buried at 'Ekkialsbakki' which has usually been taken to refer to the banks of the river Oykel. Skene, however, suggested that Ekkialsbakki should be located further south, perhaps on the banks of the Findhorn; that Sueno's Stone had been erected to commemorate the story of Sigurd and Maelbrigte; and that one of the scenes on the Stone portrayed Sigurd riding home with Maelbrigte's head at his girdle. Skene also suggested that the panel below the cross showed two figures, Sigurd and Maelbrigte, 'engaged in apparently an amicable meeting' before the conflict.

More recently Euan Mackie has accepted the argument that Sueno's Stone is 'a Pictish monument, or cenotaph, commemorating a great victory — depicted on the back — over the Norsemen; the identity of the enemy is suggested by the traditional name of the stone.'[26] Mackie suggests that the object depicted in the middle of the central panel on the reverse of the Stone, above five severed heads, is a broch (Romilly Allen, for what it is worth, decribed the object in question as 'a quadrangular Celtic bell'[27]). 'It is quite possible,' Mackie writes, 'there was a well preserved broch on or near the battlefield which was shown on the stone.' This may be so, but Mackie surely strains credulity when he suggests that the broch in question is Dun Alascaig on the south shore of the Dornoch Firth, over thirty miles from the Stone in a direct line. 'Perhaps', says Mackie, 'the presumed defeat of Sueno took place there.'[28]

I myself put forward another interpretation to the Scottish Society for Northern Studies in 1979, and the Conference of Scottish Medieval Historians in 1981. In common with other observers I took the view that Sueno's Stone commemorated an actual event. There is an urgency about the great battle scene on the reverse of the Stone which suggests an immediate secular purpose. There are, in any case, no obvious parallels

*Fig.6.6    Sueno's Stone. West face: detail of panel below cross. (Crown Copyright: Historic Scotland)*

for the iconography of the battle scene, with minor exceptions. The motif of the severed heads tallies only too well with accounts of warfare in Scotland and Ireland in which the heads of the slain figure as trophies. The Annals of Ulster refer to this custom on several occasions.[29] In 865 AD [*recte* 866] they record a victory by Aed son of Niall over the Foreigners [Scandinavians] at Lough Foyle 'and twelve score heads were taken thereby'; in 926 AD a victory by Muirchertach 'of the Leather Cloaks', son of Niall, over the Foreigners when 200 were beheaded; and in 933 AD a victory by the same Muirchertach over the Foreigners and the Men of Ulster, in which again twelve score heads were taken.[30] In Scotland, the Chronicle of Melrose records the end of a MacWilliam rising in 1215 with the presentation of heads as gift by the victor, Ferchar Mac an tSagairt, to the new king, Alexander II:

> in quos irruens Machentagar hostes regis valide prostravit
> quorum capita detruncavit et novo regi nova munera praesentavit.[31]

As late as the seventeenth century the bard of Keppoch, Iain Lom Mac-Donald, avenged the murder of the young chief of Keppoch and his brother, and took the heads of the murderers to MacDonell of Glengarry at Inverlochy castle. The heads were washed *en route* at a well by Loch Oich, still known as *Tobar nan Ceann* (The Well of the Heads) and marked by a monument.

I suggested that Sueno's Stone did indeed commemorate a real battle in which a great victory had been won, but that the vanquished were not Scandinavians but Picts. I put forward the hypothesis that the Stone marked the final victory north of the Mounth by the Scots over the Picts. The victorious leader may have been a king of the dynasty of Kenneth mac Alpin, perhaps even Kenneth himself. Alternatively, he may have belonged to the stock of the Mormaers of Moray, ancestors of Macbeth, who claimed descent from the tribe of Loarn in Dalriada, and may have infiltrated north and west by way of Laggan or the Great Glen. On this view, Sueno's Stone would commemorate a battle which took place in the mid-ninth century, although its erection need not have been exactly contemporary.

I also put forward, very tentatively, an interpretation of the panel on the obverse side of the Stone beneath the cross (Fig.6.6), which Skene thought might represent Sigurd of Orkney meeting Maelbrigte, and Cordiner supposed to be Malcolm II and Sueno (above p.105). This panel has suffered considerably from the elements or defacement, or both, and it is difficult now to make out the scene which it depicts. Lachlan Shaw, following Gordon, described it as bearing 'two human figures of a Gothish form.'[32] Romilly Allen called it 'a group of five men, one in the centre, the two tall figures facing each other and bending over him, and two smaller ones at the back.'[33] Given the key position of the panel beneath the great cross one might expect it to represent a scriptural scene, and this perhaps remains the most probable explanation. Nevertheless, it has not yet proved possible to identify the scene as such, nor to point to a clear iconographic parallel in Scotland or Ireland. It is therefore possible that this panel, like the battle scene on the reverse of the Stone, represents an actual event. If so, it must be one of considerable significance. I pointed out that the scene

*Fig.6.7    Seal of the Abbey of Scone: the inauguration of the king of Scots. (Crown Copyright: RCAHMS)*

on the panel, indistinct though it is, bears a striking resemblance to that on the common seal of the Abbey of Scone, thought to represent the inauguration of the medieval kings of Scots (Fig.6.7). Could the panel represent the ceremonial inauguration of the king of Scots after the final defeat of the Pictish monarchy?

Gaelic rulers in Scotland and Ireland (and the Isle of Man) were inaugurated, rather than crowned and anointed, in a ceremony which has pre-Christian origins.[34] A late description of such a ceremony occurs in Hugh Macdonald's seventeenth century 'History of the Macdonalds':

I thought fit to annex the ceremony of proclaiming the Lord of the Isles ... There was a square stone, seven or eight feet long, and the tract of a man's foot cut thereon, upon which he stood, denoting that he should walk in the footsteps and uprightness of his predecessors, and that he was installed by right in his possessions. He was clothed in a white habit, to shew his innocence and integrity of heart, that he would be a light to his people, and maintain the true religion. The white apparel did afterwards belong to the poet by right. Then he was to receive a white rod in his hand,

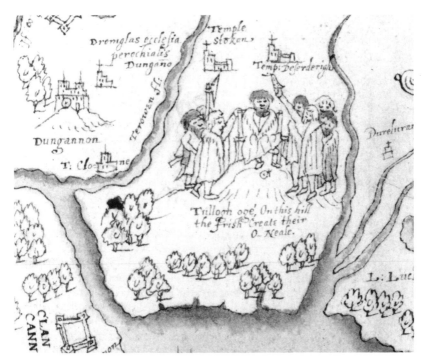

*Fig.6.8    The inauguration of O'Neill at Tullaghoge (c.1600). (Copyright: National Maritime Museum)*

intimating that he had power to rule, not with tyranny and partiality, but with discretion and sincerity. Then he received his forefathers' sword ... signifying that his duty was to protect and defend them from the incursions of their enemies in peace or war, as the obligations and customs of his predecessors were.'[35]

In Ireland the ceremony of inauguration continued until the sixteenth century, and is described in similar terms. There is a late representation of the inauguration of the O'Neill on the 'Stone of the Kings' at Tullaghoge in Tyrone (Fig.6.8).[36] In Scotland the kings of Scots continued to be inaugurated in the traditional manner until the fourteenth century. Alexander II and Robert the Bruce both petitioned the Pope for the privilege of being crowned and anointed. Alexander's request was refused but Bruce's was granted. However, permission arrived too late for king Robert himself, and the first Scottish king to be crowned and anointed was his son David II.[37] There can be little doubt that the kings of Kenneth mac Alpin's line or, for that matter, the Mormaers of Moray, would have been inaugurated in the traditional manner appropriate to Gaelic dynasts.

The Scone seal (Fig.6.7) is the only known depiction of a royal inauguration in Scotland. Professor Duncan, describing the inauguration of Alexander III in 1249, commented on the seal as follows:

The seal clearly shows that the king was vested in his robe by a bishop and unmitred cleric, the Bishop of St Andrews and the Abbot of Scone respectively. Behind both of these are secular figures, two earls whose identities are indicated by the shields of arms under the king's feet — Fife, the king, Strathearn — and who had presumably enthroned him. Three figures are shown above them; one is a cleric offering to the king a small house, a reliquary shrine, for the taking of an oath; another may be a layman and holds something long, narrow and two-dimensional, the rolls of the king's genealogy; the function of the third figure is not clear.'[38]

The parallels between the panel on Sueno's Stone, the Scone seal and the representation of the inauguration of O'Neill may not be exact, but they are sufficiently close, especially given their widely differing dates of execution, to prompt reflection. My suggestion, therefore, was that Sueno's Stone commemorated a great battle in the north, presumably near Forres, between Scots and Picts, which marked the end of Pictish power and the supplanting of the Pictish royal line by a new dynasty of Scottish rulers. The new rulers were inaugurated after the fashion of Gaelic dynasts in a ceremony of profound religious and political significance which may be depicted in the panel below the cross. This would suggest a date c.850-950 AD for the erection of the Stone, a date compatible with the art historical evidence.

When I put forward these suggestions in 1979 and 1981, I expressed surprise at the comparative lack of interest in the Stone. However, unknown to me, Leslie Southwick had also been working on the Stone, and later in 1981 his booklet 'The so-called Sueno's Stone at Forres' appeared. This is a model of its kind, combining description and observation with historical and art-historical research. Southwick also believes that the Stone represents a historical event and points to contemporary evidence from France and Germany which shows that great victories might be portrayed in works of art.[39] Traversing some of the ground covered earlier in this paper, he points out that the association with Sueno is spurious, and that there is no certain Scandinavian connection. He writes, 'It is not known what event the scenes of war on Sueno's Stone might represent or why it was erected', but goes on to speculate that the Stone may have been set up to commemorate a campaign against the Orkney Vikings or, alternatively, that it may celebrate a victory by the rulers of Moray over 'the Scottish Kings south of the Mounth.'[40] The dissociation of the Stone from a necessary Scandinavian connection is welcome, but the suggestion that it commemorates a victory over the kings of Scots may be doubted. Even allowing for the thesis of two kingdoms north and south

110

of the Mounth in the ninth and tenth centuries, with the dynasty of Kenneth mac Alpin in the south (and this has not won universal accept-ance), it seems unlikely that the kings of Scots, when they eventually gained full control, would have allowed a monument celebrating their earlier defeat to survive. Southwick considers the panel beneath the cross to be 'too defaced to attempt a reasonable interpretation'.[41]

Three years later two further interpretations of the Stone appeared. Anthony Jackson considered the Stone within the broader framework of the Picts and their monuments. Jackson's background lies in social anthropology, and he sought in his *Symbol Stones of Scotland*, published in 1984, to combine the insights of that discipline with his observation of the sculptured stones of Pictland to put forward a model of Pictish society.[42] In a chapter on Sueno's Stone, Jackson put forward a suggestion similar to my own, namely that there was no valid reason to associate the Stone with Sueno, and that the Stone might well commemorate a victory over the Picts. Some traces of earlier explanations of the Stone remained in Jackson's insistence that it celebrated a great *Christian* victory: Christian Scots against *pagan* Picts. Victory of Scots against Picts there may have been, but to stigmatise the northern Picts as still pagan in the ninth century is at variance with the historical record.

Jackson, however, went much further in his interpretation. He wrote that 'closer examination of the grouping of figures [in the battle scene] shows that the number 7 plays a crucial role in the actual composition.'[43] He believed that the defeated side could be shown to 'have 28 ($7 \times 4$) plus 14 ($7 \times 2$) dead, making a total of 42 ($7 \times 6$) as opposed to the winners 56 ($7 \times 8$). This makes a grand total of 98 figures or ($7 \times 14$ or $7 \times 2 \times 2$), which is a large number of 7's.' He pointed, in particular, to the two sets of seven decapitated bodies, which he believed must represent seven royal Pictish lineages, one for each province of Pictland. According to Jackson, however, these scenes of execution referred not to a single event but to two separate occasions. Building on later tradition which spoke of a treacherous massacre by Kenneth mac Alpin of Pictish notables after a banquet at Scone, Jackson suggested that the scene depicted towards the foot of the Stone recorded that event and showed the decapitated bodies of the murdered leaders of the seven Pictish lineages lying under a tent. The scene in the central panel, however, depicted a later judicial execution of seven lineage leaders in northern Pictland after a great victory of Kenneth mac Alpin against the Picts which was the immediate cause of the erection of Sueno's Stone. This panel 'is the heart of Sueno's Stone and depicts the execution of the Paramount king of Northern Pictland while his six confrères lie bound and beheaded. This judicial execution is accompanied by the tolling of a bell [Mackie's broch] and a fanfare of trumpets. The central position of the bell in the composition suggests that this was also a triumph for Christianity in putting down the pagan Picts.'[44]

111

Jackson suggests that the line of five figures at the top of the central panel represents the victorious Kenneth mac Alpin with five Scottish southern provincial kings. He also most ingeniously deduces the composition and line of command of the rival Scottish and Pictish armies from the carvings on the Stone, commenting that it appears that the northern Picts had no infantry and the southern Picts no cavalry, and speculating on the reasons for this. In a final paragraph which considers the scene beneath the cross, Jackson suggests, again like myself, that this may portray a royal coronation [recte inauguration], with king Kenneth as the central figure.[45]

In his paper delivered at Forres and reproduced in this volume, Jackson adheres to and elaborates on his earlier interpretation. He argues that when the Stone was re-erected it must have been put up back to front, and consequently now faces in the wrong direction. He re-iterates his belief that the Stone was erected to commemorate the victory of southerners over northerners, and suggests that it 'was erected by Kenneth MacAlpin to tell the Picts *in their own symbolic code* that they were vanquished.'[46] He points again to the crucial position of the object, be it bell (as he suggested earlier), broch or fort, in the dead centre of the monument. He repeats the theory that the scene below the cross represents a 'coronation' scene, and suggests that the elongated figures on either side of the central figure may represent the Scottish national saints Columba and Andrew. He concludes, 'It [the Stone] is a *definite statement about the end of a particular era* — the end of the dominance of the Pictish lineages in the royal line of succession to the kingdom of the *Picts*. There can only be *one* man for whom this was an all-important message: Kenneth MacAlpin, the first king of *both* the Picts and the Scots.'[47]

A quite different, but no less ingenious interpretation of Sueno's Stone by Professor Archibald Duncan also appeared in 1984.[48] In a short article on the kingdom of the Scots in the Dark Ages, Duncan noted the fate of one of Kenneth's successors as king of Scots, Dubh, who reigned from 962 to 966. According to contemporary sources, Dubh was killed at Forres in 966 by the men of Moray. 'These events must have been the subject of some long-lost Gaelic epic or lament,' writes Duncan, 'of which we hear an echo in a brief Latin annal telling that Dubh lay slain under the bridge of Kinloss and that the sun did not shine until his body was recovered for burial.'[49] Duncan suggests that the 'remarkable monument ... with the irrelevant name Sueno's Stone' commemorates this event. He believes that the central figure 'with a helmet and a quilted coat' at the top of the middle panel of the battle scene (whom Jackson took to be Kenneth mac Alpin) is king Dubh, surveying the field of battle. Beneath, a church bell watches over the bodies of the slain. Below again, six men on horseback are in full flight. 'But the battle continues with three fighting couples on each side of an arc which is the bridge of Kinloss', writes Duncan, his 'bridge' being

Jackson's 'tent'. 'Beneath the bridge lie more dead bodies and severed heads; one of the heads, that of Dubh, is framed to stress its importance.'[50] Duncan suggests that the panel below the cross, tentatively interpreted by Jackson and myself as a royal inauguration, and by Skene as the meeting of Sigurd and Maelbrigte, may represent the burial of king Dubh near the spot where the Stone was erected.

Although Duncan's account is radically different from that of other recent interpreters, it shares with them the assumption that Sueno's Stone depicts a real Dark Age battle. So convinced is Duncan of this that he uses the iconography of the Stone to illustrate contemporary army service and military apparel: 'The technology of war is faithfully represented here, but so too are the ranks of society and their obligation to fight for a leader.'[51]

The case for associating Sueno's Stone with a real Dark Age event has been greatly strengthened by an interpretation recently offered for the Aberlemno kirkyard stone (Fig.6.3) by both Southwick and Graeme Cruickshank. Alexander Gordon's unconvincing association of this stone with the origin legend of the Hays of Errol has already been noted (p.100). In an extended footnote to his work on Sueno's Stone, Southwick put forward an alternative explanation.[52] He suggested that the Aberlemno stone told a story in three stages, moving from top to bottom. A distinction should be made between the five long-haired, bare-headed warriors depicted on the left of the stone (as one faces it), and the four helmeted warriors on the right. Those on the left he thought might represent Picts and those on the right Northumbrians. He suggested that the figure at the top right was in full flight, having cast away his sword and shield. The helmeted figure at the bottom right was shown dead on the field of battle, his corpse 'carrion for the raven like the knight in the border ballad "The Two Corbies" '. Perhaps, Southwick suggested, the Aberlemno stone was meant to represent a conflict between Pictland and Northumbria.

In his *The Battle of Dunnichen*, an earlier version of which was published in 1985 as *Nechtansmere 1300: a Commemoration*, Graeme Cruickshank suggests a very similar interpretation.[53] He too interprets the stone as representing a conflict between Picts and Northumbrians, in which the former were victorious. He notes that a helmet with a prominent nasel, like those depicted on the stone, has been found in York and dated to the eighth century. The figure at the bottom right, his corpse the prey of ravens, would have been readily understood by contemporaries, argues Cruickshank, as a symbolic representation of defeat. Cruickshank suggests that the Aberlemno stone was erected, not long after the event, to commemorate the defeat of the Angles of Northumbria and the death of their king Ecgfrith at the hands of the Picts in 685 AD at the battle of Dunnichen (or Nechtansmere), fought only four miles from Aberlemno. The fallen figure at the foot may even be Ecgfrith himself. This interpretation seems entirely credible and has won some cautious acceptance.[54] If the stone in the kirkyard at Aberlemno was erected to commemorate a real battle, the arguments for associating Sueno's Stone likewise with a historical event are considerably enhanced.

The display board set up beside Sueno's Stone in 1992 by Historic Scotland suggests that the Stone may have been carved in the ninth or tenth centuries. It notes three possible theories for its erection: to commemorate a battle in which the Picts were vanquished by the Scots under Kenneth mac Alpin; to commemorate a battle between a 'Picto-Scottish' force and marauding Norsemen; or to commemorate the death of king Dubh in 966 AD. It notes that the name of the Stone was invented in the eighteenth century and 'has no bearing on the origin of the monument. Only the stone itself and its location can give any hint of why and when it was created and on whose orders.' The 1991 number of *Discovery & Excavation in Scotland* notes that 'excavation to date has not produced firm evidence for a date of erection, method of erection, or purpose'.[55] The mystery remains.

### Acknowledgements

I am most grateful to Historic Scotland for permission to reproduce Figs.6.1,2 and 6; to the Royal Commission on the Ancient and Historical Monuments of Scotland for permission to reproduce Figs.6.3, 4, 5 and 7; and to the National Maritime Museum for permission to reproduce Fig.6.8.

### Notes

1. Alexander Gordon, *Itinerarium Septentrionale, or a Journey Thro' most of the Counties of Scotland and those in the North of England* (London 1726) 158.
2. Quoted in R Douglas, *Annals of the Royal Burgh of Forres* (Elgin 1934) 312.
3. Joseph Anderson and J Romilly Allen, *Early Christian Monuments of Scotland* (Edinburgh 1903).
4. Ibid., pt.ii, 149-50.
5. A good modern description of the Stone is to be found in Leslie Southwick, *The so-called Sueno's Stone at Forres* (Moray District Library Publications 1981), discussed below p.110.
6. See Southwick, preface.
7. Lachlan Shaw, *History of the Province of Moray* (1775) ed. J F S Gordon (London and Glasgow 1882) iii, 106.
8. W Douglas Simpson, *The Ancient Stones of Scotland* (London 1965) 118.
9. Ibid.
10. Duncan MacMillan, Curator of the Talbot Rice Gallery, University of Edinburgh, himself a native of Moray, suggested a parallel with Trajan's Column in conversation; for comparisons with the Bayeux Tapestry see Southwick, *So-called Sueno's Stone* 15 and 17, and Duncan 'Kingdom of the Scots' in *The Making of Britain: The Dark Ages* ed.Lesley M Smith (London 1984) (discussed below, p.112) @ 140.
11. *The Monuments of Forres* (Grampian Regional Council, n.d.).
12. See above, note 1.
13. *Itinerarium*, 152ff.
14. Ibid., 159.

15. Ibid.
16. Lachlan Shaw is sceptical (*Province of Moray* iii, 106-7).
17. *Johannis de Fordun, Chronica Gentis Scotorum* ed.W F Skene (Edinburgh 1871-2) book iv, chapters 35, 39-40.
18. *Itinerarium*, 150.
19. Ibid., 151.
20. G W S Barrow 'Scotland's Norman Families' in *The Kingdom of the Scots* (London 1973) 325, citing Sir Anthony Wagner 'The origin of the Hays of Erroll' in *Genealogists Magazine*, 1954, 1955.
21. The quotation is from Thomas Pennant's *Tour in Scotland* 2nd ed.(London 1776) ii, 173, cited in Stewart Cruden's *The Early Christian & Pictish Monuments of Scotland* (HMSO 1957) 3. Pennant was following in the footsteps of Gordon and Boece.
22. *Itinerarium*, 162.
23. Ibid.
24. Charles Cordiner, *Remarkable Ruins and Romantic prospects of North Britain* (London 1795) 'The Forres Pillar'. Cordiner was building on earlier writers such as Pennant. For Burghead see Shepherd 'Picts in Moray' in this volume. There is no evidence for an extended Scandinavian occupation of Burghead.
25. W F Skene, *Celtic Scotland* 2nd ed.(Edinburgh 1886-90) i, 337-8.
26. Euan W Mackie, *Scotland: An Archaeological Guide* (London 1975) 204.
27. *Early Christian Monuments* ii, 150.
28. Mackie, 205.
29. *The Annals of Ulster (to AD* 1131) edd. Sean MacAirt and Gearoid Mac-Niocaill, pt.i, text and translation (Dublin Institute of Advanced Studies 1983).
30. The word 'heads' (*cenn*) appears in the original annal for 933 but has been accidentally omitted in the translation.
31. *The Chronicle of Melrose* (facsimile edition) edd.A O Anderson and others (London 1936) 60.
32. *Province of Moray* iii, 106.
33. *Early Christian Monuments* ii, 150.
34. For a recent discussion of the ceremony of inauguration in Ireland see Katharine Simms, *From Kings to Warlords* (Bury St Edmunds 1987), ch.3 'Inauguration-ceremonies, Titles, and the Meaning of Kingship'; for inauguration in the Lordship of the Isles see J W M Bannerman 'The Lordship of the Isles' in *Scottish Society in the Fifteenth Century* ed.Jennifer M Brown (London 1977) 224-5; also A A M Duncan, *Scotland: The Making of the Kingdom* (Edinburgh 1975) 115-6, 526, 552-6; and W D H Sellar 'Celtic law and Scots Law; Survival and Integration' (1989) 29 *Scottish Studies* 4 and note 5.
35. H Macdonald 'History of the Macdonalds' in *Highland Papers* ed.J R N Macphail (Scottish History Society, Edinburgh 1914-34) i, 23-4.
36. The vignette of the inauguration of O'Neill occurs in Dartmouth Map no.25 in the National Maritime Museum, Greenwich. It is described in *Ulster and other Irish Maps* ed.G A Hayes-McCoy (Stationery Office, Dublin 1964). I am most grateful to Ian Fisher, RCAHMS, for this reference, and to the Museum for granting permission to reproduce.
37. *Scotland: The Making of the Kingdom* (Edinburgh 1975) 526, 553-4; and Ranald Nicolson, *Scotland: The Later Middle Ages* (Edinburgh 1974) 124-5.

38. *Scotland: The Making of the Kingdom* 555-6.
39. *So-called Sueno's Stone* 15-16.
40. Ibid., 15, 18.
41. Ibid., 9.
42. Anthony Jackson, *The Symbol Stones of Scotland: a social anthropological resolution of the problems of the Picts* (Kirkwall 1984).
43. Ibid., 168.
44. Ibid., 170. Cordiner (see note 24) seems to have been the first to suggest that the Stone might portray a formal execution.
45. Ibid., 173.
46. 'Further Thoughts on Sueno's Stone', above p.94.
47. Above, p.95.
48. Duncan 'Kingdom of the Scots' (above note 10).
49. Ibid., 139-40.
50. Ibid., 140.
51. Ibid.
52. Southwick, 19, note 23.
53. Graeme Cruickshank, *The Battle of Dunnichen* (Pinkfoot Press, Balgavies, Angus 1991). A further booklet by Cruickshank entitled *The Aberlemno Battle-Scene* is promised shortly.
54. Anna Ritchie, *Picts* (HMSO, Edinburgh 1989) 22-7, considers the association of the Aberlemno kirkyard stone with the battle of Dunnichen to be very plausible.
55. 1991 *Discovery & Excavation in Scotland* ed.Colleen E Batey with Jennifer Ball (Council for Scottish Archaeology 1992) 38.

# THE HISTORICAL MACBETH
## Edward J Cowan

'Some of our writers relate a number of fables, more adapted for theatrical representation, or Milesian romance, than history'.[1] Thus George Buchanan, himself no stranger to fabulism, writing of one of the most famous of the sons of Moray in 1582. William Shakespeare took the hint. Within twenty four years Banquo stood on a blasted heath in a thinning mist to enquire 'How far is't called to Forres?'.[2] The answer, never given in the play, is a journey of over half a millennium along a tortuous route, frequently shrouded in Celtic mists. When the play was first produced in 1606 it was edited to accommodate the short attention spans and fidgeting predilections of its distinguished audience, King James VI of Scotland who had recently succeeded to the English throne, and his brother-in-law King Christian of Denmark.[3] It was designed to instruct and flatter James Stewart — perhaps the most flatterable, if least instructible of monarchs. It was written in the shadow of a spectacular series of Scottish witch trials just over ten years earlier when James' cousin Francis Stewart, Earl of Bothwell, had been accused of attempting to conjure, through witches' spells, the destruction of the king himself.[4] If the witches failed in their objective with regard to James, Shakespeare succeeded admirably in destroying the historical MacBeth.

Yet another review of MacBeth's life and times may seem superfluous given the already considerable literature on the subject. Virtually everyone who has ever pontificated on medieval Scottish history has had something to say about this essentially obscure mormaer of Moray 'snorting with the indigested fumes of the blood of his sovereign'[5] while others have tried to rescue him from 'the fabulist school of fawning sycophants who invented their lies centuries after his death'.[6] One invention was the incredible concoction, *The Secret History of MacBeth* which first appeared in 1708 and was reprinted by Peter Buchan in 1828. In this piece of political pornography compiled by some anonymous opponent of Stewart absolutism, MacBeth's over-vaulting ambition is reflected in his monstrous sexual appetite as allegedly related by his one-time faithful, but now repentant henchman, Angus. The true hero of the tale is clearly Archibald ninth earl of Argyll (executed 1685) since his namesake, as a 'hater of tyrants' and 'leader of the patriots', led the attack on MacBeth.[7] In 1797 it could be stated that 'the story of the Usurper's defeat, flight northward, and death at Lumphanan is known to every reader conversant in the history of Scotland'.[8] He has been compared by a crazed clansman to Lord Kitchener and President Wilson, with a quotation from *The Canadian Boat Song* thrown in for good measure.[9] The 'Priestess of Tradition with her sovereign contempt of historic detail' has been invoked on his behalf.[10] One valiant admirer tried to make an Arthur out of his hero. When MacBeth received his fatal wound 'his charger galloped away among the hills with the bleeding monarch and no man saw him die'.[11] On film he has been depicted as American gangster in *Joe MacBeth*, Japanese warlord in *Throne of Blood* and as Orson Welles. In print the distortionists have continued their clamour from spuriously historical treatments[12] to utterly preposterous fiction.[13] The folkloristic aspects of MacBeth's story have been lucidly expounded [14] but a highly respected modern historian uneasily contrasts 'a harsh, brutally violent Iron Age quality (which) characterized the struggles of these warlike mormaers' — of Moray, such as MacBeth — with the attitudes of 'those who were devoted to consolidating and preserving a new kind of Scottish kingdom'.[15] Words such as usurpation, violence, brutality or chaos flow confidently from the pens of errantly confident beholders. Arguably the years of MacBeth's rule 1040-1057 were no more violent than the seventeen years which preceded James VI's succession to the English throne; in highlighting order, while minimizing violence, recent commentators on James VI's reign have hopelessly overstated their case.[16]

There are three main collections of sources for the career of MacBeth. Firstly, what might be broadly described as the contemporary evidence: annals and poems written in the eleventh and twelfth centuries. Secondly, the hitherto overlooked material in the Icelandic sagas, notably *Orkneyinga Saga* which sheds considerable light on the topic in question. Thirdly, there are the accounts preserved in native Scottish medieval chroniclers and historians, the men responsible for transmitting the legend of MacBeth. Further evidence is to be gleaned from surviving genealogies and fragmentary records of donations and land grants. Finally and foreshadowed in the earlier histories, there has evolved since the eighteenth century an antiquarian tradition which associates historical sites with MacBeth's career and which is probably, in the main, quite bogus. What these sources cumulatively relate is a tale only partially full of sound and fury, and signifying nothing less than the remarkably successful reign of a mormaer of Moray who, through time, was to be regarded as the last great Celtic king of Scots.

The attempt to redeem 'that dead butcher and his fiend-like queen' must begin at the very dawn of Scottish history in order to refute Shakespeare's claim that MacBeth was a tyrant and a foul usurper. As is well known the first Scots or *Scotti* crossed to modern Argyll from Ireland under Fergus Mór mac Erc in the fifth century A.D. At least three clans or kindreds (*cenéla*) were established in the west, namely the Cenél nGabráin, Cenél Loairn and Cenél nOengusa. The kingship of Dalriada although held mainly by the Cenél nGabrain sometimes passed to the Cenél Loairn. In a

118

movement now attested only in the genealogies the Cenél Loairn gradually expanded their territory from Lorn through the Great Glen to Moray, and from this kindred MacBeth himself claimed descent.[17] MacBeth's lineage was thus royal and impeccable. A further related point to be noted is that the Scottish kings in the tenth and eleventh centuries practised an alternating system of succession, sometimes called tanistry or collateral succession.[18] There was also in eleventh century Scotland some form of gradation of kingship similar to that of Ireland where there were three grades — the *rí* king of a single *tuath* or tribe, the *ruiri* a 'superior king' recognized as such by the kings of two or more other tribes and a 'king of kings' the *rí ruirech*.[19] The last-named has sometimes been identified with 'High-King' though the designation has been challenged.[20]

In a Scottish context the terminology is confusing because the eleventh century was itself a period of transition and scribes were clearly fumbling with new, equivalent and/or alien vocabularies. The *Annals of Ulster* seem to designate the Scottish *rí ruirech* as *rí Alban* (AU 1034) or as *airdrigh Alban* (AU 1058). They used the Pictish term *mormaer* — 'great steward' to designate the *ruiri* or king of the middle rank (AU 1032).[21] In the sagas *mormaer* is rendered *jarl* and he would soon become *comes* or earl in Scottish records as well. The annals, however, indulge in terminological confusion where the lesser king or *rí* is concerned. In Scotland *rí* was rendered variously as *toisech* or thane.[22] Such competing terminology is not unimportant and in the present state of our knowledge is perhaps incapable of resolution; the main point to grasp is that it is the major source of confusion over the designation of individual members of the House of Moray and indeed of members of rival kindreds in the eleventh century; such confusion should be understood even if it is not comprehensible!

Armed with such information it should be possible to make some sense of the fortunes of individuals who belong to MacBeth's kindred or *derbfine* (see genealogical table, Fig.7.1). The *Annals of Tigernach* relate that Findlaech mac Ruaidri, Mormaer of Moray, was killed by the sons of his brother Maelbrigte in 1020. The *Annals of Ulster* call him *rí Alban*, so testifying to the importance of the House of Moray at this period; he is said to have been slain by his own people *a suis occisus est*. The death (*not* the slaughter) of one of Findlaech's slayers, Malcolm mac Maelbrigte, is noted in 1029.[23] He is known to have granted lands to the monastery of Old Deer, Aberdeenshire.[24] Malcolm's brother, Gillacomgain mac Maelbrigte, Mormaer of Moray was burned to death along with fifty of his men three years later (AU 1032). It is not recorded who committed this deed. A clue may be afforded by the later medieval tradition that when MacBeth killed Duncan he married Duncan's widow, 'Dame Grwok'.[25] MacBeth did marry Gruoch but historically she was the widow of Gillacomgain. The confusion may have arisen because MacBeth was responsible for avenging

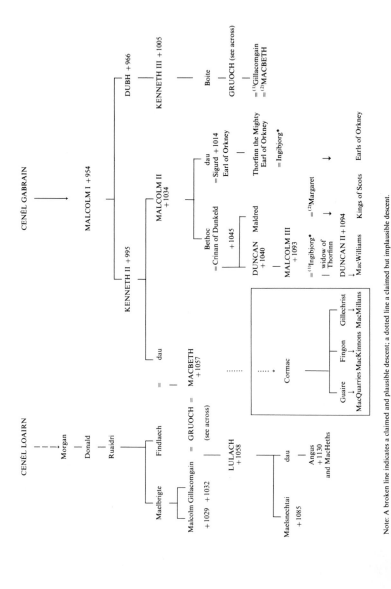

Note: A broken line indicates a claimed and plausible descent; a dotted line a claimed but implausible descent.

Fig.7.1  The House of Moray and succession to the Scottish kingship.

120

his father's killing by firing Gillacomgain's residence, a not uncommon method of despatching one's enemies at this period.[26] The noble notion, advocated by some critics that Gruoch would never have consented to marry her husband's killer is negated by contemporary Irish and Scandinavian evidence. Well over a hundred years after this episode Svein Asleifsson considered burning the house which sheltered his enemy even though it contained his own wife and children! [27] Incinerated spouses were not necessarily a deterrent to subsequent married bliss.

'It will have been collected from the foregoing particulars that not all was peace in the North in yon days'.[28] Such strife would not have been out of place anywhere else in Britain, or for that matter in Europe, at this period, but the particular problems among the men of Moray may have been symptomatic of fragmentation within the kindred. Such developments, as we know from other periods of Gaelic history, were most likely to take place when the clan as a whole was threatened by an external aggressor. Such existed in the powerful Norwegian earldom of Orkney to the north. It is also quite possible that Malcolm II, like many a later King of Scots, was not averse to dipping a royal spurtle into the cauldron of internecine strife. 'The honour of all the west of Europe' died in 1034 after a long reign. As the poem the *Duan Albanach* has it:

Thirty years verses proclaim
Maelcholuim was King of the Mounth[29]

Reference to the Mounth was significant for it stressed that Malcolm ruled both north and south of the Grampians which historically had divided the kingdoms of the northern and southern Picts. Malcolm had at least managed to co-exist, however uneasily, with the men of Moray who acknowledged him as *ruiri* or overking, and probably as *rí ruirech*. Several references suggest that peace with the men of the north was bought for the price of a marriage between Malcolm's sister and Findlaech — the parents of MacBeth.[30] The important marriage between Malcolm's daughter Bethoc and Crinan lay abbot of Dunkeld produced Duncan who succeeded his grandfather almost certainly against the wishes and interests of the Moray kindred. Another daughter married Earl Sigurd of Orkney who was killed at the battle of Clontarf in 1014.[31] Their son was the great Earl Thorfinn the Mighty of Orkney of whom more anon. What is to be noted is that these descendants of Malcolm II all belonged to the same *derbfine* or noble family. This was to prove highly significant.

The *St. Andrews Register* records a grant of Kirkness, Portmoak and Bogie to the Culdees of Lochleven by MacBeth and Gruoch, described as *Rex et Regina Scottorum*. Perhaps too much should not be read into this designation; at least one commentator thinks it significant the Gruoch is called queen and not consort.[32] Yet the wording may somehow reflect the strength of Gruoch's own claims. The Lochleven grant states she was the

121

daughter of Bodhe.[33] The identity of Bodhe (or Boite) is problematical though he was probably the son of Kenneth III. The grandson of Boite mac Kenneth or Cinead was killed by Malcolm II in 1033 (AU).[34] We should be hesitant to ascribe too many motives of revenge when much closer kinsmen were cheerfully slaughtering one another but if there was prolonged rivalry between the descendants of the two Kenneths then Gruoch was clearly in the anti-Malcolm II camp. By marrying Gruoch MacBeth merged several claims to the kingship; his own as the son of Findlaech[35] and those of his wife through previous kings. He also acquired custody of Lulach, son of the marriage between Gruoch and Gillacomgain. Gruoch is the most conspicuous female in medieval Scottish History with the exception of St. Margaret, truly her *alter ego*. Her importance and reputation may stem from the strength of the claims combined in the person of *Gruoch Regina*.

What then, is known of the career of MacBeth from contemporary, or near-contemporary sources? After a reign of six years (1034-1040) *Donnchad mac Crinan rí Alban* (Duncan, son of Crinan, king of Scotland) was killed by his own people, *a suis occisus est* (AU). One account states that he was slain 'at an immature age' which cannot be strictly true since he had fathered at least three sons.[36] The 'pure and wise' Duncan was slaughtered at Pitgaveny near Elgin; in 1235 Alexander II used part of the burgh rents to endow a chaplaincy in the cathedral providing masses in perpetuity for the souls of his ancestor. Marianus Scottus (1028-1083), an Irishman also known as Maelbrigte the Hermit, who completed his *Chronicon* in Mainz in 1073, states that Duncan was killed *a duce suo MacBethad* on 14 August 1040. No other contemporary source shares this specific attribution in which the Latin *dux* is probably best translated as 'war-leader', an apt description of one of the functions of the mormaer. Marianus enjoyed immense popularity throughout Europe in the Middle Ages and his material was used by most chroniclers worthy of the name. It is tempting to believe that all accounts of MacBeth's personal involvement stem from this single assertion though as mormaer of Moray he undoubtedly had to shoulder some of the blame for a regicide that took place within his own province.

Of MacBeth's seventeen year rule there is not a great deal to report. Several Irish annals record in 1045 a battle between the Scots themselves in which Duncan's father, Crinan lay abbot of Dunkeld and 'nine score fighting men' were killed. English accounts (which are very confused at this point) suggest that a warband under Earl Siward of Northumbria also participated. Nowhere is MacBeth mentioned by name although the episode is generally interpreted as a rebellion by forces loyal to the family of Duncan, sometimes known anachronistically, but conveniently, as the House of Dunkeld.[37] 1050 found MacBeth on pilgrimage to Rome where according to Marianus 'he scattered money like seed to the poor'. Irish and English accounts agree that in 1054 a great battle was fought between the Scots and the English. Earl Siward is credited with the defeat of MacBeth and with the restoration of Malcolm Canmore to his kingdom. Well over three hundred years later (circa 1420) Andrew Wyntoun related that the battle was fought at Dunsinnan or Dunsinane in the parish of Collace, Perthshire. MacBeth was eventually killed in 1057 by Malcolm Canmore; according to twelfth century tradition, in Lumphanan, Aberdeenshire. A verse in the *Chronicle of Melrose* states that in MacBeth's reign, *fertile tempus erat* — there were productive seasons 'but Duncan's son, named Malcolm, cut him off by a cruel death in Lumphanan'.[38]

Northumbria in the mid eleventh century might almost be viewed as the Moray of England. The men of the English north were regarded by Edward the Confessor as aliens, a bastard breed of Britons, Anglo-Saxons and Scandinavians whose shared sense of identity did not preclude a little internecine distraction. Siward had risen to prominence under Cnut; he was 'a Danish parvenu' who became earl of York in 1033 and who conquered Northumberland nine years later, consolidating his position, as he would have done in a similar position in Scotland, by marrying the comital heiress, in his case Aelfleda daughter of Ealdred earl of Northumbria.

Siward's considerable energies were diverted by the aggressive actions of Scottish kings, who were intent upon exploiting English weakness caused by the Scandinavian presence, through advancing the Scottish border to the south at Northumbrian expense. Malcolm II unsuccessfully attempted to take Durham in 1006. In 1018 he won a significant victory at Carham, in which battle his ally Owen the Bald king of the Cumbrians of Strathclyde, was killed. The ancient kingdom of the Cumbrians extending all the way from Loch Lomond to Stainmore had long been a thorn in Northumbria's side; after the demise of Owen it became a painful lance in a bleeding wound since the heirs of the Scottish kings, certainly in the cases of Duncan and Malcolm Canmore, were given the title of king or prince of the Cumbrians.[39] In alliance with his Cumbrians Duncan also besieged Durham in 1040; indeed his lack of success may have contributed to his overthrow later that same year.

When MacBeth triumphed Duncan's sons fled the kingdom. A more important figure at this juncture was possibly Maldred brother of Duncan; this individual was married to Ealdgyth daughter of Earl Uhtred of Northumbria and granddaughter of King Ethelred. Their son was to be Cospatric earl of Northumbria and later earl of Dunbar. There was a distant relationship with Siward who was married to Uhtred's granddaughter by his first marriage, while Maldred was the husband of a daughter of Uhtred's third marriage. The demise of the House of Dunkeld played straight into Siward's hands for he could barter assistance to recover a kingdom against security on his frontier. It has been convincingly suggested that his prime pawn was Maldred and that the expedition of 1045, backed by Maldred's father Crinan, was designed to place Maldred in the kingship of the Scots.[40] It was not to be. In an unnamed battle Crinan was killed. English accounts, mostly late, imply several expeditions by Siward as well as retaliation by MacBeth. There is also some evidence that Siward attempted to exert ecclesiastical pressure by having two Scottish bishops ordained by the Archbishop of York.[41] MacBeth also afforded shelter to exiles, for when Earl Godwin temporarily displaced Edward the Confessor in 1052 certain Normans in his retinue, fearing Godwin's wrath, fled to Scotland, presumably in the expectation that they would provide assistance against the Northumbrians.[42] Siward attempted abortive diplomatic overtures in 1053 but the following year more traditional methods triumphed at a great battle on the Day of the Seven Sleepers, 27 July 1054.[43] Siward's force was supported by supply ships. The battle was hard-fought; in it fell Siward's son Osbeorn, and his nephew, as well as Dolfin son of Thorfinn from Cumbria. MacBeth was defeated, his Normans killed, while he fled northward to Moray. Malcolm became king though it was to be three years before he finally despatched MacBeth. Siward returned home with 'booty such as no man had before obtained', a statement which one commentator soberly views as 'a remarkable testimony to the excellence of MacBeth's government and the soundness of whatever economic policy he may have followed';[44] a year later the 'giant' of Northumbria died at York. In later years the propaganda department of Edward I would anachronistically claim that Malcolm Canmore had become the vassal of the English king. It is salutary to recall, however, that Malcolm himself eventually died in battle while attacking the Northumbrian frontier. They were worthy opponents these warriors of pre-feudal Britain — MacBeth, Siward and Malcolm. In their ranks should be placed at least one other — Earl Thorfinn the Mighty of Orkney.

A major source for the history of Northern Scotland in the eleventh century is *Orkneyinga Saga* or *Jarla Sogur*, the saga of the earls, a version of which was written down shortly before 1192.[45] It mentions by name some six hundred men and women and over one hundred and fifty place-names in the British Isles. Historians still manifest some reluctance in utilising the saga corpus — the great Icelandic vernacular prose narratives — in their investigations and this is not the place to discuss their credits and demerits.[46] The unknown author of *Orkneyinga* betrays the strengths and weaknesses of the genre. He made great use of skaldic poetry, or the compositions of the skalds, poets who were mainly Icelandic and who like their Celtic counterparts, the bards, were as capable of immortalising a man's ignominy as they were of celebrating his great deeds. Arnor Thordarsson — earl's skald (*jarlaskald*) — for example, composed in honour of his great patron Thorfinn the Mighty of Orkney.[47] Naturally the sagaman was mainly interested in the powerful earls of Orkney and his knowledge of Scottish affairs was often pretty hazy. Nonetheless his localism is often more rewarding to the historian than the wilder assertions of contemporary, and equally hazy, English chroniclers.

However the hand behind *Orkneyinga Saga* is described — as that of scribe, author, editor or compiler — he was committing the oral medium to vellum. Notoriously in that medium the exploits of one great hero are transferred without comment to another, the deeds of lesser mortals absorbed by the better known heroes. The sagaman, like the Irish annalists, was understandably confused by the plurality of Scottish kings. Like many subsequent commentators he conflated Malcolm mormaer of Moray who died in 1029 with Malcolm II. He related that Earl Sigurd Hlodverson of Orkney married a daughter of Malcolm King of Scots — *Scotakonungr* — probably Malcolm II. The offspring of this marriage included Earl Thorfinn the Mighty, one of the greatest heroes in the saga (cap.13). The saga also mentions Malcolm Longneck (*langhåls*) i.e. Canmore and his son Duncan (cap.33). Thus only two Scottish kings for the period 1005-1094 are not mentioned by name; these are Duncan I and MacBeth. At the period which coincides with their rule a mysterious individual, not recorded in any other source, appears in the saga. This is the famed Karl Hundason whose identity has exercised the minds of many historians.[48] Most commentators have gone astray in attempting to identify this individual by assuming that the name, which means 'man son of a dog', bears pejorative connotations, that it was a term of abuse. This view cannot be sustained. No nominal criticism is implied in other individuals called Karl; for example Karl of Moer during a brief appearance in *St Olaf's Saga* is a 'manly fellow ... of noble lineage, a man of great enterprise, an athlete and resourceful in many ways'.[49] In the *Tain Bo Cuilnge* Cu Chulainn is the 'Hound of Ulster' named for a magnificent hunting hound and the Celtic equivalent of the lion.[50] There was thus no disgrace in the name. The sagas abound in abusive appellations as calculated as they were offensive; Karl Hundason is innocuous.

Duncan was considered an obscure king by a number of annalists in both England and Ireland. It would not be surprising therefore if he were similarly treated in *Orkneyinga*, particularly since, apart from visiting Pitgaveny to be killed, he presumably operated in a southern rather than a northern orbit. If Duncan was overlooked in the saga then Karl Hundason would appear to be MacBeth. There is further reason for such an identification.

Both *Orkneyinga Saga* and *Njal's Saga* describe battles fought between the Orkneymen and the native earls. *Orkneyinga* (cap.2) relates that 'a Scottish jarl called Finnleik' challenged Earl Sigurd to fight him at Skitten. Sigurd fearing the odds against him consulted his mother who was a sorceress. She contemptuously told him that 'if I thought you might live forever I'd have reared you in my wool-basket'. Armed with a raven banner (fatal to whoever carried it) and stung by maternal taunts Sigurd went on to defeat Finnleik. At least three well respected authorities[51] have suggested that this was probably the same battle as that described in *Njal's Saga* (caps.85, 86) as having been fought at Duncansby Head. On this occasion Earl Sigurd, assisted by Kari and the Njalssons confronted Earl Hundi and Earl Melsnati. Admittedly Skitten (now Kilimster north west of Wick) is ten miles south of Duncansby Head but such a short distance would not detain a sagaman, particularly since Duncansby would be a more familiar place-name to the author of *Njal's Saga*. Several battles have migrated over greater distances in the more recent past. In *Njala* the raven banner is absent but the same story — 'all those who bear it get killed' — is told of it at the Battle of Clontarf (cap.157). At Duncansby Sigurd was victorious as in the *Orkneyinga* version. Melsnati is the same name as Maelsnechtai, a name recorded for the Moray kindred. Much more significant, however, is the identification of Hundi and Finnleik or Findlaech, for the son of Hundi must be the son of Findlaech and hence, MacBeth.

If this identification is accepted then *Orkneyinga Saga* sheds considerable light on MacBeth's career, albeit conceived in the eyes of the sagaman as a minor adjunct to that of Earl Thorfinn. The latter was five years old when his father Sigurd was killed at Clontarf. Malcolm II is said to have given Thorfinn Caithness and Sutherland and to have conferred the title of earl upon him (cap.13). The earlier part of the earl's career was absorbed in a power struggle with his brothers for control of Orkney, two thirds of which he controlled by the time Karl Hundason appeared on the scene in succession to Malcolm II whose support for Thorfinn was said to have greatly strengthened the latter's position in Orkney. Karl (or if we may presume) MacBeth demanded tribute from Thorfinn for his earldom of Caithness. Refusal led to reciprocal attacks. MacBeth attempted to establish his nephew Mutatan or Muddan as earl or mormaer in Caithness, an individual who is almost certainly the eponymous of the Celtic-Norse family known as Moddan of the Dale.[52]

Moddan was driven out of Caithness while Thorfinn resided at Duncansby 'keeping five well-manned longships with him' (cap.20). MacBeth responded by personally leading a fleet of eleven ships to the north, despatching Moddan with an army overland so planning to encircle Thorfinn. The saga contains a graphic description of what ensued. MacBeth landed in Caithness, unknown to Thorfinn who set sail for Orkney. 'They were so close to each other that MacBeth and his men were able to make out the sails of Thorfinn's ships' as he was crossing the Pentland Firth, to cast anchor off Deerness. There MacBeth took the Orkneymen completely by surprise. Naval battles involved the ships grappling each other to create a floating platform, on which to all intents and purposes a land battle was fought. Thorfinn urged his men on with assurances that 'the Scots would never stand up to the pressure'. The hard fought and bitter conflict was celebrated by Arnor Jarlaskald:

> Made clear then to King Karl
> the close of his iron-fate,
> east of Deerness, defied
> and defeated by warrior-kin.
> Confronting the foe, Thorfinn's
> fleet of five ships
> steered, steadfast in anger
> against Karl's sea-goers. Ships grappled
> together; gore as foes fell,
> bathed stiff iron, black
> with Scots' blood;
> singing the bows spilt
> blood, steel bit; bright
> though the quick points quaked
> no quenching Thorfinn[53]

MacBeth, however, *was* quenched, jumping overboard to scramble on to another ship and retreating to the Moray Firth to recruit fresh troops.

Thorfinn and his foster-father Thorkel pressed their advantage by plundering the shores of the Moray Firth. Thorkel Fosterer was then despatched with an army to dispose of Moddan. He 'was able to travel in secrecy for all the people of Caithness were faithful and loyal to him'. At Thurso Thorkel sliced off Moddan's head as he leapt from his burning house. He then rejoined Thorfinn and the two once again confronted MacBeth, who was supported by reinforcements from Ireland, at Tarbat Ness. Resplendent in golden helmet Thorfinn was conspicuous as he 'outfaced the Scots king'. According to the saga the rout was so total that there were reports that MacBeth had been killed in the battle. Thereafter the sky, or indeed Fife, was the limit, for Thorfinn is said to have carried fire and sword all through Scotland to the shores of the Forth, plundering, pillaging and seizing hostages. The campaign ended gloriously if inconclusively, as Thorfinn went on to even greater feats of conquest in the Hebrides, Galloway and Ireland.[54] And now MacBeth is out of the saga, that is, assuming he had ever been in it!

It was perhaps in gratitude for Thorfinn's withdrawal from Fife that MacBeth and Gruoch 'with the utmost veneration and devotion' granted Kirkness (appropriately a Scandinavian place-name), Portmoak and 'Mactorfin's Bogie' — was MacBeth now haunted by the name Torfinn? — to Lochleven. The premise is as dubious as the notion that Thorfinn ever raided Fife but the saga does shed an interesting beam on otherwise totally undocumented aspects of MacBeth's career. It suggests that Thorfinn was embroiled in the same strife which was potentially destroying the kindred of Moray. These men did not require enemies when they had kinsmen. The saga shows the Orcadians and the Moraymen at loggerheads over a period of almost two hundred years, preserving as it does personal names known to have been used by the Moray kindreds. Maelbrigte of the poisoned tusk had despatched an earlier Earl Sigurd of Orkney in truly treacherous Celtic fashion killing a man by whom he had already been decapitated (cap.5). An earlier Jarl MacBeth (Magbjóðr) defeated an earlier Earl of Orkney at an earlier battle of Skitten (cap.10). The late Nora Chadwick made the fascinating suggestion that lines in the awesome poem *Darraðarljoð*, which was probably composed in Caithness, related not to the battle of Clontarf but to the power struggles between the men of Orkney and the native mormaers.

> Lands will be ruled
> By new peoples
> who once inhabited
> outlying headlands [55]

By one of those quirks in which two threads are spliced in the same historical tapestry, Thorfinn also went on pilgrimage to Rome (*OS* cap.31). It is not recorded whether he booked passage with MacBeth. Since the Second Coming had failed to transpire in 1000 A.D., 1050 was a good year to visit the Eternal City. Persistent doubts about the authenticity of MacBeth's pilgrimage are needless. King Dyfnwal of Cumbria had visited in the tenth century. In 1028 Sitric king of Dublin and his neighbour Flannacan king of Brega set off for Rome together. Flaithbertach Ua Néill king of Ailech went in 1030, King Cnut the following year and the King of Gailenga and his wife in 1050. Duncan MacBrian, king of Ireland and King Echmarcach of Dublin died in Rome in 1065.[56] MacBeth returned to further problems with Siward and Northumbria. Thorfinn, having received papal absolution for all his sins, gave up his viking expeditions to devote 'all his time to the government of his people and country and to the making of new laws'. At Birsay 'he built and dedicated to Christ a fine minster, the seat of the first bishop of Orkney' (cap.31). The suggestion made long ago by Skene that MacBeth and Thorfinn somehow partitioned Scotland between them is as anachronistic as it is erroneous.[57] Despite his grandiloquent obituary Thorfinn never held 'nine Scottish earldoms, the whole of the Hebrides and a considerable part of Ireland' (cap.32). Thorfinn's alleged achievements owe not a little to the contemporary activities of Sven and Cnut of Denmark and to the imperialistic ambitions of Harald Hardrada of Norway. The Orcadian empire never extended south of Strathoykel on the Scottish mainland and its tenure on the Hebrides was tenuous. Had he not been distracted by struggles with his own kinsmen in the earldom or involved in political intrigue with the kings of Norway Thorfinn might have displaced MacBeth. As it was the son of Findlaech more than held his own. If the two did travel together to Rome then each held the other hostage for the safety of their territories in their joint absence. They were, after all, civilized men of the world.

It may be reasonably objected that the name Karl Hundason bears not the remotest resemblance to the name MacBeth. The latter literally means 'son of life',[58] but this may be thought to be an ecclesiastical name and it does not preclude the possibility, indeed the probability, that MacBeth had another name or names. MacBeth would presumably be favoured by the monastic scribes and annalists who preserve most of what is known of him. On the other hand name changes are not uncommon. In *Orkneyinga Saga* King Sigurd of Norway gave Kali Kolsson the title of earl and the (new) name of Rognvald because it was considered lucky (cap.61). Much later than the eleventh century competing names for individuals are confusing — consider the designation of clan chiefs — and the subject requires more study. The use of nick-names also compounds the problem.

Scottish history, asserted the learned Roderic O Flaherty, 'is no more than a fabulous modern production founded on oral tradition'. Elsewhere he observed that there were certain individuals in the Scottish king list 'such as their mother never felt the travails of their birth but were hatched in historians' brains'.[59] The legend of MacBeth was born, or at the very least nurtured, in the works of several medieval chroniclers and historians. The first major Scottish chronicler was John of Fordun who completed his *Chronica* about 1380. He depicts Duncan as an easy going and popular king, 'murdered through the wickedness of a family, the murderer of both his grandfather and greatgrandfather, the head of which was Machabaeus or MacBeth son of Finele'[60]. The murderers then drove Duncan's sons out of the kingdom. Their supporters were harshly treated — 'some he delivered over to death, others he thrust into loathsome dungeons, others he reduced to utter want'. MacDuff Thane of Fife, nowhere mentioned in eleventh century sources, became a notable target for MacBeth's wrath and he escaped to join the exiled Malcolm Canmore in England. Fordun supplies a long account of a debate between MacDuff and Malcolm in which the latter claims that he cannot return to Scotland because he is unfit to be a king, lustful and sensuous as he is, a thief, a liar and a deceiver. This test of MacDuff's integrity was, of course, to become the basis of *MacBeth* Act IV Scene III.[61] Malcolm then, with the assistance of Siward of Northumbria, returns to Scotland and MacBeth is defeated. Fordun has no mention of Dunsinnan or Birnam but he depicts MacBeth as retreating ahead of the advancing army before he is killed at Lumphanan.

An incomparably more amusing source is Andrew Wyntoun's interminable metrical chronicle of Scotland composed in vernacular Scots about 1420. Wyntoun was a canon regular of the priory of St. Andrews and he became prior of St. Serf's, Loch Leven, in Fife. He doubtless knew of MacBeth and Gruoch's benefactions. He was a great Fife chauvinist and the William MacGonagall of his age. Wyntoun very likely drew upon material in the now lost great register of St. Andrews, specifically the *Historia* which in turn had incorporated earlier oral tradition.[62] His great value lies in his preservation of rival traditions about MacBeth and his notable adversary, Malcolm Canmore.

According to Wyntoun MacBeth had a dream in which

> He sawe thre wemen by gangand
> And thai wemen than thoucht he,
> Thre werd systers mast lyk to be.
> The fyrst he hard say gangand by
> Lo yonder the Thane of Crumbachty. [Cromarty]
> The tothir woman sayd agayne
> Off Morave yonder I see the Thane.
> The thryd than sayd I se the king
> All this he hard in his dremyng.

Wyntoun then inserts a passage obviously culled from existing records since the content can be checked from earlier extant sources:

> All this tyme was gret plenté
> Aboundand bath in land and sé.
> He was in justice rycht lawchfull
> And till his legis all awfull.
> Quhen Leo the Tend was Pape off Rome
> As pylgryme to the curt he come
> And in his almus he sew sylver
> Till all pure folk that had myster; [need]
> And all tyme oysyd he to wyrk
> Profitably for Haly Kyrke.

So far so good but Wyntoun cannot resist communicating certain strange tales about the conception of MacBeth:

> Bot as we fynd be sum storys
> Gottyne he wes on ferly wys. [marvellous]

MacBeth's mother, unnamed — it was not until Hector Boece wielded his inventive pen that she was revealed as Doalda or Donalda — had a great penchant for wandering in the woods. One day she became enamoured of a handsome stranger that she met by chance and before the word 'haughmagandie' could be uttered, he had fathered a child upon her. His pleasure taken he informed the lady that he was none other than the Devil himself but he bade her 'no be fley'd (scared) o that' and assured her with reference to her unborn son,

> na man suld be borne off wyff
> off powere to reive him hys lyff [remove]

When he became king MacBeth decided to build a great house 'apon the hicht of Dunsynane' and he gathered oxen from all over Angus and Fife to haul timber for the construction. When the oxen of MacDuff, thane of Fife, did not work hard enough the king threatened to place their owner in the yoke in their stead. MacDuff wasted no time. When he

> Makbeth herd speke
> That he wald put in yhok his neke,
> Off all hys thowcht he mad na sang
> Bot prewaly oot off the thrang
> Wyth slycht he gat ....
> And als swyne as he mycht se
> Hys tyme and oppurtunitye,
> Oot of the curt he past and ran.

In due course he had a similar debate with Malcolm to that described by Fordun.

There were also, however, stories about the peculiar circumstances of Malcolm's conception. Wyntoun the churchman had something of a hang-up where the sexual mores of the Scottish royal family were concerned. Malcolm was the illegitimate son of Duncan by his 'lemman lewyd', the daughter of the miller of Forteviot, and Duncan's desire to place Malcolm on the throne had caused MacBeth's revolt in the first place.

Malcolm and MacDuff returned to Scotland, 'past owre Forth Syne straucht to Tay' and up the water to Birnam where, wondering how to tackle MacBeth in his stronghold, they learned of his fantastical notion that he would never be defeated,

> (Until) wyth his ene he suld se
> The wode brocht off Brynnane
> to the hill of Dunsynane

This gave them the idea of cutting boughs. MacBeth saw the wood advancing, took to flight across the Mounth and was killed in Lumphanan.[63]

It is a relatively straightforward matter to explain how the MacBeth myth arose. Malcolm Canmore established a strong dynasty which produced some outstanding kings and which survived until the eve of the Wars of Independence. However, the Men of Moray continued to plague these kings. The nephew of Maelsnectai mac Lulach, Angus earl of Moray, was killed in rebellion against David I in 1130. Irish annalists noted that the battle was between the 'men of Scotland and the men of Moray' the latter being slaughtered. A supporter of Angus mormaer of Moray — Malcolm MacHeth, almost certainly a kinsman, carried the banner of resistance into the reign of Malcolm IV and beyond. This man's story has not so far been adequately investigated. He identified closely with the forces of reaction, the anti-feudal faction which included the great Somerled of Argyll and Harald Madaddsson earl of Orkney. His actions led to the transplantation of the men of Moray in the reign of Malcolm IV, but the struggle continued under Donald MacHeth and later under Kenneth MacHeth who was killed resisting Alexander II in 1215. The MacHeths in turn were associated with the MacWilliams, another disaffected kindred.

Remoteness of location, rebellion and revolt, and possibly even reality, conferred a kinship with MacBeth upon these two kindreds. The last of their line was a young child of MacWilliam descent who in 1230 had her brains dashed out on the mercat cross at Forfar.[64]

Elsewhere in Europe the Normans earned a well deserved reputation for behaving little better than thugs encased in steel. The ruffians on the Scottish frontier were the match of their counterparts on the Welsh marches or in Ireland. The chronicler of Lanercost considered the episode of 1230 'a somewhat-too-cruel vengeance for the blood of the slain' but the perpetrators of the deed were desperate men in a desperate time. Faced with such prolonged resistance the House of Dunkeld, or the Canmore dynasty as it is sometimes called, resorted to other methods of defence by mounting a deliberate campaign to blacken MacBeth's name. The means at its disposal was that of the *fili* or bard, the court poet who was commissioned to manufacture the libels which Wyntoun preserves. The bards, like their counterparts in the Norse world, the skalds, excelled in venom and scurrility. It is no coincidence that *skald* produces the English word *scold*[65] while in the fifteenth century William Dunbar wrote 'wondor laith wer I to be ane baird, flyting to use richt gritly I eschame'. That some kind of a flyting did indeed develop is suggested by the account of Malcolm Canmore's lowly mother;[66] clearly the Moray bards reciprocated. The Celts, after all, were as effective at battling with words as with swords.

It is of considerable interest that the stories about MacBeth drew upon existing motifs in Celtic and Old Norse literature. The dream motif is very common in Celtic stories and Norse sagas (as it is admittedly in many other literatures). The three weird sisters derive directly from the Norns or Fates in Old Norse mythology; in Norse they were *spákonur*, *spaewives* in Scots, who could predict the future. The story of MacBeth's father is basically a Celtic *compert* or conception tale and so is that relating to Malcom's birth. MacBeth thus joins the ranks of other 'fatherless' heroes — Taliesin in the *Mabinogion*, Ambrosius Aurelianus and St. Mungo. The cutting of the boughs at Birnam is borrowed from the traditional Celtic motif of the travelling wood known in Welsh as the *Cat Godeu*, the battle of the trees, which is also found in Germanic literature as early as the eighth century, notably in the *Gesta Francorum* of Gregory of Tours. The idea of a seemingly impossible condition or conditions being fulfilled before the hero can be killed is an example of *geis* (pl. *gessa*) which has many parallels in both Irish and Old Norse tales.[67] At one time there were probably many more traditions about MacBeth and his opponents in circulation. Fortunately for posterity at least some of the effusions of the bards have been preserved by the medieval chroniclers.

Dunsinnan Hill is still where it was in MacBeth's day, in the beautiful Howe of Strathmore (Fig.7.1). The hill is crowned by most impressive ramparts of a dark-age fortress, one of the largest enclosed areas of any

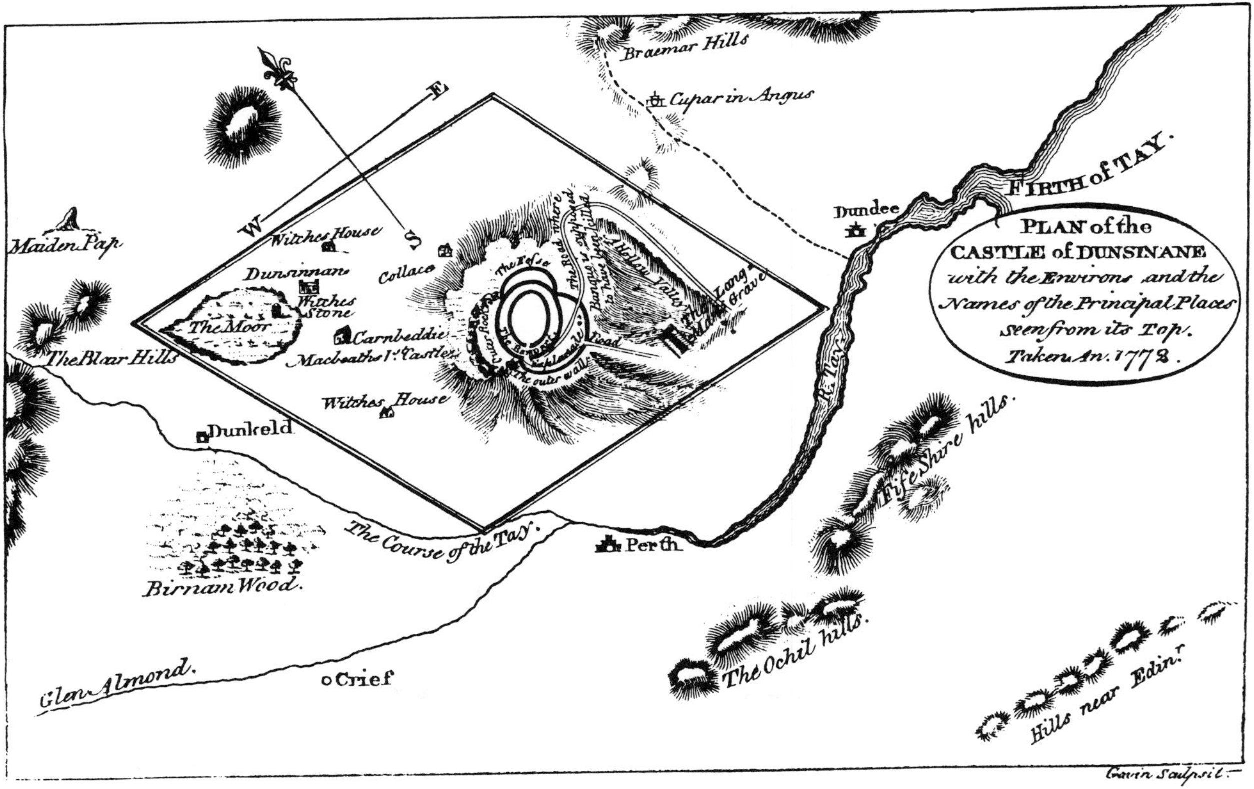
PLAN of the
CASTLE of DUNSINANE
with the Environs and the
Names of the Principal Places
seen from its Top.
Taken An. 1772.
FIRTH of TAY.
Braemar Hills
Cupar in Angus
Dundee
R. Tay.
Maiden Pap.
The Blaar Hills
The Moor
Witches House
Dunsinnan
Witches Stone
Collace
Carnbeddie
Macbeaths 1st Castle
Witches House
Dunkeld
Birnam Wood.
The Course of the Tay.
Perth
Fife Shire hills.
The Ochil hills.
Hills near Edinr.
Glen Almond.
o Crief
W
S
E
Gavin Sculpsit.

Fig.7.2 Plan of the Castle of Dunsinane, 1772.

surviving Scottish fortification from the period. From the summit the woods of Birnam can clearly be seen to the west along the Tay valley. To the east the city of Dundee and the Firth of Tay are clearly visible.[68] Northwards the great mass of the Grampians conceals the hill tracks and glens that would lead MacBeth to Lumphanan. In the vicinity are a number of sites associated with our hero — Carnbeddie, supposedly MacBeth's Castle; MacBeth's stone, a large chunk of whinstone some twenty tons in weight which could only have been lifted by a veritable Cu Chullain; and the tumulus of Belle Duff where the dead were supposedly buried. The vicinity was surveyed by Sir John Sinclair in 1772, satisfactorily proving to himself the highly improbable thesis that Shakespeare had actually visited the place to do a little field work.[69] There are similar attributions in MacBeth's Cairn and Cairn Baddy in Lumphanan.[70] The route of retreat from Dunsinnan to Lumphanan has been minutely traced via Brechin, across the Fir Mounth Road to Aboyne, through Cromar to the slopes of Mortlich where MacBeth's well marks a place of refreshment during his last great battle.[71] All of these sites almost certainly post-date Shakespeare. The Scots were a literate lot and many a canny soul must have invented sites for the credulous tourist.

Considering the amount of propaganda in circulation about MacBeth in the centuries following his death and the prolonged resistance to the central monarchy on the part of the Men of Moray it is perhaps surprising that the name itself remained fairly common until about 1300 when, as a forename it seems to disappear.[72] It was not MacBeth of Moray who left his name on MacBeth's Castle up Manor Water in Peebleshire; the name clearly was not avoided as was that, for example, of John, considered unlucky at a later date, since fairly impressive lists of the name's occurrence have been compiled.[73] It is perhaps even more surprising that in the fifteenth century a number of clans claimed descent from none other than MacBeth. Such was the boast of, among others, the MacQuarries, MacKinnons and the MacMillans. Epigraphical confirmation for such genealogical claims has recently been uncovered.[74] It is, however, difficult to believe that this descent is actually genuine[75] involving as it does such hoary questions as 'How many children had Lady MacBeth'?[76] We can discount the tradition that a standing stone in the parish of Tough marks the spot where MacBeth's son died[77] but what is not in doubt, as above indicated, is that strenuous efforts were made to exterminate anyone remotely related to the king. Lulach son of Gruoch and Gillacomgain was killed in Strathbogie in 1058,[78] wrongly regarded by some as MacBeth's son rather than his step-son[79]. He stands at the head of a bloody procession extending all the way to the child at Forfar in 1230, a chronicle of carnage written by those 'devoted ... to a new kind of Scottish kingdom'. If a son of MacBeth had survived to procreate it is almost inconceivable that he would have escaped notice. On the other hand the fifteenth century clans associated with the Lordship of the Isles knew perfectly well what MacBeth represented. To them he was the last great Celtic king of Scots, a challenge to the encroachment of centralising authority and a mirror of their own aspirations.

Did William Shakespeare, then, perpetuate a wilful and unforgivable fraud in his treatment of MacBeth? The answer, like so much in Scottish history, is poetically ambiguous. Shakespeare clearly intended, in presenting his play, to warn James VI and I of the danger of tyranny, reminding him that 'a good and virtuous nature may recoil in an imperial charge' — the kingly office may corrupt. Few kings have had to suffer so much advice as the unfortunate James. George Buchanan harped on the danger of power overextended, reinforcing the idea that the king was bound by a contract with his subjects. The presbyterian ministers, headed by Andrew Melville, played the same tune. It was a relief for 'God's sillie vassal' to flee to England only to receive more lectures from the scribbler of Stratford. Yet Shakespeare did hit the mark, though he chose the wrong target. The Scots throughout the centuries did control their kings more rigorously than other nations. This tradition derived from an ancient, and by no means exclusively Celtic belief, in sacral kingship. If the country was ruled by a good king, if he had the power of truth, his personal prosperity would be reflected in the well-being of his subjects and kingdom. Conversely the bad king would bring war, famine, pestilence and poverty upon his kingdom and the solution then, the way to restore prosperity or normality, was quite simply to kill the king.

It is a superb irony that Shakespeare makes precisely the same point — MacBeth's unnatural act assures that the times are out of joint:

> Thou seest the heavens as troubled with man's act,
> Threatens his bloody stage: by th' clock 'tis day,
> And yet dark night strangles the travelling lamp:
> Is't night's predominance, or the day's shame,
> That darkness does the face of earth entomb,
> When living light should kiss it? (Act II Scene IV)

A falcon was killed by a mousing owl. Duncan's horses ate each other. Shakespeare strengthened his drama by borrowing the witches of Forres from the tenth century reign of King Duff but to similar effect he totally suppressed Duncan's 'softness and over much slackness in punishing offenders'.[80] Historically virtually nothing is known of Duncan save his abortive siege of Durham in 1040, the very year in which he was removed, possibly on account of the 'immaturity' with which he is credited by Marianus Scottus. Shakespeare in a superb example of dramatic irony was guilty of a colossal historical inversion in his treatment of MacBeth. The single most important fact that has been preserved about the king is enshrined in the *Chronicle of Melrose* in a line borrowed from a Latin poem composed within a generation of MacBeth's death — in his time *fertile tempus erat.*[81] In his time there were productive seasons, a perfect reference to the idea of sacral kingship, rendered by Wyntoun:

> All his tyme was gret plenté
> Aboundand bath in land and sé.

MacBeathadh the famed[82] was also celebrated in similar vein by the Prophecy of St. Berchan:

> ... the ruddy-faced king will possess the kingdom of high-hilled Scotland.
> After the slaughter of the Scots, after the slaughter of the foreigners, the liberal king will possess Scotland.
> The strong one was fair, yellow haired and tall.
> Very pleasant was that handsome youth to me.
> Brimful of food was Scotland, east and west,
> During the reign of the ruddy, brave king.[83]

Historically it was most likely Duncan who was sacrificed for good seasons. What James knew, thanks to George Buchanan, and what Shakespeare presumably did not, was that if MacBeth truly had been the tyrant depicted in the play, he would have been removed by his own people — no assistance from England would have been required. MacBeth strutted his hour upon the Scottish stage of kingship for seventeen years. He contained the House of Dunkeld, fought off the might of the earldom of Orkney and resisted the southern threat posed by Earl Siward and his Northumbrians. His kingdom was sufficiently secure to permit him to visit Rome. He was to be remembered as the great champion of the Men of Moray and latterly of Gaelic Scotland. But above all, in his time there were productive seasons.

## Notes

1. James Aikman, *The History of Scotland Translated from the Latin of George Buchanan* 4 vols. (Edinburgh 1827) i, 336.
2. Robert Douglas, *Annals of the Royal Burgh of Forres* (Elgin 1934) relates the story that one Alexander Duff, a native of Forres who emigrated to the United States, was summoned by the President who was anxious for information about the 'blasted heath'. Since this was in the 1880s he was a little late for Abe Lincoln who opined 'I think nothing equals *MacBeth*. It is wonderful ...' (*Complete Works* vol. IX).
3. Henry N Paul, *The Royal Play of MacBeth* (New York 1948) 317-31, 399-402. The latest editor of *MacBeth* considers it unlikely that the play was ever designed for court performance [Nicholas Brooke, *Tragedy of MacBeth* (The Oxford Shakespeare, 1990)].
4. Edward J Cowan 'The Darker Vision of the Scottish Renaissance; the Devil and Francis Stewart' in *Renaissance and Reformation in Scotland* edd. Ian B Cowan and Duncan Shaw (Edinburgh 1983); Peter Stallybrass 'MacBeth and Witchcraft' in *Focus on MacBeth* ed. John Russell Brown (London 1982).

Existing investigations of 'topicality' or attempts to uncover the contemporary model for MacBeth are not convincing eg. Sir James Fergusson, *The Man Behind MacBeth and Other Studies* (London 1969), Arthur Melville Clark, *Murder Under Trust or The Topical MacBeth and other Jacobean Matters* (Edinburgh 1981); but the obvious candidate in the crowded gallery of rogues and miscreants in Jacobean Scotland is clearly Bothwell.

5. John S Keltie, *History of the Scottish Highlands* 2 vols. (Edinburgh 1875) i, 54.

6. Somerled MacMillan, *A Vindication of MacBeth and His Claims* (Ipswich, Mass.1959) 3.

7. P Buchan, *The Secret History of MacBeth* (Peterhead 1828) 19, 66. This remarkable production would repay further study. It enraged poor John MacBeth (*MacBeth King, Queen and Clan* (Edinburgh 1921) 13-19) but its pages preserve rare specimens of Scottish erotica and such hitherto suppressed historical nuggets as the assertion that 'Banquo was a latitudarian in love but never asked a man to pimp for his sister' (p. 85). Just why Peter Buchan, the well known ballad collector, should have thought it worth reprinting is a mystery.

8. *Stat.Acct.* xx, 246.

9. John MacBeth, *MacBeth King Queen and Clan* (Edinburgh 1921) 32, 66.

10. Ruaraidh Erskine of Marr, *MacBeth* (Inverness 1930) 77.

11. *MacBeth King Queen and Clan* 64.

12. Peter Berresford Ellis, *MacBeth High King of Scotland 1040-57* (London 1980).

13. Dorothy Dunnett, *King Hereafter. A Novel* (New York 1982).

14. Nora Chadwick 'The Story of MacBeth' (1949) *Scottish Gaelic Studies* vi, pt.1, and (1951) *S.G.S.* vii, pt.2.

15. G W S Barrow 'MacBeth and Other Mormaers of Moray' in *The Hub of the Highlands* (Inverness Field Club 1975) 113, 122.

16. Gordon Donaldson, *Scotland James V to James VII* (Edinburgh, London 1965); Maurice Lee, *Government by Pen. Scotland under James VI and I* (Urbana 1980); Jenny Wormald, *Court, Kirk and Community. Scotland 1470-1625* (London 1981); Keith M Brown, *Bloodfeud in Scotland. Violence, Justice and Politics in an Early Modern Society* (Edinburgh 1986).

17. John Bannerman, *Studies in the History of Dalriada* (Edinburgh 1974) 108ff, 132; David Sellar 'Highland Family Origins — Pedigree Making and Pedigree Faking' in *The Middle Ages in the Highlands* (Inverness Field Club 1981) 104.

18. Alfred P Smyth, *Warlords and Holy Men. Scotland AD 80 - 1000* (London, 1984) 218ff.

19. D A Binchy, *Celtic and Anglo-Saxon Kingship* (Oxford 1970) 31; Bannerman, *Dalriada* 134.

20. Francis John Byrne, *Irish Kings and High Kings* (London 1973) 42.

21. *Annals of Ulster to AD 1131* [AU] edd. Sean MacAirt and Gearoid MacNiocaill (Dublin 1983).

22. See K Jackson, *The Gaelic Notes in the Book of Deer* (Cambridge 1972) 110ff. *The Book of Deer* contains a clear example of one who was both *ruiri* and *rí* — Muiredach, 'it is he who was mormaer and toisech' (pp.30, 33, 112). The identification of toisech and thane is, of course, the source of all those thanages which clutter up the legend of MacBeth. See G W S Barrow 'Pre-feudal

Scotland: shires and thanes' in *The Kingdom of the Scots* (London 1973). Symeon of Durham describes Crinan, lay abbot of Dunkeld, as Crinan the thane (Anderson, *Early Sources of Scottish History* (Edinburgh, 1922) ii, 41. A confused reference in the *Anglo-Saxon Chronicle* names Malbeth (? Mac-Beth) as a 'king' who submitted to King Cnut, along with Malcolm II in 1031 (Anderson, *Scottish Annals from English Chroniclers* (London, 1908) 82-3).

23. A O Anderson, *Early Sources of Scottish History* [*ES*] 2 vols (Edinburgh 1922) i, 571.

24. Jackson, *Book of Deer* 31, 34, 52.

25. Andrew Wyntoun *The Orygynale Cronykil of Scotland* (Historians of Scotland, Edinburgh 1872) ii, p.128.

26. The burning of Njal is the central episode in *Njal's Saga*. Moddan of Caithness is smoked out in *Orkneyinga Saga* [*OS*] (cap.20), while Frakokk and her associates were burned to death by Svein Asleifsson (cap.78). That such time-honored methods were by no means redundant by the late 16th century is attested by such ballads as 'The Burning of the Bonnie Hoose o Airlie' and 'The Burning of Frendraught'.

27. *OS* cap. 95; Edward J Cowan 'Caithness in the Sagas' in *Caithness. A Cultural Crossroads* ed. John R. Baldwin (Edinburgh 1982) 37.

28. Erskine, *MacBeth* 42.

29. Kenneth Jackson 'The Duan Albanach' (1957) 36 *SHR* 133.

30. *ES* i, 580.

31. *OS* cap.12.

32. MacMillan, *MacBeth* 9.

33. A C Lawrie, *Early Scottish Charters prior to AD* 1153 (Glasgow 1905) 5-6, 231-2.

34. Anderson notes a reference, which he suggests may mark a stage in the feud which continued through MacBeth's reign, in the *Annals of the Four Masters*, 999 — 'Dungal Kenneth's son was killed by Gillacomgain Kenneth's son', an intriguing juxtaposition of patronymics (though hopefully different *patres*) which doubtless appealed to the annalist (*ES* i, 520). AU 1035 notes that the granddaughter of Gilla Caemgein son of Cinaed and her husband Cathal together with his hound were killed by the son of Cellach son of Dunchad. The *Scottish Chronicle* (Anderson's Chronicle King List A) a generally reliable source [see E J Cowan 'The Scottish Chronicle in the Poppleton Manuscript' 32 *Innes Review* (1980)] states that Malcolm mac Donald (943-954) 'went with his army into Moray and slew Cellach' (*ES* i, 452). Another Cellach is mentioned as reigning in the 960s. As Barrow 'MacBeth', p.3 notes the *Annals of Tigernach* 976 record 'three mormaers of Scotland - Cellach son of Findguine, Cellach son of Bard and Duncan son of Morgand' (*ES* i, 480). Cellach may indeed be a Moray name as Professor Barrow suggests and the events of 1035 may be somehow linked to those of 999. For some reason the Irish annalists remained very interested in the activities of the Men of Moray right through until the 12th century. [However, there may be some confusion here between the names Gilla Comgain and Gilla Caemgain - Ed.]

35. Shakespeare derived the name of MacBeth's father, Sinell (Brooke, *Tragedy of MacBeth* i, 3, 71) from Holinshed where 'S' has clearly been rendered for 'F'.

36. *ES* i, 581
37. *ES* i, 583-4; AO Anderson, *Scottish Annals from English Chronicles AD* 500 *to* 1286 (London 1908) 84.
38. *ES* i, 600-02.
39. William E Kapelle, *The Norman Conquest of the North. The Region and its Transformation* 1000-1135 (Chapel Hill 1979) 27-49.
40. Ibid., 42-4.
41. Ibid., 44.
42. Frank Barlow, *Edward the Confessor* (London 1970) 126.
43. The Day of the Seven Sleepers, 27 July, is named for seven young men who defied the Emperor Decius at Ephesus. They hid in a cave in Mount Coelius subsequently sealed up. Over two hundred years later they were awakened from their slumber miraculously believing they had slept only one night. A festival was established in their honour (R Chambers, *The Book of Days* 2 vols. (Edinburgh, 1864) ii, 127; *The Catholic Encyclopedia* 15 vols. (New York 1909) loc. cit.). Some aspect of the story may have influenced the legend of MacBeth.
44. R L G Ritchie, *The Normans in Scotland* (Edinburgh 1954) 7.
45. Peter Foote 'Observations on Orkneyinga Saga' and Paul Bibire 'The Poetry of Earl Rognwald's Court', in *St. Magnus Cathedral and Orkney's Twelfth-Century Renaissance* ed. Barbara E Crawford (Aberdeen 1988) at 197 and 212 respectively. For *Orkneyinga Saga* see A B Taylor, *The Orkneyinga Saga. A New Translation with Introduction and Notes* (Edinburgh, 1938); *Orkneyinga Saga. The History of the Earls of Orkney* trans. Hermann Palsson and Paul Edwards (Harmondsworth 1978); and *Orkneyinga Saga* ed. Finnbogi Gudmundsson *Islenzk Fornrit* (Reykjavik, 1965).
46. Cowan 'Caithness in the Sagas' 25-7.
47. Lee M Hollander, *The Skalds* (Ann Arbor 1945) 177-88.
48. Almost all commentators have interpreted Karl Hundason as a name of abuse. Skene identified Karl with Duncan who is nicknamed *Ilgalrach*, diseased, in some Irish sources (WF Skene, *Celtic Scotland* 3 vols (2nd ed. Edinburgh 1886-90) i, 400-404). Many have followed him eg. Ellis, *MacBeth* 46ff. A B Taylor, 'Karl Hundason "King of Scots"' *PSAS* lxxi (1936-7) 334-341 which suggests tht Karl was an otherwise unknown *regulus* of Argyll is quite unconvincing.
49. Lee M Hollander, *Heimskringla. History of the Kings of Norway* (Austin 1964) 429.
50. Two other persons named Hundi are mentioned in the saga. Hundi or Hvelp a son of Earl Sigurd was taken hostage by Olaf Tryggvason (cap.12), an episode also noted in *Heimskringla* (Hollander p.351). Once again the name Whelp need not be considered in a pejorative sense. The other reference occurs in the name Holdbodi Hundason, a great chieftain in Tiree (caps.66,67).
51. Anderson, *ES* i, 499; Taylor, *OS* p.356; and Chadwick 'MacBeth' (1951) 5.
52. Cowan 'Caithness in the Sagas' 33.
53. *OS* cap. 20.
54. A most suggestive skaldic verse referring to Thorfinn is translated by Taylor (p.173) as follows:
    The Man of the Sword

Seeking Scotland's throne,
Ever won victory.
Fire flamed fiercely,
Fast fell the Irish host
And flower of Welsh manhood (cap.22)

This translation has been eagerly embraced by Ellis, *MacBeth* 42. However there is nothing in the original text which would justify the first part of Taylor's translation. Thus the passage:

Ymisst vann sás vnni
írsk fell drott, þás sótti,
Baldrs eða brezkar aldir.
brá eldr Skota veldi (Gudmundsson p.59)

is less misleadingly rendered by Palsson and Edwards,

The warrior laid waste
now the Welsh, now the Irish
now feasted the Scots
with fire and flame (*OS* cap.22)

55. *Njals Saga* cap.157; Chadwick 'MacBeth' (1951) 22.

56. Kathleen Hughes, *The Church in Early Irish Society* (London l966) 256; *ES* i, 592.

57. William F Skene, *Celtic Scotland. A History of Ancient Alban* 3 vols, (2nd ed. Edinburgh, 1886-90) i, 405.

58. John Bannerman, *The Beatons: a medical kindred in the classical Gaelic Tradition* (Edinburgh 1986) 1.

59. Roderic O'Flaherty, *Ogygia or a Chronological Account of Irish Events* trans. Rev. James Hely (Dublin 1793) 226.

60. For this and what follows see Johannis de Fordun *Chronica Gentis Scotorum* [*Chron.Fordun*] i, 187-206, iv, 174-94. Fordun's assertion might actually be correct. The Men of Moray and the stench of treachery are linked in notices of the killings of Malcolm I (954) and Kenneth II (995). To each that sinister phrase is applied — *a suis occisus est*, almost a code in the annals (*ES* i, 451-4, 511-16). In Walter Bower's *Scotichronicon* [*Chron.Bower*] MacBeth's murder of Duncan furnishes an excuse for a homily on kingship (vol.2, edd. John and Winifred MacQueen (Aberdeen 1989) caps.49-55, pp.419-441).

61. *MacBeth*'s recent editor 'does not know' where Holinshed 'found the dialogue between Malcolm and MacDuff' (Brooke, p.70)

62. Chadwick 'MacBeth' (1949) 199.

63. Wyntoun, ii pp.122-41. *Berchan's Prophecy*, a problematical source, contains the line 'In the middle of Scone he (MacBeth) will vomit blood, on the evening of a night, after a wound' (*ES* i, 601). It has been suggested that the passage should be interpreted to mean, not that MacBeth died at Scone, which would contradict every other account, but that he was surprised at Scone, was wounded and escaped. The legend of Birnam Wood does seem to support the idea of a surprise attack (Erskine, *MacBeth*, 74-5; Ellis, *MacBeth*, 92-3).

64. The troubled history of the MacHeths may be traced through the pages of Anderson, *Early Sources*. The *Chronicle of Holyrood* notes that in 1163 *rex Malcolmus Murevienses transtulit*, king Malcolm transferred the men of Moray (Anderson, *Scottish Annals from English Chroniclers* 142-3, 190). Fordun

expanded this to a full blown transplantation — 'Malcolm collected an army and transferred the rebel nation of Moray to the other districts, on both sides of the mountains, so that not one remained; and placed in Moray a peaceful population' (*Chron.Fordun* i, 256-7). Mackay historians cited this reference to explain the arrival of their supposed ancestors, the MacHeths, in Sutherland. The eponymous of the MacHeths is alleged to be Aed husband of Lulach's daughter [Angus Mackay, *The Book of Mackay* (Edinburgh, 1906) 21], which if true would neatly link the MacHeths into the MacBeth kindred, but the matter is contentious.

65. Bibire, 212.
66. cf. David Sellar 'Marriage, Divorce and Concubinage in Gaelic Scotland' in (1981) 51 *Transactions of the Gaelic Society of Inverness* 1978-80, 475-6.
67. Chadwick 'MacBeth'.
68. George Stevens, *MacBeth, Earl Siward and Dundee. A contribution to Scottish history from the Rune Finds of Scandinavia* (Edinburgh 1876) argued on the basis of a runic inscription from East Gotland that the battle of Dunsinnan was actually fought at Dundee. His arguments do not convince.
69. *Stat.Acct.* xx, 241-6.
70. *Stat.Acct.* vi, 388; *NSA* xii, 1082-4.
71. Erskine, *MacBeth* 74-8.
72. Bannerman, *Beatons* 1.
73. MacBeth, *MacBeth King Queen and Clan* 93-5; George Chalmers, *Caledonia* 4 vols. (Edinburgh 1807) i, 412.
74. Kenneth Steer and John Bannerman, *Late Medieval Monumental Sculpture in the West Highlands* (Edinburgh 1977) 103.
75. Sellar, 'Highland Family Origins' (above, note 17) 106.
76. L C Knights 'How many Children had Lady MacBeth?' in *Explorations* (London 1946).
77. *Stat.Acct.* viii, 269.
78. *ES* i, 602-4.
79. Ibid., i, 604; O'Flaherty, *Ogygia* 263.
80. Raphael Holinshed, *The Scottish Chronicle or a Complete History and Description of Scotland* (Arbroath 1805) 293-7, 336.
81. *ES* i, 601.
82. Jackson 'Duan Albanach' 133.
83. Ellis, *MacBeth* 63.

*Lochindorb, (G. Stell).*

# THE WOLF OF BADENOCH
## Alexander Grant

Some six hundred years ago, on 17 June 1390, the province of Moray experienced the most dramatic of the acts of violence which punctuate its history. 'The men of lord Alexander Stewart, son of the late king [Robert II] ... in the presence of the said lord Alexander, burned the whole town of Elgin and the Church of St Giles in it, the hospice beside Elgin, eighteen noble and beautiful mansions of canons and chaplains, and — what gives most bitter pain — the noble and beautiful church of Moray, the beacon of the countryside and ornament of the kingdom, with all the books, charters and other goods of the countryside preserved there.'[1] As well as being the son of Robert II, the lord Alexander was earl of Buchan, lord of the earldom of Ross and lord of Badenoch; but, as the chronicler Walter Bower put it in the early 1440s, he 'was vulgarly called The Wolf of Badenoch'. We cannot be sure if that was a contemporary nickname, but it certainly sums up his effect on the province of Moray. Although Elgin cathedral was subsequently repaired, so that its present state cannot be blamed on the Wolf, viewing the modern ruins does help bridge the six centuries and gives a vivid sense of the outrage which he and his men — 'wyld wykkyd Heland-men' — committed.[2]

Alexander Stewart first appears in Badenoch, the main Highland part of the province of Moray, twenty years earlier, when he was probably in his late teens. On 14 August 1370 he issued letters patent from Ruthven (the *caput* of Badenoch) in which he undertook to protect all the men and lands of the bishop of Moray, especially in Strathspey and Badenoch, and ordered his friends and men to look after the bishop's men and lands as if they were his own. Surprisingly, the document is dated about six months before Alexander's formal grant of Badenoch. The explanation is probably that (judging by the review of landholding after David II's 1367 Act of Revocation), Alexander's father, Robert Stewart, himself held Badenoch in the 1360s. He had probably acquired it through his second marriage, in 1355, to the widow of the last Randolph earl of Moray; since Badenoch was part of the Randolph earldom, it may have come to Robert as her widow's terce. Despite the query about it in 1367, it apparently stayed in Robert Stewart's hands for the rest of David II's reign — and Robert presumably allowed his third son Alexander to exercise lordship in it on his behalf.[3]

In 1370 Alexander's position in Badenoch was unofficial; he is plain 'Alexander Senescallus' in his undertaking to the bishop. But once his father had succeeded David II on the throne (22 February 1371), his position was formalised. On 30 March 1371 he was granted the lordship of Badenoch together with the lands, forest and castle of Lochindorb.

That constituted a major part of the earldom of Moray, but Alexander perhaps wanted more. The first chamberlain's account for Robert II's reign records receipts of only £11 from Moray, 'and no more from the fermes or grains of the said earldom because lord Alexander Stewart, the son of the king, has taken possession of them.'[4] Three of his brothers were already earls; Alexander may have had designs on the earldom. It would have been difficult, however, for his father to give it to him, because of the claims of the Randolph heirs-general. In 1371 these were George Dunbar, earl of March, and his brother John. Both had supported Robert II significantly at the beginning of his reign and deserved to be rewarded; accordingly, Robert made John Dunbar earl of Moray in March 1372. But John did not get the whole Randolph earldom: Alexander's extended lordship of Badenoch was excluded, and so were Lochaber (held by John MacDonald, lord of the Isles) and Urquhart, a large barony stretching westwards from the southern half of Loch Ness, which went to Alexander's younger brother David. John Dunbar was compensated with land in Aberdeenshire, and married one of King Robert's daughters.[5]

The division of the Randolph earldom of Moray which began when Robert Stewart acquired Badenoch was thus consolidated. The 1372 earldom consisted of the southern coastal plain of the Moray Firth, from the mouth of the Spey to Inverness, plus the region around upper Loch Ness; but within this all the land of the sheriffdom of Nairn was held by the earls of Ross.[6] Thus in practice John Dunbar's territory was restricted to the fairly small modern shire (now district) of Moray, and the area around Inverness and Loch Ness. This was the most fertile and economically valuable part of the province of Moray; but politically and strategically, without most of its hinterland, it looks extremely weak, open to attack from the Highland areas to the south, and especially from the lordship of Badenoch. (The loss of Lochindorb, formerly the earldom's main stronghold, no doubt explains why John Dunbar built the great hall at Darnaway, discussed elsewhere in this volume by Mr Stell.)

Badenoch was the first in a series of grants made to Alexander in the early part of his father's reign. During the 1370s he expanded his lands to the west of Loch Ness by leasing Urquhart from his brother, and extended his Grampian possessions eastwards with the barony of Stratha'an, which is the valley of the river Avon, on the eastern side of the Cairngorms running down to the river Spey.[7] Then, following several smaller acquisitions from Caithness to Aberdeenshire and Perthshire,[8] in June 1382 he more than doubled his territory by marrying Countess Euphemia of Ross, a few months after the death of her first husband. On his marriage, he was granted the earldom of Ross, then the largest earldom in Scotland, for life, and joint ownership of the rest of Euphemia's inheritance: chiefly the isle of Skye, the thanage and castle of Dingwall, the barony and sheriffdom of Nairn, and the barony of Kineddar in Aberdeenshire. He became an earl: Kineddar consisted of part of the lands of the old earldom of Buchan, to which Euphemia was an heiress, and therefore Alexander took the title earl of Buchan.[9] These territories carried great administrative and judicial powers, especially Badenoch, which Alexander held with the semi-royal powers of regality. In addition, he was sheriff of Inverness, which covered the modern (pre-1975) shire and the whole area to the north of it. And, in October 1372, Robert II appointed him royal lieutenant north of the Moray Firth and in Inverness-shire outside Moray; that placed him above the earls of Ross, Sutherland and Caithness, and (at least in theory), the Gaelic chiefs of the north and west.[10]

This accumulation of territory and offices clearly made Alexander Stewart supreme in the North. With Badenoch, Ross, Nairn, Urquhart and Stratha'an he had far more territory than the earl of Moray, and he had his official positions, sheriff of Inverness and royal lieutenant, as well. Consider also his main castles: Ruthven, dominating the main north-south route through the Highlands; Lochindorb, dominating Strathspey; Urquhart, dominating the middle of the Great Glen; Inverness (held as sheriff), dominating 'the hub of the Highlands'; and Dingwall, dominating the routes to the north. All in all, Alexander's position in the early 1380s looks to have been as powerful as, or even more powerful than, that held by anyone else in the whole history of the Highlands, at least since the time of Macbeth.

It is reasonable to assume that Alexander's rapid rise to such power would have been resented by the other local magnates. His main neighbours, however, were equally new arrivals on the scene. In the 1370s Ross was held by Euphemia Ross's first husband, Sir Walter Lesley, formerly a courtier of David II, who had no firm base in the region. Similarly the slimmed-down Moray had gone in 1372 to the southern incomer John Dunbar. Both men's interests probably lay elsewhere: Walter Lesley spent much of the 1370s abroad, while John Dunbar was prominent in Border warfare.[11] Neither seems to have mounted — or to have been able to mount — any challenge to Alexander Stewart.

He was challenged, however, by the local ecclesiastical potentate, Bishop Alexander Bur of Moray. In the medieval Highlands, bishoprics were generally closely linked with earldoms: Dunblane and Strathearn, Dunkeld and Atholl, Rosemarkie and Ross. On the other hand in Moray, where there was no earldom in the twelfth and thirteenth centuries, the bishops were much more independent, like their colleagues of St Andrews and Glasgow. In the Wars of Independence Bishop David Murray — whose famous support for Robert Bruce may partly have been due to antipathy towards the Comyn lords of Badenoch — is an example of this. But when Robert I created the great earldom of Moray for Thomas Randolph, the bishopric of Moray, like all the other ecclesiastical and lay lordships in the province, was put under the earl's overlordship, regality jurisdiction, and military leadership.[12] Robert I's grant, however, was limited to the heirs-male of Randolph's body, and so technically it lapsed when the male Randolph line died out in 1346. That is almost certainly what Bishop Bur believed; throughout a long episcopate (1362-1397), he seems to have been obsessed with asserting his bishopric's former independence. Aspects of this, for instance 'following the earl's banner', were issues in his quarrel with John Dunbar, earl of Moray, during the 1380s. Earlier, in 1365, he persuaded David II to allow him to have full (in practice, regality) jurisdiction over his tenants in Strathspey and Badenoch, to the exclusion of the royal justiciar and other officers. And when he in effect recognised Alexander Stewart as *de facto* lord of Badenoch in 1370, he insisted on Alexander's promise not to summon the bishop's men to his courts, nor to impose exactions on them, nor to raise them for any army — all points which echo Thomas Randolph's superiority over the bishopric.[13]

The agreement with Alexander Stewart, however, was made before the formal grant of the lordship of Badenoch in March 1371. According to Robert II's charter, Alexander was to hold the lands of Badenoch in regality and in every way as Thomas Randolph, earl of Moray, had held them, which presumably included superiority over the episcopal territories.[14] No doubt Bishop Bur protested, and that might explain the curious fact that the version of the grant of Badenoch recorded in the *Register of the Great Seal* has no mention of regality rights nor of Thomas Randolph's powers; instead, Alexander was to hold Badenoch simply as John Comyn and his predecessors had held it, in the thirteenth century.[15] But since that more limited grant did not stop Alexander from exercising regality jurisdiction, it is reasonable to assume that it likewise did not inhibit him from regarding himself as having the same powers as Thomas Randolph. At any rate during the 1370s Alexander seems to have been trying to force Bishop Bur to recognise his superiority over the episcopal lands in Badenoch and Strathspey. This caused a long-running struggle, which can be partly reconstructed from documents recorded in the *Register of the Bishopric of Moray*.

The evidence starts with the notarial account, produced for the bishop, of a 'test case' in Alexander's chief court for Badenoch, held on 10 October 1380 at the standing stones of Easter Kingussie.[16] Bishop Bur had been specially summoned, to show on what grounds he held certain episcopal lands in Badenoch. He turned up with a sizeable following, but remained outside the court and made the following declaration: his appearance did not mean that he recognised Alexander Stewart's jurisdiction, but he happened to have heard that he had been cited, and wished to protest; he held his lands directly of the crown, and some months earlier had asserted this before the king and the royal council in Inverness. Alexander replied that he needed proof that the episcopal lands were held directly of the crown; otherwise the case would proceed. The bishop then tried to have the dispute transferred to the royal courts. He offered a pledge to the sheriff of Inverness; offering a pledge, generally a sum of money, to the convenor of a court was the normal way to initiate a lawsuit. But the sheriff of Inverness was Alexander Stewart himself, and he refused to accept the bishop's pledge. Next the bishop appealed to the justiciary court. The justiciar, then Sir Alexander Lindsay of Glenesk,[17] was not present, but William Chalmers the justice clerk was. Chalmers was also, however, Alexander Stewart's secretary, and once again the bishop's pledge was rejected. The bishop also offered the pledge to Patrick Crawford, sheriff of Banff, who had just arrived; but he was probably one of Alexander Stewart's men, and in turn refused the case. The only other royal representative present was Robert Galbraith, the king's macer, and he did accept the pledge. But that did not stop the case from continuing in the Badenoch regality court, which found against the bishop, and the episcopal lands in Badenoch were declared forfeit. The bishop reacted by declaring that any action against them by Alexander's officials was a trespass against the royal dignity and the liberties of the bishopric of Moray, risking severe royal penalties and, being sacrilege, the most severe ecclesiastical punishments. Nevertheless, the first round had gone to Alexander.

Next day, however, informal procedures replaced formal ones. The bishop had long discussions with Alexander in Ruthven castle. Eventually, Alexander declared that he was now 'fully informed' about the case, and on the advice of his council — including William Chalmers, Patrick Crawford, and another of Alexander's followers, Sir William Fotheringham — he agreed that the judgement against the bishop should be revoked. William Chalmers cut the record of the case out of the court roll, and ceremonially burned it before a crowd of local landowners and clergy. Round two had gone to the bishop, and the previous day's formal proceedings are revealed as largely shadow boxing. The bishop would have known his appeals were futile, but had to go through the proper procedures. Conversely Alexander must have known of the bishop's appearance at Inverness before his father and a council headed by his two elder brothers; it is hard to believe, indeed, that Alexander himself would not have been present, or at least near-by, at the time.

Moreover, Bishop Bur was probably successful in the royal council, at least informally (the council did not have formal jurisdiction over lawsuits concerning land tenure). This is indicated in a statement by Alexander dated 28 October 1381. He said he had occupied certain lands in Badenoch, believing them to belong to the lordship; but now he had been persuaded by his legal experts and councillors, and by documents produced by the bishop of Moray, that the lands really belonged to the bishop. Therefore he instructed them to be delivered to the bishop, and ordered his officers never to claim them again. If Alexander had accepted the bishop's documents, no doubt the king and council had, too; Alexander had probably simply been stalling. And crown sympathy for the bishop is demonstrated by letters patent of 7 March 1382 giving him supreme jurisdiction over all crimes, including pleas of the crown, committed by the bishop's tenants; this re-enacted the similar grant made by David II in 1365, and cancelled any regality jurisdiction which Alexander Stewart might have claimed over the episcopal territories.[18]

Yet while round three had gone emphatically to the bishop, to see Alexander as surrendering absolutely is an oversimplification. What he had claimed in 1380 and acknowledged as the bishop's in 1381 appears to have been the original ecclesiastical lands in the region, held by the bishops of Moray before there was a feudal lordship of Badenoch, and (in some cases at least) quit-claimed by the first Comyn lord of Badenoch in the early 1230s.[19] Bishop Bur's defence in 1380, on the other hand, included not only these lands but also the territory of Rothiemurchus. Now Rothiemurchus had been granted directly to the bishops of Moray by Alexander II, which means it was outside the lordship of Badenoch, certainly as defined under the Comyns; that perhaps explains why Alexander did not claim it in 1380.[20] In round four of their contest, however, Bishop Bur actually conceded Rothiemurchus. On 20 April 1383 it was leased for the lifetimes of Alexander and two heirs of his body; in return Alexander promised to protect the bishop and the bishop's lands, and keep them free of malefactors. This was a significant gain for Alexander; Rothiemurchus was considerably larger than the other lands at dispute, covering six davochs (compared with a total of sixty davochs for the whole of Badenoch).[21] It also contained Loch an Eilean, on the island of which lies 'the most famous castle of Badenoch', traditionally attributed to the Wolf of Badenoch;[22] if the attribution is valid, that would help to show the importance Alexander attached to Rothiemurchus. Be that as it may, things do seem to have been swinging back towards Alexander. He had perhaps also been pressurising Bishop Bur in the Inverness sheriff court; in October 1383 the bishop appealed to the justiciary court, challenging the judgement given against him by the sheriff of Inverness (Sir William Fotheringham, presumably Alexander Stewart's deputy), because the bishops of Moray had always been exempt from citations to the Inverness sheriff court.[23]

After this, the *Register* indicates a three-year lull. Then, on 2 February 1387, Alexander met the bishop in the house of an Inverness burgess, and made an agreement over the rent of Rothiemurchus, which he had not been paying in full; but other issues, including the episcopal teinds due from the proceeds of the justiciary and sheriff courts held by Alexander, were not settled. As that indicates, by this time Alexander was justiciar — chief justice — of Scotland north of the Forth. The office had been vacant since the death of Sir Alexander Lindsay in 1381. We do not know when Alexander Stewart was appointed, but circumstantial evidence suggests it was not until after 1385, and that the office had been vacant until then. The reason for the hiatus is unclear. Perhaps the vacancy suited Alexander — for example, there would have been no justiciar to hear the bishop's appeal in 1383 — but subsequently he decided the office could be advantageous. That may be implied in the letters issued by Bishop Bur after the Inverness meeting. These grant a four-merks feu of the lands of Abriachan and others, north of Urquhart, to 'the magnificent, noble and powerful lord Alexander Stewart earl of Buchan, lord of Ross and Badenoch, lieutenant of the lord our king and justiciar in the land north of the river Forth, in return for the multiple benefits, aids and assistances he has rendered unto us and our church, and will render faithfully in the future.' Bishop Bur, it might seem, had decided he had nowhere else to go for help, and therefore had given up. The contest appears to have ended in a draw, with the bishop maintaining the principle that his lands were outside the lord of Badenoch's overlordship, while Alexander gained Rothiemurchus and Abriachan.[24]

Thus, judging from the *Moray Register*, the mid 1380s, while not marked by such spectacular gains as the years 1371-82, apparently went well for the lord of Badenoch. Other evidence suggests that, too. In October 1384 Alexander had a royal charter of the barony of Abernethy (now Nethy Bridge) to the north of Badenoch, with regality rights which removed it from the earldom of Moray; and in October 1386 the earl of Moray granted him the barony of Bona (now Dochfour), at the head of Loch Ness. These acquisitions, together with those of Rothiemurchus, Abriachan, Stratha'an and Urquhart, are all on or near the fringes of Badenoch, and suggest perhaps a deliberate policy of, in effect, expanding the boundaries of the lordship on the part of Alexander. Meanwhile relations between the earl and bishop of Moray had deteriorated badly — which no doubt helps to explain the bishop's willingness to compromise in 1387.[25]

The *Acts of The Parliaments of Scotland*, however, tell a very different story. The council-general of April 1385 witnessed a widespread attack on Alexander Stewart, which had probably been facilitated by the partial coup d'état of the previous November, in which Robert II had been made to transfer responsibility for everyday justice to his eldest son John, earl of Carrick. Alexander's brother David complained that Alexander was wrongfully detaining the barony of Urquhart, which had been temporarily leased to him; the king and his eldest sons, the earls of Carrick and Fife, recommended family arbitration, but David's response shows that he did not anticipate an amicable settlement. At the same time, Sir James Lindsay of Crawford pursued a hereditary claim to the lordship of the earldom of Buchan. He stated that King Robert refused to deliver Buchan to him at pledge — in other words give him temporary possession while the question of ownership was settled — and he now sought this from Carrick and the council. It was agreed that this should be determined at the next council-

149

general in June; that Alexander Stewart was to be summoned to make his counter-claim; but that whether or not he appeared, the question of who should have Buchan at pledge would be decided. Meanwhile it was to be taken into crown hands, and was not to go at pledge to Alexander; if the king had sent contrary instructions, these were to be overridden. Thirdly, following a complaint by the earl of Moray, Carrick was instructed to order Alexander to search his lands for Finlay 'Lauson' and the sons of Harald 'Foulson' (both surnames are presumably anglicised forms of Gaelic patronymics), who had killed some of Moray's men. Finally, the council-general ordered that because of the general lawlessness of the north, Carrick should go there in person with enough manpower to ensure that justice was properly done. Although that was not aimed specifically at Alexander Stewart, as the king's lieutenant in the north he was probably being indirectly blamed for the breakdown of law and order. All four measures demonstrate a widespread perception that Alexander could not be bothered with the due processes of law; and, from the Buchan case, there is an inference that King Robert was favouring him.[26]

Three years later, in November 1388, Alexander was again attacked in a council-general. 'It was decided ... that whereas Alexander Stewart son of the king, to whom the king had granted and committed the office of justiciar for the parts north of the river Forth, has at various times been accused before the king and before the council of being negligent in the execution of his office, in that he did not administer that office where and when he should, but wherever justice ayres were held he was useless to the community, and that having often been summoned and expected he did not appear, he deserved to be removed and ought to be removed from that office.'[27] Unfortunately, as discussed above, we do not know when Alexander became justiciar, but it was almost certainly after 1385. It should follow that King Robert personally appointed Alexander as justiciar *after* the initial attack on him, and indeed after the king had given up his judicial responsibilities. This indicates that Robert II was not the aged cipher so often described. But it also shows his continuing favouritism towards Alexander, who no doubt saw the justiciarship as a means both of outflanking the cases brought against him in 1385 and of gaining an advantage in his dispute with the bishop of Moray.

Yet if things seem to have gone Alexander's way in 1386 and 1387, it is now clear that that was only temporary; he suffered a major reverse in November 1388. Not only was he strongly censured and dismissed from the justiciarship, but his elder brother the earl of Fife — the ablest of all Robert II's sons — became warden of the kingdom. Under Fife, the effort to bring justice to the north which Carrick had been told to make in 1385 does seem to have started. In April 1389 his son Murdoch Stewart became justiciar, on condition that Fife himself gave assistance with sufficient power. Accordingly Fife led an expedition to Inverness the following

150

autumn. On 27 October 1389 he settled the bishop of Moray's other long-running dispute with Earl John Dunbar. Among many items, Bishop Bur purged himself of complicity in the killing of Sir David Barclay, almost 40 years earlier, which suggests he may not have been a completely blameless character; and, more relevantly here, the earl agreed to take no action against the bishop for making some of the earl's men swear an oath to lord Alexander Stewart, 'because he [the bishop] did this for the best'.[28]

Less than a week later, on 2 November, another important quarrel was apparently settled, again in Inverness, this time concerning Alexander Stewart himself.[29] Alexander had abandoned his wife, Euphemia Ross, and was living with a lady called Mairead daughter of Eachann ('Mariota filia Athyn', or 'Mariette Nighean Eachainn').[30] Now he promised to return to Euphemia as her man and husband and with her possessions, to treat her honourably without threat of death, and not to use his men[31] illegally against her. Euphemia seems to have been treated badly, and it might seem surprising that she wanted Alexander back. The phrase about her possessions may be the key; Alexander had probably been denying her any of the revenues of Ross. Whatever the case, it was no doubt a political settlement rather than a marital one, involving not only Alexander but also the earl of Sutherland, who agreed to be the chief surety that Alexander would keep his promise.[32] And, although he is not expressly mentioned, the earl of Fife was no doubt involved too, for he had dealt with the earl and bishop of Moray only a day or so earlier. But marital discord was a Church matter, and the actual settlement was ordered by the ecclesiastical authorities: the bishops of Moray and Ross. Since Alexander Stewart's previous dispute with Bishop Bur had been over superiority in secular affairs, it is hard to believe that the bishop did not relish asserting his spiritual power — albeit, presumably, with the backing and perhaps at the instigation of the earl of Fife.

Alexander must have been humiliated. And within a few months Bishop Bur rubbed salt in the wound. On 22 February 1390 he made an indenture with Thomas Dunbar, eldest son of the earl of Moray, who had replaced Alexander as sheriff of Inverness. Thomas undertook to defend the bishop's possessions and men, for the rest of the bishop's life, against all malefactors, caterans (Highland bandits), and everyone else except the king; in return the bishop was to pay Thomas an annual fee. The indenture does not mention Alexander by name, but it obviously related to him. The bishop may have been seeking protection against Alexander's revenge for his humiliation at Inverness; or he and Thomas Dunbar may have been indulging in one-upmanship at Alexander's expense. Whatever the explanation, the indenture was the last straw for Alexander. The *Moray Register* describes it as 'The useless and damnable provision for the lands and tithes of the church of Moray, from which followed their final destruction'. Thomas Dunbar proved incapable of fulfilling his promises (and indeed

151

the indenture was annulled by Robert III six months later). In late May 1390 — not long after the death of Robert II, which may have been another consideration — Alexander Stewart attacked Forres, destroying the town, the choir of St Lawrence's church, and the archdeacon's house; and, as we have seen, on 17 June the city, churches and cathedral of Elgin were given to the flames.[33]

For the past century and a half, the teinds of Rothiemurchus parish had gone to provide the lighting ('*ad luminarie*') of Elgin cathedral.[34] It is tempting to speculate whether, after 1383, Bishop Bur might have emphasised this responsibility to the new tenant of Rothiemurchus Alexander Stewart — and whether, in June 1390, Alexander grimly saw himself as fulfilling the responsibility once and for all. The fire destroyed the cathedral's interior and the roofs of the nave, choir and chapter house. Surviving masonry in the nave and choir shows scorch marks and evidence of extensive repairs to the upper levels, while the west front, central crossing and great tower were all damaged and had eventually to be rebuilt. The canons of Moray were summoned, together with expert masons, to decide on the repairs and their financing. The Avignon pope Clement VII was approached, and gave some of his revenue from the Scottish Church for the next ten years. Bishop Bur also petitioned the parliament following Robert III's coronation in August 1390. He may have hoped for a tax, but found parliament unresponsive. In December an appeal to the king was more successful, for Robert III provided £20 a year to the Elgin building fund from 1391 until 1397, when Bishop Bur died. Much more was no doubt raised from other sources, and the cathedral was gradually repaired — though the central tower was only completed in about 1420, and the west front a decade or so later.[35]

Bishop Bur wanted political support as well. On 19 August Robert III, with the advice of his council, cancelled the protection agreement with Thomas Dunbar because the bishop's lands had been devastated. At the same time he prohibited Alexander Stewart and the earl of Moray from seizing the bishop's castle of Spynie. But there is no written evidence of more positive action against Alexander. The explanation probably is that the sacrilegious attack on the cathedral was a matter for Church courts, and given the bishop's quarrel with Alexander over jurisdiction he would not have wanted to go to the lay courts. Instead the full ecclesiastical penalty of excommunication was pronounced upon Alexander. Then, in his December appeal to Robert III, Bishop Bur put his case in the king's hands. This, however, was not so much a criminal prosecution as a suit for damages; what the bishop wanted (in addition to finance) was political pressure to make the perpetrators of the outrage provide reparation.[36]

That, it appears, was what happened. 'And after this [the burning of the cathedral] lord Alexander Stewart, on the special commission of the lord Bishop Alexander Bur, and in the presence of the lord king, the earl of

Fife, and lords William Keith, Malcolm Drummond lord of Mar, Thomas Erskine, and many others, in Perth before the doors of the church of the Friars Preacher, and afterwards before the high altar, was absolved by lord Walter Trail, bishop of St. Andrews, from the sentence of excommunication; on condition that he at once made satisfaction to the church of Moray and sent to the Pope for absolution, otherwise the former sentence of excommunication would apply again.'[37] This clearly indicates that combined ecclesiastical and secular pressure had been applied effectively to Alexander. He perhaps appears to have got off lightly; in presumably the most widely-read account of the affair his absolution at Perth is depicted as an empty charade.[38] But he was eventually buried in Dunkeld cathedral, which indicates that the excommunication was not reimposed, and so the conditions must have been met. Unfortunately, we cannot tell what the 'satisfaction to the church of Moray' amounted to. What is striking, however, is the way the settlement at Perth corresponded with traditional methods of settling feud in medieval Scotland.[39] In return for submission and compensation by the offender, peace was made without involving the secular law courts. Since ecclesiastical law had been broken, however, the Pope had to agree to lifting the excommunication; that parallels the Scottish crown's practice of pardoning those who broke its laws on condition that their victims were satisfactorily compensated.

The evidence of the later parts of the *Moray Register* suggests that the ceremony at Perth did settle the feud between Alexander Stewart and Bishop Bur. After 1390, it contains only one direct reference to Alexander, a royal command to him to hand over Spynie castle to Bishop Bur's successor in 1398. Alexander is unlikely to have held Spynie in 1390, because Bishop Bur's protests would surely have been recorded; he probably only had it (on the king's behalf) during the episcopal vacancy. There is one other echo of the previous conflict, an appeal to the justiciar by the new bishop against a judgement by Sir William Fotheringham, lieutenant of 'the lord sheriff of Inverness' — perhaps Alexander Stewart — that he owed suit to Inverness sheriff court. But this dispute did not escalate; the justiciar, Murdoch Stewart, appears to have sympathised with the bishop, and no more is recorded on the matter.[40]

Between 1391 and 1397, Bishop Bur may have been afraid to provoke Alexander Stewart. But what did re-emerge was the problem of Alexander's marriage, one of the stimuli for the attack on Elgin cathedral. In 1392, following Euphemia Ross's petitions, papal letters stated that 'the marriage has been the cause of wars, plundering, arson, murders, and many other damages and scandals, and it is likely that more will happen if they remain united'; therefore the bishops of St Andrews, Glasgow and Aberdeen were commissioned to investigate Alexander's adultery and grant Euphemia her separation.[41] The ending of his marriage lost Alexander the earldom of Ross and the accompanying territories.

153

At much the same time he lost Urquhart, which was in crown hands from 1391. Also, the earl of Moray's grant of Bona barony was cancelled; in 1394 Thomas Dunbar, earl of Moray following his father's death in 1391, granted it and other lands to Alasdair MacDonald of Lochaber, in return for seven years' protection. Why Thomas Dunbar wanted this is not spelled out; the obvious guesses are either that he needed it against Alexander Stewart, or that Alasdair simply forced it on him (the latter is more probable, since Alasdair had also made an agreement with and received lands from Sir William Fotheringham). In either case, this clearly indicates a change of power in the region; Alexander's star was waning fast. The last years of his career may even have seen his withdrawal from the Moray region. In 1402 he appears as baillie of the earldom of Atholl; in 1404, when some Inverness-shire territory was mortgaged to him, the transaction took place in Perth; and when he died in 1405, he was buried behind the high altar of Dunkeld cathedral — an ironic resting-place for the Wolf of Badenoch.[42]

Yet while the feud between Alexander Stewart and the bishop of Moray died down in the 1390s, dramatic Highland violence did not. Early in 1392 according to Walter Bower, 'there was a fight at Glen Brerachan [near Pitlochry] where the noble Sir Walter Ogilvie sheriff of Angus and his brother Walter de Lychton were killed by caterans whose leader was Duncan Stewart a bastard son of Sir Alexander earl of Buchan. Some sixty of the sheriff's worthy men were slain with him while resisting acts of robbery in Angus.' As the fuller account by Andrew Wyntoun shows, this fight (located by Wyntoun at Glasclune, near Blairgowrie) was virtually a full-scale battle. The government took it extremely seriously, outlawing twenty-two of the raiders and their followers, including, in first place, Duncan and Robert Stewart. There is no reason for not identifying these with two of Alexander's sons by Mairead the daughter of Eachann — and they may also surely be identified with 'the thre sonnes of Schir Alisander Stewart the qwylkis ar now in prisoun in the castel of Stryuelyng' in January 1399, who were to 'be kepit fermly and nocht be deliuerit but consail general or parlement'. They were indeed, probably among the 'certain prisoners' held in Stirling from 1396 to 1402. The violence by Alexander Stewart's sons was thus, in the end, dealt with effectively, just as Alexander's own violence was — something that is often forgotten in accounts of 'weak' Scottish government in the 1390s. And the fact that his sons were in crown captivity in the later 1390s might help account for Alexander's own quiescence during that decade.[43]

But what lay behind the raid by Alexander's sons? Did Alexander encourage them, as retaliation for his enforced submission at Perth? Were they acting on their own initiative, taking over their father's challenge to the political community? Or was it simply that, after Perth, their father could no longer hold them and other local chieftains in check? No certain answers can be given. But according to Wyntoun, the raid originated not with Alexander or his sons but in a 'hey grete dyscorde' between Sir David Lindsay of Glenesk, who was wounded in the battle and whose lands included Strathnairn to the north of Badenoch, and the 'Duncansons', that is Clan Donnachaidh or Robertson. Although Wyntoun was reticent about Alexander Stewart — he did not name him in the account of the burning of Elgin, for example — his explanation seems plausible, since Lindsay had inherited much of his lands from his mother, whose sister was married to 'Robert of Atholl', a chief of Clan Donnachaidh, and one of the first named among the twenty-two outlawed in 1392.[44] Thus it may be considered unlikely that the initiative for the raid came from Alexander himself. Yet whatever the case, it seems clear that Alexander either would not, or could not, restrict his sons; he had, in other words, simply opted out of any responsibility for maintaining peace in northern Scotland. Such a conclusion is indicated, too, by the other Highland drama of the 1390s, the clan fight at Perth in 1396. This judicial battle settled a feud between two clans from the Moray/Badenoch region. Had Alexander Stewart been exercising regional lordship at all effectively, the feud should have been pacified earlier; and he should at least have been involved in its bloody dénouement at Perth. But he is conspicuous by his absence; the fight was arranged by two other local magnates, Thomas Dunbar, earl of Moray, and Sir David Lindsay of Glenesk.[45]

Perhaps, in the 1390s, Alexander deliberately chose not to exercise effective regional lordship, in order to show how bad the situation would be without him: *après moi le déluge*, so to speak. But there is no clear evidence of his acting as an effective lord at any time in his career.[46] And indeed the fact that, having acquired Ross through marriage in 1382, he allowed the marriage to collapse and thereby lost the largest earldom in Scotland, suggests gross incompetence by normal magnate standards. Marriage was the common way for late medieval nobles to acquire extra land; once married, the heiresses did not usually slip from their husbands' grasps, no matter how unhappy the marriages were. Thus the first earl of Douglas (d. 1384) married the heiress to the earldom of Mar, deserted her in favour of her sister-in-law, but still remained earl of Douglas and Mar until his death. Or consider the first earl of Huntly (d. 1470), who had his first marriage to an heiress annulled, but made her grant him most of her lands. By comparison, Alexander Stewart of Badenoch does not cut a very effective figure. Indeed the only late medieval Scottish parallel for his loss of Ross is the case of Thomas Fleming, second earl of Wigtown, who surrendered his earldom in 1372 because he could not control its inhabitants.[47]

Was that, perhaps, Alexander Stewart's problem, not just in the 1390s but throughout his career? What, for instance, went wrong for him in Ross? There may have been a belief within the earldom that it should rightfully have been held not by Euphemia's husband but by the male representatives of the Ross kindred. In the 1360s Euphemia's father, the last earl of the original line, tried to entail the earldom on his brother, the laird of Balnagown, but David II refused to allow it. In reaction, the Rosses of Balnagown seem to have looked to the MacDonalds of the Isles, and, later, even to have supported Donald of the Isles at the time of Harlaw in 1411.[48] Euphemia's father had already married a sister of John MacDonald, lord of the Isles, and subsequently her daughter by Sir Walter Lesley married John's son Donald. That marriage gave Donald his claim to Ross, but it was almost certainly contracted in the 1380s or '90s, and probably reflects Ross opposition to Alexander Stewart. Now the early seventeenth-century *Brieve Cronicle of the Earlis of Ross* states of Euphemia's son that he 'was callit Alexander Ross als lang as his mother leivid, and theirfter was callit Alexander Leslie.' And although her daughter had a Lesley father and a MacDonald husband, on her seal she called herself 'Margaret de Ross domina insularum', while on her tomb she is 'Mariota de Ross Insularum Domina'.[49] There are, here, strong signs of identification with the Ross kindred by Euphemia and her daughter. It is worth speculating that this identification reflects the attitudes within Ross in the late fourteenth century — and that it was coupled with hostility towards Alexander Stewart of Badenoch. No doubt Alexander's treatment of Euphemia made things worse — but the evidence of this comes from Euphemia's side, and it could have been provoked by difficulties which Alexander may well have encountered in the earldom.

The fundamental problem with Alexander's situation in Ross was that he (like Sir Walter Lesley before him) had no kinship base within the earldom. But that also applied to the lordship of Badenoch — and indeed he may have had problems of control there as well. For how long had the great feud which culminated in the 1396 clan battle at Perth been running? When, in 1385, Alexander was told to have his lands searched for Finlay 'Lauson' and the sons of Harald 'Foulson', who had killed men of the earl of Moray, does this imply that Alexander was behind the killings, or does it mean that Alexander had done nothing about them? Similar letters had already been sent to him in 1382 by the king and the earl of Carrick, following complaints by the bishop of Aberdeen about attacks on his lands by Farquhar Mackintosh ('Farchardo Mctoschy'), who probably came from Badenoch (and perhaps Rothiemurchus). Again, does that mean that Alexander was feuding with the bishop of Aberdeen, or that he had failed to respond to the bishop's demands for action against one of the inhabitants of Badenoch? Since there is no other evidence of feuds between Alexander and the earl of Moray or the bishop of Aberdeen (and in the latter case, at least, it could reasonably be expected to survive in the episcopal muniments), it is probably safer to assume that in both cases Alexander was simply being negligent. And that, of course, tallies not only with the examples of his inaction later in the 1390s, but also with the evidence from the *Acts of the Parliaments*: in both 1385 and 1389 the general burden of the attacks on Alexander is not that he actively did wrong, but that he normally did nothing at all.[50]

In fairness to Alexander, it should be emphasised that it was an exceptionally difficult task which he had undertaken (or had been given: we do not actually know whether Alexander positively wanted to be a power in the Highlands, or whether he had in effect been sent there by his father). Badenoch would have been a particular problem, because it cannot have experienced effective on-the-spot lordship since the destruction of Comyn power by Robert I during the Wars of Independence. As with the original regality of Moray and with other similar lordships and earldoms, the purpose of Alexander's regality powers was probably to compensate for his lack of any kin-based authority over it; but that must have been significantly weakened by the bishop of Moray's refusal to accept his superior jurisdiction. That, no doubt, is why he quarrelled with the bishop rather than with the earl of Moray. With their separate regality jurisdictions, Alexander Stewart and John Dunbar were no threat to each other, and could exist side-by-side in peace; but Bishop Bur's insistence on the liberties of Elgin cathedral must have undermined both men's positions. It is not surprising that they both quarrelled with him — but the problem for Alexander, in Badenoch, was probably much more serious, just as his reaction was eventually much more devastating. It is ironic that the chapel in Elgin cathedral's northern transept was dedicated to St Thomas Becket; Becket had died two centuries earlier over much the same kind of issue.[51]

Nothing, of course, can excuse what Alexander did at Elgin six hundred years ago. But the implication of the preceding paragraphs is that the attack was made out of weakness, not strength. For all the difficulties involved in controlling the Highland regions, it could be done, as was demonstrated by his own son, Alexander, earl of Mar, who according to Bower 'ruled with acceptance nearly all the north of the country beyond the Mounth'. The MacDonald lords of the Isles, too, seem very different as Highland potentates to Alexander Stewart.[52] It is worth adding that the MacDonald advance eastwards began with Alasdair of Lochaber in the 1390s along the shores of Loch Ness, into an area which Alexander had either lost or relinquished. Thus it may be concluded that the 'Wolf of Badenoch' was a failure as a Highland chief, just as he was a failure as a Scottish earl; perhaps he simply did not understand how to exercise effective power. But his obvious pride and furious temper naturally exacerbated his failures — and, as so often happens in such cases, it was a physically defenceless target that was hit. Little wonder that Walter Bower described him as 'insolent and malign', and that all subsequent historians have echoed that comment in one way or another. But the most accurate

157

summing-up of the 'Wolf of Badenoch' is probably the scathing dismissal made by the 1388 council-general: *'Inutilis fuit communitati'* — 'he was useless to the community'.[53]

## Notes

1. *Registrum Episcopatus Moraviensis* (Bannatyne Club 1837) [*Moray Reg.*] p.381.
2. *Scotichronicon ... Walteri Boweri*, ed. W Goodall (Edinburgh 1759) [*Chron. Bower* (Goodall)] ii, 416 (lib. xiv, cap. lvi); Androw of Wyntoun, *The Orygynale Cronykil of Scotland*, ed. D Laing (Edinburgh 1872-9) [*Chron. Wyntoun* (Laing)] iii, 55. It should be added here that my suggestion, in A Grant, *Independence and Nationhood: Scotland 1306-1469* (London 1984) 208, that the nickname 'Wolf of Badenoch' 'was self-bestowed, ... for his heraldic crest was a wolf', is incorrect; as various friends have pointed out, the crest is a boar's head, not a wolf's.
3. *Moray Reg.* no.154, and pp.472-3; *The Acts of the Parliaments of Scotland* (Edinburgh 1814-75) [*APS*] i, 528-9; *Regesta Regum Scottorum* [*RRS*] v, *The Acts of Robert I* (Edinburgh 1988) no.389. But Robert II's possession of Badenoch did not include the regality jurisdiction which the Randolphs had had; that was controlled by David II in the 1360s: *RRS* vi, *The Acts of David II* (Edinburgh 1982) nos.348, 374.
4. *Moray Reg.* 472-3, in which the grant of Badenoch is stated to be in regality, but cf. *Registrum Magni Sigilli Regum Scottorum* [*RMS*] i (Edinburgh 1912) no.558; *The Exchequer Rolls of Scotland* (Edinburgh 1878-1908) [*ER*] ii, 363. For the association of Lochindorb with Badenoch in the 13th century, see G W S Barrow 'Badenoch and Strathspey, 1130-1312. 1: Secular and Political', *Northern History*, VIII (1988) 8-9.
5. *RMS* i, nos.405, 389, 627. For Dunbar support for Robert II in 1371 see *Chron. Wyntoun* (Laing) iii, 8. David was Alexander's half-brother, son of Robert's second wife, the widow of the earl of Moray; does the grant of Urquhart represent her wish that part at least of Moray should go to *her* child? Interestingly, Urquhart was entailed on the heirs of David's body, with reversion to Alexander.
6. Cf. *RMS* i, app. I, no.8.
7. *APS* i, 553; *RMS* i, nos.559, 600; Scottish Record Office [SRO], MSS Register House Charters, RH6/167.
8. *RMS* i, nos.601, 674, 675, 676, 677, 678; *Illustrations of the ... Antiquities of the Shires of Aberdeen and Banff* (Spalding Club 1847-69) iv, 376.
9. *RMS* i, nos. 736, 737, 741, 742. There was, however, no formal grant of the earldom of Buchan, nor of any of the small bits of territory and superiorities which were still associated with that title; that, presumably, is why Sir James Lindsay of Crawford, a descendant of the Comyn earls, brought a lawsuit over Buchan in 1385: *APS* i, 551-2, and see below, p.149.
10. *Moray Reg.* no.185; *RMS* i, no.556. He was sheriff in 1380, but when he was appointed is unclear.
11. *The Scots Peerage*, ed. J B Paul (Edinburgh, 1904-14) vii, 239-40; vi, 298-301.
12. *RRS* v, no.389.
13. *Moray Reg.* nos.169, 163, 147, 154.

14. SRO, MSS Register House Transcripts, RH1/s.d. 30:3:1371; printed, 'ex apographo in archivis publicis Edin.' in *Moray Reg.* pp.472-3.
15. *RMS* i, no.558.
16. *Moray Reg.* no.159.
17. See the list of justiciars in H L MacQueen 'Pleadable Brieves and Jurisdiction in Heritage in Later Medieval Scotland' (Edinburgh University Ph.D. thesis, 1985) appendix B, at p.331.
18. *Moray Reg.* nos.161, 186 (wrongly attributed to Robert III's reign).
19. Alexander challenged the bishop over lands in Laggan ('Logachnacheny') and Insh ('Ardinche'), the kirkland of Kingussie, the lands of the chapels of Raitts and Dunachton ('Nachtan'), and the bishop's land of Kincardine; and he conceded the bishop's possession of Laggan, Insh, and the chapel lands. Laggan, Insh and the Kingussie kirkland must correspond with the davochs at 'Logykenny' and 'Ardynch' and the six acres beside Kingussie kirk which Walter Comyn quit-claimed and granted to the bishop of Moray (ibid., no.76), while Kincardine will be the bishop's half-davoch, the bounds of which were agreed by Comyn in 1234 (ibid., no.85). The chapels at Raitts and Dunachton are part of the pre-parochial structure, and so, no doubt, is the attachment of lands to them. Cf. the bishop of Moray's reservation of (among others) the davoch of Laggan and the half davoch of Kincardine *'pertinente ad mensam nostram'* from his endowment of the canons of Elgin cathedral in 1239 (ibid., no.41). For a general discussion of early medieval ecclesiastical structures in the region, see G W S Barrow 'Badenoch and Strathspey, 1130-1312. 2: The Church', *Northern History*, IX (1989) 1-15. As this article indicates, the episcopal lands in the region seem to have consisted of half-davochs in the various parishes (or, earlier, shires and thanages). In the four parishes which, strictly speaking, made up Badenoch, however, the bishop had a whole davoch in Laggan and another in Insh, and very little in Kingussie and Alvie; but the total of two davochs to four parishes is consistent with the overall pattern, and so this might represent some earlier rearrangement.
20. *Moray Reg.* no.29. Unlike the neighbouring parish of Kincardine (also outside Badenoch proper), Rothiemurchus had not been held by the Comyns.
21. Ibid., no.162, and (for the davochs), no.29 and p.473. The rent was £8 a year for Alexander's life, £16 a year for his two heirs; and (a face-saver for the bishop?) Alexander also owed suit to the bishop's chief court.
22. Barrow 'Badenoch and Strathspey: Secular and Political', p.9 and note 99.
23. *Moray Reg.* nos.162, 164.
24. Ibid., nos.167, 168. If Alexander had been justiciar much earlier, that would surely have been mentioned in the bishop's 1383 appeal (ibid., no.164), and in the parliamentary attacks on him in 1385 (*APS* i, 551-3) which are described later in this paper; cf. MacQueen 'Pleadable Brieves' 331.
25. *RMS* i, no.790, and SRO, MSS Maitland Thomson Transcripts, GD212/11/1, s.d. 7:1:1384, for the regality over Abernethy; SRO RH6/184; *Moray Reg.* nos.163, 169.
26. *APS* i, 550-3; and, for the political dimension, Grant, *Independence and Nationhood* 180-1.
27. *APS* i, 556.
28. *APS* i, 557; *Moray Reg.* no.169.

29. Ibid., no.271.
30. G W S Barrow 'The Sources for the History of the Highlands in the Middle Ages' in *The Middle Ages in the Highlands* ed. L McLean (Inverness 1981) 16-17. There is no evidence for the identification in *Scots Peerage* vii, 159, of Eachann with Iye Mackey of Strathnaver.
31. These are described as '*homines suos nativos nobiles et alios*', which presumably means 'serfs, nobles and others' — but if so, it is probably the last specific reference to *nativi* as serfs in Scotland. Could it perhaps mean 'natives', i.e. Gaelic Highlanders?
32. Sutherland was probably by then Alexander's son-in-law, married to a daughter of Mairead (*Scots Peerage* viii, 329-30). The only other evidence for Alexander's dealings with the earls of Sutherland is a crown payment of £7 5s. 4d. in 1373 'pro expensis faciendis versus Dunrebyn' (*ER* ii, 414).
33. *Moray Reg.* nos.170, 172, and p.381.
34. Ibid., no.65.
35. Ibid., nos.298, 266, 173; *ER* iii, 276, 316, 348, 376, 403, 430; H B Mackintosh and J S Richardson, *Elgin Cathedral* (guide book, 2nd edn. HMSO 1980); see also D MacGibbon and T Ross, *The Ecclesiastical Architecture of Scotland* (Edinburgh 1896-7) ii, 121-45.
36. *Moray Reg.* nos.172, 173, and cf. p.382.
37. Ibid., pp.382-3.
38. See chapter XXV of Nigel Tranter's historical novel *Lords of Misrule* (London 1976), the first in his *A Folly of Princes* trilogy.
39. See J Wormald 'Bloodfeud, Kindred and Government in Early Modern Scotland' *Past and Present* 87 (1980) 54-97.
40. *Moray Reg.* nos.178, 179, 180.2
41. *Calendar of Papal Letters to Scotland of Clement VII of Avignon* (Scottish History Soc. 1976), 174, 181.
42. *ER* iii, 274, 277, 317, 376; *Moray Reg.* no.272; W Fraser, *Memorials of the Family of Wemyss of Wemyss* (Edinburgh 1888) ii, no.33; SRO, MSS Mar and Kellie, GD124/1/1128; *ER* iii, 634; MacGibbon and Ross, *Ecclesiastical Architecture* iii, 45-6.
43. Walter Bower, *Scotichronicon* ed. D E R Watt, viii (Aberdeen 1987) [*Chron. Bower* (Watt)] 7; *Chron. Wyntoun* (Laing) iii, 58-60; *APS* i, 579-80; ibid., i, 573; *ER* iii, 436, 490, 553.
44. *Chron. Wyntoun* (Laing) iii, 58; W F Skene, *Celtic Scotland* iii (2nd edn, Edinburgh 1890) iii, 309-10. Skene's analysis of the 22 men outlawed in 1392 links most of them with various parts of Alexander Stewart's territories, but not completely convincingly, and places more emphasis on the Lindsay inheritance. For the view that Alexander Stewart was the raid's main organiser, see I F Grant, *Social and Economic Development of Scotland before 1603* (Edinburgh 1920) 482-3, but there is no strong evidence for this. For Lindsay possession of Strathnairn, see *RMS* i, no.764, and SRO, MSS Forbes, GD52/1044. ·
45. *Chron. Bower* (Watt) viii, 7-8; *Chron. Wyntoun* (Laing) iii, 63-4. Cf. Skene, *Celtic Scotland* iii, 310-18. Lindsay's involvement was probably in support of the opponents of 'Clan Qwhele', who as '*omnes Clanqwevil*' had been outlawed

for taking part in the 1392 raid. The identification of 'Clan Qwele' and their enemies 'Clan Kay' does not seem to have been settled satisfactorily.

46. The only evidence of any constructive act of lordship by Alexander in the Highlands is the remission he gave in November 1372, as 'justiciar within the *abten* of Dull' (North Perthshire), to Andrew Baxter and 20 others who were accused of crimes in Glencairnie and Drummochter against Robert Duncanson and his men, presumably Clan Donnachaidh; this was probably a piece of local dispute settling, though it might not have endeared him to Clan Donnachaidh (SRO RH1/2/134). Otherwise the few documents in his name which survive are merely routine. The contrast with his mid-15th century successor as the dominant power in the Highlands, Alexander MacDonald, earl of Ross and lord of the Isles, is striking; see *Acts of the Lords of the Isles*, edd. J and R W Munro (Scottish Hist. Soc., 1986) nos.21-50.

47. *Scots Peerage* iii, 152-5; iv, 524; viii, 523-4. Fleming's surrender of Wigtown is in *RMS* i, no.507.

48. *Scots Peerage* vii, 236-43; *Ane Account of the Familie of Innes* (Spalding Club 1864) 70-2; SRO, MSS, J. and F. Anderson, GD297/194, 195. See also, more generally, J Munro 'The Earldom of Ross and the Lordship of the Isles' in *Firthlands of Ross and Sutherland* ed. J R Baldwin (Edinburgh 1986) 59-67; and A Grant 'Scotland's "Celtic Fringe" in the Late Middle Ages: The MacDonald Lords of the Isles and the Kingdom of Scotland' in *The British Isles 1100-1500* ed. R R Davies (Edinburgh 1988) 127, 138.

49. *Ane Brieve Cronicle of the Earlis of Ross* ed. W R Baillie (Edinburgh, 1850) 9; K A Steer and J W M Bannerman, *Late Medieval Monumental Sculpture in the West Highlands* (Edinburgh 1977) 148-9.

50. *APS* i, 550-3, 556; *Registrum Episcopatus Aberdonensis* (Maitland Club, 1845) i, 136-8.

51. Mackintosh and Richardson, *Elgin Cathedral* 14; W L Warren, *Henry II* (London 1973) chapter 13.

52. *Chron. Bower* (Watt) viii, 293. For the dynamics of MacDonald lordship, see J W M Bannerman 'The Lordship of the Isles' in *Scottish Society in the Fifteenth Century* ed. J M Brown (London 1977) 209-40.

53. *Chron. Bower* (Goodall) ii, 383, *APS* i, 556.

*Fig.9.1 View by J C Nattes and J Fittler, 1799 (from Scotia Depicta (1819), plate 10).*

162

# THE GREAT HALL AND ROOF
# OF DARNAWAY CASTLE, MORAY

## Geoffrey Stell and Michael Baillie

In March 1987 it was learnt that 'Randolph's Hall' the great hall of Darnaway Castle, was in the final stages of redecoration, and that the internal scaffolding erected for this purpose would afford a rare opportunity of examining at close quarters the medieval roof over the hall.[1] Accordingly, a detailed survey of the accessible portions of the roof was carried out by the Royal Commission on the Ancient and Historical Monuments of Scotland, while Mike Baillie of the Palaeoeceology Centre, The Queen's University of Belfast, was invited by Moray Estates to carry out a dendrochronological analysis. This paper presents the results of these two surveys.

## History

An early royal manor and hunting lodge, Darnaway, though not mentioned by name, was included in Robert Bruce's grant of the regalian earldom of Moray to his trusted nephew, Thomas Randolph, in 1312.[2] The ownership and building history of Darnaway followed the subsequent descent of the earldom, though the keepership of the castle passed through various hands. The earldom itself was transmitted in reduced extent to the Dunbars through marriage with the daughters of Thomas Randolph, who died in 1332. The male succession of the Dunbars came to an end in 1429, and Elizabeth Dunbar's marriage in 1434 brought it into the orbit of the burgeoning Douglas empire until their forfeiture in 1455. Thereafter, the earldom intermittently became, in the gift of the crown, a royal appanage for the members of the ruling Stewart family, particularly their natural sons, James IV's illegitimate offspring by Janet Kennedy, and James V's by Margaret Erskine, from whom the present Lord Moray is descended.[3]

The estate was renowned as a vast and nationally important source of building timber, mainly of oak. Darnaway oaks are known to have been used for the roof of the cathedral church of Dornoch in 1291, but most references belong to the later 15th and 16th centuries when the forest of Darnaway was at the crown's disposal and appeared in royal records.[4] The felling and transport of Darnaway oaks to Leith was a regular and systematic process in this period, some of them possibly going towards the construction of the king's ships including James IV's, 'The Great Michael', others possibly destined for the roofs of the great halls of Edinburgh and Stirling Castles. It is thus appropriate that one of the other very few great medieval timber roofs in Scotland should survive in the heart of this ancient and important forest.

Direct documentary evidence about the use and building history of the castle itself is not plentiful. The first castle and a hall, presumably derived from the royal hunting lodge, is traditionally ascribed to Sir Thomas Randolph himself in the early 14th century. The first documented building episode dates from the middle of the 15th century when Archibald Douglas was reported to have strengthened and extended Darnaway and Lochindorb.[5] Building works continued under royal auspices in the later 1450s, and again during the reign of James IV.[6] The subsequent history of the building has not yet been pursued in detail, but, judging simply from later views, it seems reasonably clear that the castle was enlarged and embellished between the 16th and 18th centuries. The view by T Griffin, engraved and published by J Walker in December 1800, for example, shows wall-head and corbelling details that belong to the 16th century. At this date also, as the *Statistical Account* testifies, the hall still had a balcony, with a music gallery above, extending across the full width of the building.[7] Bishop Pococke in 1760 'was told that underground rooms had been taken from it [that is, the hall] by raising the floor, and consequently its height is much lessened'. He recorded also that 'To Tarnaway Castle a large house has been built in the castle style, and there are fine woods with ridings in them'.[8] The view by John Claude Nattes in 1799 (Fig.9.1) shows the relationship of the hall to the later accretions rather more distinctly and in an appropriately wooded setting. Interesting features to note include the large tower with a first-floor entry and squared angle-turrets.

During the twenty years between the drawing of this sketch and its publication in 1819[9] great changes took place in the appearance and character of the house at the hands of the 9th earl of Moray; in the fashion of the times he was also a great tree planter. Between 1802 and 1812 medieval Darnaway was largely effaced behind the mansion redesigned by the architect, Alexander Laing.[10] (Fig.9.2) Laing, who died in 1823, was an Edinburgh mason turned architect, whose buildings were characterised by what has been described as a plain, masculine Georgian style. Darnaway was one of his biggest undertakings.

Laing had worked on various schemes since at least 1796, all of which, despite the dilapidated condition of some parts of the castle fabric, respected the venerable antiquity of the great hall. In 1794, for example, workmen complained to the earl's agent that 'attempting to repair [the roof of the wardrobe room] or put in any new baulks might bring the whole thing down about their ears'.[11] The building accounts show various payments for drawings, including elevations of the great hall; in 1805 Laing designed a new window for the hall, and in 1807 a new doorpiece from the salon, and a new hall fireplace.[12] The *Statistical Account* makes it clear that there had been two large fireplaces, one at the S end, now occupied by a later window, and the other in a side-wall, probably in the position of the existing fireplace.[13]

*Fig.9.2    View from NE, 1965.*

The foundation stone of the new works was laid on 19 June 1802, and on 2 November 1802 Alexander Stronach, presumably of the famous family of Easter Ross/Moray Firth builders of that name, was paid for taking down the roof of the old hall.[14] If, as this evidence clearly implies, the medieval roof was dismantled and re-assembled on reconstructed walls, it was handled extremely well and re-erected in an authentic manner. There is evidence of later modifications in the N and S end trusses of the existing roof where the reflex curves of the inner braces are the most obvious signs of later renewal; the decorative carvings have also clearly been reworked and the date 1810 incised on the S truss.[15] The overall effects of the restoration and reconstruction did not impress all commentators, however. According to William Rhind,[16] 'The present modern mansion was erected by the late Lord Moray but the roof, and all that remained of the ancient hall, was very properly preserved. Unfortunately, the restoration of this magnificent hall has not been conducted on the strictest antiquarian principles,' probably a reference to the removal of the S fireplace and the insertion of the window. 'This hall, no doubt,' he mused, 'often dined several hundred persons; when its floor, according to the times, was strewed with rushes or heather, as many hundreds of plaided warriors and hunters may have soundly slept many a night after the fatigues or revelries of the

*Fig.9.3   Great hall from E, 1965.*

day.' The idea that great halls served as glorious medieval barrack-blocks dies hard, but it would be churlish to censure the otherwise strict Rhind for allowing his historical imagination to have some freedom.

**Structural analysis**
As it now stands, the hall is a large rectangular building aligned N-S; at the N end it is attached to the house, and at the S the ground falls away steeply (Fig.9.3) Internally, it measures 26.6m in length by 10.7m transversely within side-walls 1.8m and gable walls no more than 1.5m in thickness. The windows are of arch-pointed, almost rounded, form with simple Y-tracery and a high transom. In addition to the inserted window in the S wall, there are three windows in the E side-wall and two in the W, the fireplace in the W side-wall being set behind a dummy window. The lower roof members (the 'hammer beams') are some 9m above the existing floor-level (which has probably been heightened) and the roof itself is just over 8m in height overall. The floor is about 1.5m above ground-level, so externally, from ground to ridge the hall stands to an impressive 18.5m overall. At the wall-head there is a crenellated parapet, and the roof is covered with sarking boards and slates.

*Fig.9.4    Great hall roof, 1965.*

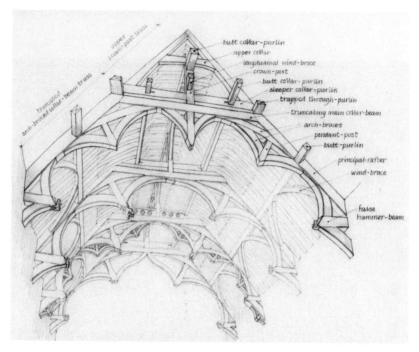

The labels on the sketch read:

butt collar-purlin
upper collar
longitudinal wind-brace
crown-post
butt collar-purlin
sleeper collar-purlin
trapped through-purlin
truncating main collar-beam
arch-braces
pendant-post
butt-purlin
principal-rafter
wind-brace
false hammer-beam

upper crown-post truss
truncated arch-braced collar-beam truss

*Fig.9.5   Great hall roof; annotated sketch by A Leith and G D Hay, 1974.*

The roof structure (Figs.9.4, 5 and 6) consists of seven principal roof trusses forming six main bays which vary between about 3.7m and 4m in length and contain six pairs of common rafters. The end-bays, where the trusses have been partly reconstructed, are only 1.2m and 0.7m at N and S ends respectively with, correspondingly, two and one pairs of common rafters. It is possible that the removal of the galleries has involved a foreshortening of each bay, possibly by as much as two or three metres each. In its original form the 8-bay roof may well have been some 6 m longer.

Overall, the trusses form a series of stiffened or braced Gothic arches, pitched at about 53° and with a 10.7m span; uninterrupted with lower tie-beams, they fulfil the purpose but are not of quite the same form as English late medieval hammer-beam roofs. The roof is made up mainly of pegged and tenon-jointed members, but not all the rafter-holes are explicable in terms of the existing jointing. The members are generally of large scantling, the principals being 0.3m by 0.45m at base, the collars 0.3m by 0.2m, and the crown-posts 0.2m square; the principals are thicker at the wall-heads and the collar-beams expand slightly towards their centres. Carpenters'

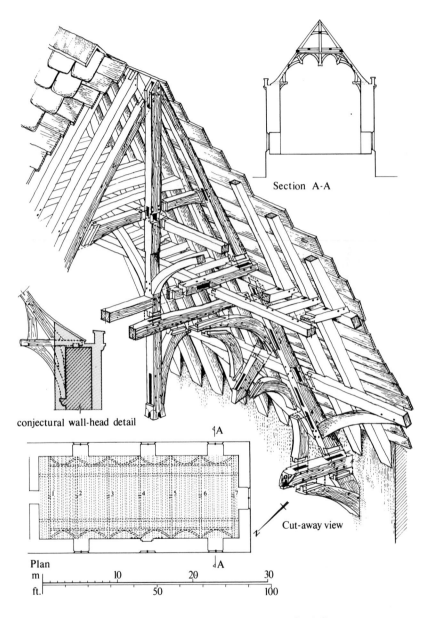

Section A-A

conjectural wall-head detail

Cut-away view

Plan

m

ft.

| 10 | 20 | 30 |
| 50 | 100 |

*Fig.9.6    Great hall roof; plan, section and cut-away view by S Scott.*

169

*Fig.9.7    Roof-truss 6, main collar and cusped braces.*

assembly-marks have been scratched, probably by a race knife, on each face of most of the principal rafters; a sequence of Roman numerals from 2 to 11 is marked on the wind-braces of five central trusses on the W side, and the corresponding marks on the E side have an extra short mark or tail.

Unusually, it is a two-stage or two-tier roof, each truss being formed in two independent halves. The triangular top stage comprises an upper and lower (or sleeper) collar with a vertical crown-post, into which is tenoned a longitudinal butt collar-purlin (or collar-plate) secured by wind-braces. The sleeper collar traps two through-purlins at each side, and the crown-post is tenoned into the top of the upper collar, the pendant-post being a separate member. The purlins are made up of scarf-jointed lengths. The lower stage is a truncated arch-braced collar-beam truss. The arch-braces have angled pendant-posts, but only two of the trusses have central vertical pendant-posts, forming in effect four instead of three broad cusps. The end trusses incorporate later reflex-curved braces.

The lower horizontal members are 'false' hammer-beams, for they lack the essential characteristics of vertical hammer-posts. The wall-head is concealed but may conceivably include a form of wall-post and corbel to

*Fig.9.8   Roof-truss 3, E side, carved head.*

reinforce the lower brace and 'hammer-beam'. Overall, Darnaway is a hybrid incorporating the traditions and character of hammer-beam roofs, as well as of arch-braced collar-purlin or trussed rafter roofs with single principals.

**Carved decoration**
Two of the trusses — 3 and 6 (Fig.9.7) — exhibit a greater degree of elaboration at virtually every level. There is cusping around the upper collar, the sleeper collar-purlin is decorated with a row of quatrefoils, and there are traceried cusps formed within the arch-braces. These same trusses extend furthest down the side-walls and have the greater projection on the 'hammer-beam' ends. Different in both emphasis and treatment, they seem

171

*Fig.9.9    Roof-truss 4, E side, carved figures.*

to represent the equivalent of ornate spere trusses marking the positions of partitions or screens in an open hall, physically or symbolically demarcating the dais and service areas.

Detailed decoration is not confined to trusses 3 and 6, however, for there is a whole world of human figures, beasts, birds and naturalistic carvings inhabiting this roof. They occur mainly on the projecting ends of the false hammer-beams with others on the inner pendant-posts, some bearing slight traces of colour. Most are of rustic and fantastic inspiration, appropriate to an area of wild forest; at least a couple may be allegorical, but some may be representations of unidentified earls or their royal masters. The absence of carved armorials is somewhat surprising, and makes identification less easy.

The opposed hammer-beam ends of truss 3 have crowned male heads.

172

*Fig.9.10    Roof-truss 5, E side, carved figure.*

The one on the W has a neatly trimmed beard and ear-length hair; his crown or coronet is slightly broken. The corresponding head on the E side (Fig.9.8) is beardless with dimpled chin, is more youthful-looking and has longer tresses and a better-defined foliated coronet. It is of slightly cruder execution and there are indications that it has been reworked.

The carved heads on the beam-ends of the two end-trusses are modern. The S truss (7), which is dated 1810 on one of the pendant-posts, has on

*Fig.9.11    Roof-truss 4, E side, carved hunting scene.*

*Fig.9.12    Roof-truss 6, E side, carved birds.*

*Fig.9.13    Roof-truss 5, E side, carved beast.*

the W side, a male head wearing a form of glengarry complete with chequer band and cylindrical tassel; facing him on the E is another male head with a coronet. At the N end, W side, there is a male head wearing a tall riding helmet (cap and visor having been planted on), and on the E is a male head wearing a three-cornered hat.

Genuine medieval figure carving is represented by a cloaked and hooded pair of clerics (truss 4 Fig.9.9); the left-hand of one figure is clasping a spherical object while his right hand is intertwined with his partner's left. On the E side of truss 5 is a kneeling droll and lustful figure (Fig.9.10); he wears a head band, and his hands clutch his stomach above exaggerated genitalia. A short length of vine scroll ornament occurs beneath him. Facing him on the corresponding W beam-end, is an erect sow which has extended hind legs. One forepaw holds its stomach, the other appears to be brushing away a tear from its eye.

Further relief carved decoration occurs on the soffits of the beam-ends, the liveliest of these being a hunting scene (Fig.9.11) under the paired figures on truss 4 (E). The huntsman has one hand on a bow, probably a long bow, though the arrow is bolt-like.[17] The beast is both bear- and wolf-like with a long leonine tail bent along its back. The spirit and character of this carving, and the paired figures immediately above it, are not unlike some of those on nearby Sueno's Stone, and they might easily be regarded as Pictish derivatives. The subject-matter is appropriate to the context of Darnaway and its forest, and other wildlife is depicted, for example, on the underside of truss 6 (E). Slightly hollowed, it consists of a pair of birds pecking at a central container of fruits (Fig.9.12). Fierce zoomorphic carvings, probably intended to represent beasts of the forest in fearsome pose, are also formed on the ends of the pendant-posts in the central cusps (Fig.9.13). These are generally powerful, square-jawed, thick-set animals with prominent snarling teeth, probably bears. Those with short sharp forepaws convey a dynamic, pouncing image. As elsewhere, these carvings represent a mixture of realism and fantasy.

**Dating and comparisons**

It has long been recognised that the Darnaway hall and roof are of late medieval origin. The range of suggested dates is wide, however, extending from the time of Thomas Randolph in the early 14th century (hence the popular name of 'Randolph's Hall') through the Douglas era to the period of royal possession after 1455, particularly to the reign of James IV.

But perceptions based on circumstantial and stylistic evidence have now been considerably altered by Dr Baillie's analysis of the dendrochronological or tree-ring evidence. On this analysis, the trees used in the Darnaway roof last grew in 1387 and had been felled in the summer of that year immediately after the production of the spring growth. Given that oak must be worked whilst it is green and before it hardens, the timbers of the Darnaway roof were assembled and placed in position during the last years of John Dunbar, earl of Moray from 1372 to 1392. Younger brother of the earl of Dunbar and second son of Isabella, younger daughter of Sir Thomas Randolph, he was an active national figure who could certainly have had the means and the motive to have erected such a roof, but there is no corroborative surviving evidence which connects him with major building activity at Darnaway.[18]

Typologically, the closest surviving parallel in Scotland to the Darnaway roof is that over the Great Hall of Edinburgh Castle. This hall is slightly narrower and shorter than Darnaway, measuring 28.9m by 12.5m externally, and has undergone an even more thorough restoration and reconstruction.[19] Between 1887 and 1891 inserted floors were removed, and the roof was altered, as can be judged by comparing it with a survey done in 1754. As restored, the roof has a similar general appearance to that of Darnaway, largely because of the inserted curved bracket-like lower braces; it is also known that the hammer-beams originally ended in carved beasts. However, the Edinburgh roof incorporates many differences of detail: it was constructed with exposed wall-posts and corbels; both the original and restored versions made greater use of straight braces; it possesses short but genuine hammer-posts; it has a greater number of trusses — nine — but shorter bay-lengths, comprising four common rafters; and the lower halves of the principals have been doubled with what are usually described as kerb principals. What is not entirely clear is whether the principal rafters are also of two stages. Overall, compared to Darnaway, this is of a more rationalised trussed-rafter and collar-purlin construction but has had to make the best of poor materials; straight braces have been used instead of arched braces, and timber of comparatively slight scantling has been employed throughout.

The building or rebuilding of this hall and roof have been ascribed to the reign of James IV. Numerous payments were recorded between about 1496 and 1511, and James IV's monogram appears on one of the wall-post corbels. On the other hand, it has recently been argued on stylistic grounds that the character and ornament of the scrolled corbels correspond more closely to the French-inspired work of James V, when the same principal carpenter of the King's Works, John Drummond, was operating. It has thus been suggested that there might be two phases in the hall, the latest belonging to the 1530s.[20]

An early sketch of the original roof over James IV's Great Hall at Stirling Castle suggests that it was similar to that of Edinburgh, but otherwise there is little comparative evidence for the Darnaway roof and for its place in Scottish late medieval carpentry traditions as a whole. A few, more humble Scottish roofs incorporate some of its features. The 15th-century roof over the nave of Holy Rude Church, Stirling, for instance, has distinctive trapped through-purlins, which are also trapped between two framed members of a principal rafter.[21] The hall roof of a late 15th- or early 16th-century building at Linlithgow demolished in *c.* 1886 incorporated in simpler form and more modest scale the basic elements of an arch-braced roof truss with single principals, double collars, arch-braces, wind-braces and through- or trenched-purlins.[22]

In England hammer-beam construction developed from the early 14th century onwards in ways that suggest that it was an alternative means of spanning halls that would otherwise have been aisled.[23] The apogee of the type was the magnificent hammer-beam roof which replaced an earlier roof, possibly aisled, over Westminster Hall, London.[24] Originally built by William Rufus at the end of the 11th century, the hall was reconstructed at the end of the 14th century, probably between 1394 and 1402, and probably the brainchild of the master carpenter, Hugh Herland. Although basically of a conventional single hammer-beam type, the structure also makes use of continuous and deep arch-braces rising from the base of the corbelled wall-posts up to the collar, intersecting the hammer-beam and the hammer-posts. There are twelve major bays and two short bays set close to the end-walls. The internal clear span is about 20.55m, almost twice that of Darnaway, and at 73m it is almost three times as long.

Though the Westminster Hall roof remained atypical, the fashion for hammer-beam roofs took firm hold, particularly among the large churches of eastern England. The fashion persisted into the 16th century, one of the last of the kind being the six-truss, seven-bay hammer-beam roof above the Great Hall of Henry VIII's Hampton Court Palace, built between 1531 and 1536.[25] Overall, the internal span is 12.19m, only about 1.5m more than Darnaway, and the length, including the screens area, is 29.57m, about 3.9m longer.

Without going into further detail, it is clear that the structural characteristics of the Darnaway roof do not conform readily with those of English hammer-beam roofs, or even with those few later medieval roofs in Scotland about which there is surviving information. Its anomalous position is at once both emphasised and better understood, however, in the light of the revised dating which dendrochronology has now provided. A date of 1387 places Darnaway at least a century earlier than the assumed date of its nearest — and royal — parallels in Scotland; even in England the hammer-beam genre was still not fully developed in 1387.

**Hall design**
The related questions of the purpose, design and dating of medieval great halls in general, though relevant to an understanding of the Darnaway hall, lies beyond the immediate scope of this paper. They tend to be associated with the major castles of the monarchy and greater nobility, secular and ecclesiastical, and their incidence and character serve as a crude architectural index of medieval power politics.

In medieval castle establishments, the great hall was essentially the principal reception and banqueting room for public and ceremonial purposes, as opposed to lesser halls and chambers for more private domestic use. At one end or in the middle of the hall was the high table set on a low platform or dais, an area usually distinguished by superior windows, fittings and perhaps roof trusses. At the opposite, 'lower', end of the hall was the service area, usually screened in some way and linked to the kitchens, buttery, pantry and other services, the lobby thus formed being known as the screens passage. Although they shared certain common characteristics, halls varied in size and relative importance, and in their relationship to other domestic suites and catering facilities. Internally, some were centred around open hearths or braziers, while others had fireplaces. Usually in Scotland, they were set on the first floor above vaulted or joisted cellarage, but there are known cases of 'laich' or ground-floor halls.[26]

Elsewhere in Moray, for example, the ruins of at least one great hall are associated with the palace of the medieval bishops of Moray at Spynie. The hall in the N range is probably a second-phase, 15th-century structure for there is what might have been an earlier, 14th-century hall-gatehouse

178

on the S side. Although very ruinous, the N range retains some indications of its former grandeur; above a shouldered window-head there are corbels that were probably associated with the wall-posts of a trussed rafter roof, whilst a lower corbel, carved in the form of a dignified male head, is in a position to have corresponded to a spere truss in front of the probable dais area.

At Darnaway there is still much to be clarified about the internal arrangements, the dais and the screens, and about relationships with the services and private chambers. Further research in the Moray muniments, particularly among the papers relating to the great reconstruction in the late 18th and early 19th centuries, may advance our detailed understanding of this structure. But, whatever the results of further enquiry, the carved details of this remarkable roof will continue to cast a shaft of light on the tough, crude and mysterious world of medieval Darnaway and its dark forests.

### Notes

1. D MacGibbon and T Ross, *The Castellated and Domestic Architecture of Scotland* (1887) 304-6 and Fig.261; G D Hay 'Some Aspects of Timber Construction in Scotland' in A Fenton *et al.* (edd.) *Building Construction in Scotland, Some Historical and Regional Aspects* (1976) 28-38 and 29.
2. *Regesta Regum Scottorum* V: *The Acts of Robert I* ed. A A M Duncan (1988) no.389 (see also no.101).
3. *The Scots Peerage* ed. Sir J Balfour Paul (1904-14) vi, 292-330.
4. M L Anderson, *A History of Scottish Forestry* i (1967) 127, 202-3.
5. *Acts of the Parliaments of Scotland* [*APS*] ii, 76.
6. *Exchequer Rolls of Scotland* vi, 220, 380, 483; ibid., xii, pp.xlv-xlvi, 673; *Reg.Mag.Sig.* ii, nos.2585-7.
7. *Stat.Acct.* xx (1798) 224.
8. *Bishop Pocock's Tours in Scotland, 1747-1760* ed. D W Kemp (Scottish History Society 1887) 183.
9. J C Nattes and J Fittler, *Scotia Depicta* (1819) plate 10.
10. H M Colvin, *A Biographical Dictionary of British Architects 1600-1840* (1978 edn) 499-500.
11. Darnaway Castle, Moray Muniments, vol.v, box 11C, estate houses nos.1202 and 1204 (letter of 20 January 1794 from Mr MacGrouther to Mr Maule).
12. Ibid., vol.vi, box 18, no.701 (9 July 1805 and 16 June 1807).
13. *Stat.Acct. loc.cit*
14. Moray Muniments, vol.vi, box 18, no.701 (2 November 1802).
15. The date 1722 was also incised on the E side of truss 2.
16. W Rhind, *Sketches of the Past and Present State of Moray* (1839) 140.
17. Cf. J M Gilbert 'Crossbows on Pictish Stones' *PSAS.* 107 (1975-6) 316-7.
18. *Scots Peerage* vi, 298-301.
19. *Cast. and Dom. Arch.* i, 455-7 and Figs.396-7; RCAHMS, *Inventory of Edinburgh* (1951) no.1 at p.21; J Gifford *et al.*, *Buildings of Scotland, Edinburgh* (1984) 95-6.

20. *Buildings of Scotland, Edinburgh loc.cit.*
21. RCAHMS, *Inventory of Stirlingshire* (1963) i, no.131 at p.13, and plates 23A, 25, 26; Stell 'A Note on Medieval Timber Flooring and Roofing' in A C Riches and G P Stell (edd.), *Materials and Traditions in Scottish Buildings* (1992) 75-80.
22. *Cast. and Dom. Arch.* i, 510, 512-13; *Edinburgh Architectural Association Sketch Book* 1878-79 ii, plates 35-7 (J Russell Walker); and *The Building News* 26 February 1886 (Thomas Ross).
23. J T Smith 'Medieval Roofs: a Classification' *Archaeological Journal* 115 (1958) 111-49 at 123-4.
24. RCHM, *Inventory of London* ii West London (excluding Westminster Abbey) (1925) no.24. Thomas Pennant even described 'Randolph's Hall' as being 'timbered at top like Westminster Hall' (Thomas Pennant, *A Tour in Scotland*; 1769 (1774 edn) 152).
25. RCHM, *Inventory of Middlesex* (1937) no.2 at pp.34-5.
26. Eg. RCAHMS, *Inventory of Argyll* ii (Lorn) no.293 at p.232.

# DENDROCHRONOLOGY

## General background

In attempting to date the oak timbers from the roof of Randolph's Hall, Darnaway, two questions were being addressed. The first was clearly a question of architectural history — what date is this important roof? The second related to the geographical position of the site. The Darnaway oaks represented the most northerly group of oak timbers so far encountered by dendrochronologists in Britain. Thus the second was a tree-ring question — can timbers from the north of Scotland be dated by dendrochronology?

To set the scene for this discussion it is worth outlining how dendrochronology has developed in the British Isles. In the 1960s there were no reference chronologies and little information on cross-matching between ring patterns. Initial work related to building 'local' chronologies, for example, in the separate chronologies for the north of Ireland, Dublin, south/central Scotland,[1] Sheffield,[2] south/eastern England[3] and western England.[4]

It gradually transpired that significant cross-matching existed between most of these chronologies,[5] that is, most of the chronologies matched most others. One chronology complex which did not fit into this system, Fletcher's art-historical 'Type A' chronology — constructed using boards from panel paintings — clouded the issue as to whether dating within Britain could always be expected or whether some oak chronologies were mutually exclusive. This problem was eventually resolved when it was shown that the Type A chronologies had in fact derived from the eastern Baltic.[6] This effectively removed the only significant anomaly in British dendrochronology.

Other work, using modern site chronologies from a wide area of northern Europe, suggested that most oak trees were responding to one underlying 'signal', the effects of which were diluted by distance and site factors.[7] This was very encouraging and confidence began to develop that any replicated site chronology from anywhere in Britain could be expected to cross-date against existing chronologies. The only other factor which would influence the likelihood of success in dating was the length of the available ring-pattern. Although there are no set figures, it is generally recognised that long chronologies are required, a period of over 150 years being desirable and 200-300 being ideal.

Within Scotland a basic medieval chronology was constructed during the 1970s. This used modern (that is, living tree) timbers from Raehills near Dumfries and from the Cadzow estate near Hamilton. These long modern ring-patterns were then extended using samples from Castle of Park, Lincluden College, Caerlaverock Castle and Glasgow Cathedral. The resultant south/central Scottish chronology extended back to AD 946.[8] It was found that some timbers (for example, samples from Threave and Perth) matched satisfactorily with this chronology, while others (for example, timbers from Dumfries, Midhope and St Andrews) totally failed to match. Clearly, these latter examples raised questions about the ability to date throughout Scotland. In particular, it was not clear whether the failure was due to local factors or due to importation of foreign wood. In the only test involving modern chronologies, it was found that oaks from the River Dee, that is, as far north as Aberdeen, fitted acceptably with an overall European oak master chronology.[9]

### Darnaway enquiry

It is against this background that the attempt to date the Darnaway timbers must be viewed. Darnaway lies 100km north-west of the sampling site on the River Dee, 150km north of Perth and some 200-300km north of the main Glasgow/Dumfries sampling areas used in the construction of the Scottish chronology. It was not therefore by any means certain that ring-patterns from Darnaway would be datable against the available chronologies from Scotland, England and Ireland, or indeed against an available British Isles average chronology, produced by averaging all the available precisely dated chronologies.

The stages involved in approaching this dating problem are as follows:

1) Are the timbers oak?
2) Can samples be acquired?
3) Will there be sufficient rings?
4) Can a 'site' chronology be constructed?
5) Will the timbering represent a single phase?
6) Can samples be acquired with sapwood?
7) Can the site chronology be placed precisely in time; that is dated?

Item 6 is particularly important for accurate dating. In oak the outer band of rings beneath the bark — the sapwood — is frequently subject to insect damage or removal during woodworking processes.

Since the dendrochronologist wants to provide the date of the final growth ring before felling, that is, the closest possible date to the building process, the presence of complete sapwood is critical. If the sapwood is incomplete, an allowance can be made by adding a range of 15-50 years to the date of the last heartwood ring. This represents a dramatic reduction in dating accuracy. Worse still is the case where the sapwood is completely missing. In this case the sapwood allowance has to be added to the date of the *last existing ring*, the resultant date range forming a *terminus post quem*.

At Darnaway, the availability of access to the roof timbers in March 1987 allowed confirmation that the timbers were oak. The major replacement elements in the end bays of the roof were immediately apparent, the timbers being distinctly different in character. It was also apparent that a number of the original structural elements retained sapwood and in some instances bark. Samples were therefore removed from twelve timbers. Of these, three were thin slices removed from the exposed ends of wind-braces and nine were cores extracted using a 'Henson' type hollow corer powered by electric drill.[10] In three cases the cores were supplemented by small wedges of sapwood to ensure the retrieval of exact felling dates.

For simplicity in description of sample locations the trusses are numbered from N to S as follows:

| Truss | Samples | Numbers |
| --- | --- | --- |
| 1 | nil | |
| 2 | nil | |
| 3 | 3 | Q6752,Q6753,Q6762 |
| 4 | 1 | Q6761 |
| 5 | 1 | Q6760 |
| 6 | 5 | Q6754-6757,Q6763 |
| 7 | 2 | Q6758,Q6759 |

List of samples.

All samples were taken at the level of the false hammer-beams and were from apparently original roof elements:

Q6752: W side, false hammer-beam
Q6753: W side, S wind-brace
Q6754: W side, decorative feature below false hammer-beam
Q6755: W side, north wind-brace
Q6756: W side, arch-brace
Q6757: W side, false hammer-beam
Q6758: W side, N wind-brace
Q6759: W side, principal rafter

Q6760: E side, arch-brace below false hammer-beam
Q6761: E side, arch-brace
Q6762: E side, arch-brace
Q6763: E side, decorative feature below false hammer-beam

Of the 12 ring-patterns, three — Q6752, Q6757 and Q6763 — were short with only 34, 30 and 88 rings respectively. These proved to be undatable. The nine other ring-patterns all cross-dated and were formed into a single site chronology. Figure 9.14 illustrates the relative placement of the ring-patterns. It is clear that the main structural elements form a coherent group with the two samples with complete sapwood, Q6760 and Q6761, both ending in the same year. This consistency is backed up by the end years of Q6756 and Q6762, which were both cut from the same tree (correlation value t = 17.3). In the case of these timbers the outer sapwood was not so well preserved, due to insect damage, but could be measured to within one year of the felling date of Q6760/Q6761. The four timbers without sapwood are entirely consistent with the main group. Their staggered placement in time is accounted for by missing heartwood rings as a result of the woodworking process.

The wind-brace, Q6753, where the sapwood appears to be complete, ends five years after the main group and indicates either that the wind-braces were an afterthought or that building took several years. Only a more detailed sampling exercise, undertaken with this result in mind, would clarify this question.

Having established site chronology, the total available length of ring pattern was 424 years. This was due to the extreme age of Q6762 which contained 418 rings. Since the purpose of the dating exercise was, at least in part, to ascertain whether oaks from this new area could be dated successfully, it was decided to produce only a replicated master chronology, that is, a chronology which did not depend on a single tree at any point. The resultant replicated Darnaway chronology spanned 262 years ending at the year specified by Q6760/Q6761.

The most obvious chronology with which to compare Darnaway was the south/central Scottish chronology.[11] This produced the *highest* correlation value, using the Belfast Cross 84 program,[12] at AD 1387 (t = 5.2). This same end-year was indicated by the highest correlation against the Dublin chronology (t = 3.5),[13] and against a generalised British Isles chronology (t = 4.5)[14]. In addition when compared with the latest Belfast long chronology for the north of Ireland, the Darnaway chronology gave the highest correlation in the last four millennia at AD 1387 (t = 4.0).

This suite of correlations, combined with satisfactory visual matching, between both chronologies and individual timbers from various sites, suggests that the Darnaway chronology can be dated against available chronologies and that its end-year is AD 1387. No other consistent correlation position was indicated by the analysis.

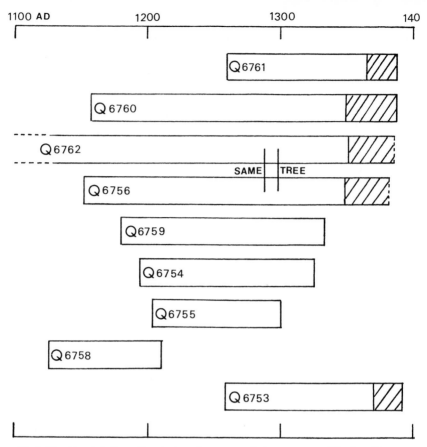

*Fig.9.14    Great hall roof; relative placement of ring-patterns. The hatching represents sapwood. There is a clear felling phase in AD 1387 with one later wind-brace, Q6753, felled in 1392.*

The results can therefore be summarised as follows. The timbers forming two of the main arch-braces of the Darnaway roof, Q6760 and Q6761, were felled in AD 1387. Three other timbers from the roof were highly consistent with this date, namely two other arch-braces, Q6765 and Q6762 from the same original tree, and one principal rafter, Q6759. Three heavily woodworked elements, namely the wind-braces Q6755 and Q6758 and a decorative feature Q6754, are not inconsistent in that they fall well back in time from the proposed felling date. Only the wind-brace, Q6753, is definitely later than the main structural elements and it last grew in 1392 on the assumption that the sapwood, which ends in that year, is complete. It is of interest that the two structural elements, which failed to date, were both false hammer-beams, Q6752 and Q6757. Both of these timbers were fast grown (wide ringed) in contrast with the majority which were very narrow ringed. This may reflect a desire for trees with very straight trunks — for which young fast grown trees would seem ideal — for the straight false hammer-beams. Trees to supply the curved arch-braces might therefore be selected from a different population.

**Conclusion**

Dendrochronological analysis indicates a clear felling phase in AD 1387 for timbers from the roof of Randolph's Hall, Darnaway. This implies that this new, most northerly, site falls within the same tree-ring remit which operates throughout Britain and Ireland. It reinforces the notion that any well replicated, long, oak site chronology should be datable against existing chronologies and lends hope to further dating exercises from the far north of Scotland.

**Notes**
1. M G L Baillie 'The Belfast Oak Chronology to AD 1001', 'Dublin Medieval Dendrochronology' and 'An Oak Chronology for South Central Scotland' *Tree-Ring Bulletin* 37 (1977) 1-12, 13-20 and 33-44 respectively.
2. R A Morgan 'Dendrochronological Dating of a Yorkshire Timber Building' *Vernacular Architecture* 8 (1977) 809-14.
3. J M Fletcher 'Dating of Art-Historical Artefacts' *Nature* 320 (1986) 466.
4. V Siebenlist-Kerner 'The Chronology, 1341-1636, for Certain Hillside Oaks from Western England and Wales' *British Archaeological Reports* (International Series) 51 (1978) 157-61.
5. M G L Baillie 'Dendrochronology for the Irish Sea Province' *British Archaeological Reports* (British Series) 54 (1978) 25-37.
6. M G L Baillie, J Hillam, K Briffa and D M Brown 'Re-Dating the English Art-Historical Tree-Ring Chronologies' *Nature* 315 (1985) 317-19; Fletcher 'Dating of Art-Historical Artefacts'.
7. M G L Baillie 'Is There a Single British Isles Oak Tree-Ring Signal?' *Proceedings of the 22nd Symposium on Archaeometry, Bradford 1982* (University of Bradford 1983) 73-82.
8. Baillie 'An Oak Chronology for South Central Scotland'.
9. Baillie 'Is There a Single British Isles Oak Tree-Ring Signal?'.
10. M G L Baillie, *Tree-Ring Dating and Archaeology* (1982) 70.
11. Baillie 'An Oak Chronology for South Central Scotland'.
12. M A R Munro 'An Improved Algorithm for Cross Dating Tree-Ring Series' *Tree-Ring Bulletin* 44 (1984) 17-27.
13. Baillie 'Dublin Medieval Dendrochronology'.
14. M G L Baillie and J R Pilcher (1982, unpublished).

**Acknowledgements**
The authors wish to record their thanks to the Earl of Moray for permission to carry out the surveys of the roof, and to Michael Chapman, General Manager and Factor of Moray Estates Development Company, for his considerable assistance in the conduct of the work. The survey by the Royal Commission on the Ancient and Historical Monuments of Scotland was carried out by Sam Scott (drawings), Jim Mackie (photographs) and Geoffrey Stell (description and analysis). This material is Crown Copyright, Royal Commission on Ancient Monuments, Scotland, and is reproduced by permission of the Commissioners.

# THE CULBIN SANDS — A MYSTERY UNRAVELLED
## Sinclair Ross

### The Culbin Sands
Along the southern shores of the Moray Firth some 50 km of the coastline are formed from unconsolidated sands and shingle of fluvio-glacial origin. The Culbin Sands lie on this coast between the river Findhorn and the river Nairn (Fig.10.1).

The whole of this stretch is covered by blown sand, with spectacular dunes reaching up to 30 m in height. Old photographs show it to have been a desert-like wilderness at the beginning of this century. Over the past 100 years, however, the sands have gradually been stabilised by afforestation and today the 28 square kms of the Culbin Sands are covered by a thriving forest.

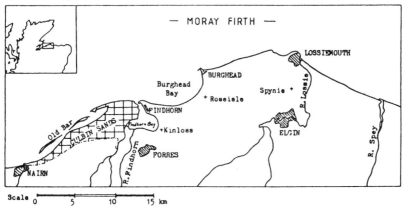

*Fig.10.1   Part of the Moray Coast showing location of the Culbin Sands.*

There are historical records of severe sand-blowing which buried stretches of farmland in Lower Moray around the close of the 17th century, but no tales so harrowing as the destruction of the Culbin Estate in 1694. This had been dramatically described by Martin and later by Bain, and, backed up by the desert scenery of Culbin, these accounts fired the imagination of all their readers.[1] From their descriptions the following synopsis of events has been compiled.

### The Barony of Culbin (popular version)
With a history going back to the beginning of the 13th century, the estate of Culbin was the finest and the most fertile in Moray. In the centre of it stood the mansion house of the Kinnairds — a large square building of dressed stones, embowered with a beautiful garden, a fruitful orchard, and

187

a spacious lawn. It was, given the social position of the Baron, and the wealth the family possessed, a centre of the culture and refinement of the time.

The estate itself was called the garden and granary of Moray. 'Stretching away in the distance in every direction were to be seen the highly cultivated fields with heavy corn; the rich meadows, dotted here and there with thriving herds; and the extensive pastures with numerous flocks'.[2] There were in all 3600 acres. To the east and west were sixteen fair sized farms and farm houses, each tenant paying on average £200 Scots in money rent, as well as forty bolls each of wheat, bere, oats and oatmeal in kind. There were numerous small crofts and huts all over the estate. The rent roll still exists.

The river Findhorn flowed past the north side of the lands in a slow, broad stream. Along its banks were rows of fishermen's huts, with their boats and fishing gear in front — all of these dwellings teeming with life and activity. The salmon fishing was particularly valuable, and the little community appears to have enjoyed a large measure of prosperity. The late frost or protracted drought might destroy the crops in other parts of the district, but so rich and deep was the alluvial soil of Culbin that the crops there never failed. One year a heavy crop of barley was reaped, though no rain had fallen since it was sown.

The great sand drift came from the west in the autumn of 1694: it came suddenly and with short warning. A man ploughing had to desert his plough in the middle of a furrow. The reapers in a field of late barley had to leave without finishing their work. In a few hours plough and barley were buried beneath the sand. The drift, like a mighty river, came on steadily and ruthlessly, grasping field after field, and enshrouding every object in a mantle of sand. In terrible gusts the wind carried the sand amongst the dwelling houses of the people, sparing neither the hut of the cottar nor the mansion of the laird. The splendid orchard, the beautiful lawn, all shared the same fate.

In the morning after the first night of drift, the people had to break through the back of their houses to get out. They relieved the cattle and drove them to a place of safety. After a lull, the storm began again with renewed violence, and they had to flee for their lives, taking with them only such things as they could carry. To add to the horrors of the scene, the sand choked the mouth of the river Findhorn, which now poured its flooded waters amongst the fields and homesteads, accumulating in lakes and pools till it rose to a height at which it was able to burst the barrier to the north, and find a new outlet to the sea, in its course sweeping to destruction the old village of Findhorn.

On returning, the people of Culbin were spellbound. Not a vestige, not a trace of their houses was to be seen. Everything had disappeared beneath the sand. From that time to this, the estate of Culbin has been completely buried by the sand. A portion of the old mansion house appeared about a hundred years later, like a ghostly spectre amidst the sand, and became an object of superstitious interest to the people of the neighbourhood, especially as one man who had bawled down the chimney, heard a voice distinctly respond to his cry. It eventually disappeared as suddenly as it came on the scene. Fruit trees have actually come out and blossomed and borne fruit in this sandy desert, only to be swallowed up again. The dovecote and chapel also reappeared, and their ruins supplied stones for neighbouring farm buildings.

As for the laird and his family, the sequel is more pathetic. Kinnaird escaped the night of the catastrophe with his wife and child, attended by a nurse. Their boy was but a few months old. Kinnaird petitioned Parliament to be exempt from the payment of land tax, on account of the greater part of his land being overrun by the sand and the remainder threatened. Shortly afterwards he was forced to sell out and applied for personal protection against his creditors. The estate was sold in 1698 and both the laird and his wife died a few years later. The faithful nurse took the child to Edinburgh and supported him and herself by needlework. When the orphaned child grew up, he enlisted in the army where he was recognised by an uncle of his who procured for him a commission. He later became Captain of a Troop of Horse but died without issue about 1743 bringing the Kinnaird line to a close.

### The Extent of the Barony of Culbin

Investigation by the writer into the coastal processes which formed the Culbin foreland[3] showed that the river Findhorn had at one time flowed into a wide estuary, flanked on its northern side by a westward-growing shingle bar which diverted the course of the river to the southwest. This was at the time of the Post-Glacial High Sea Level, when, 6500 years ago, the sea stood 5.5 m higher than today.

As the sea level fell back, the shingle bar was left high and dry as a fossil beach, the estuary dried out with vegetation and soil developing, and the old river channel became a peat-filled hollow. The estuarine soils were to become the farm lands of the Barony of Culbin. Today the outlines of the shingle ridges can be traced in the forest, and by digging down through the sand in hollows between the dunes, the extent of the soil and peat horizons can also be gauged (Fig.10.2). When mapped to scale it became obvious that a considerable discrepancy existed between the accepted extent of the old estate and the most generous estimate that could be made on the ground of the area of potentially arable land — the stretches of estuarine soils between the shingle ridges and the river. Details of carse lands flanking the river were obtained from a map of 1758[4] and an estimate of the area of soil available came to 548 ha. (1354 acres). This had to be

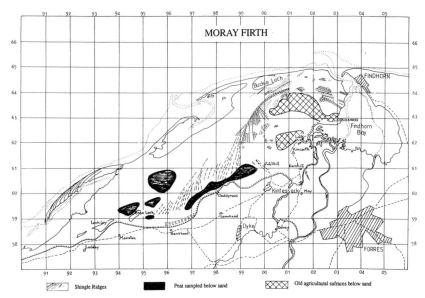

*Fig:10.2   Areas in Culbin Forest where peat and soils have been sampled below sand.*

shared between several farms, some of which were not part of the Barony of Culbin.

Much of the original information about the estate was contained in an article written in 1865 by C Fraser Mackintosh,[5] who had access to old estate papers. These were described in 1884 as totalling 68 documents,[6] but today only a few survive.[7] On researching what had been written on the Culbin Sands, some 200 papers, articles and books have been traced. These are of varying length and weight, with roughly half covering aspects of the history of the estate. The 'facts' in these accounts have often been taken verbatim from the well known lectures by Martin and descriptions by Bain, and then not uncommonly enhanced in the telling.

Only one author urged caution in the acceptance of the popular version. In 1938, the Rev. J G Murray wrote, 'It might have been expected, however, that newspaper and magazine editors would exercise a measure of discretion before publishing in their columns fantastic legends which have been repeated ad nauseam during the last quarter century. Or do they imagine that their readers will swallow "cauld Kale het again" if only it is served by a different writer each time'.[8] Fifty years later this is still fair comment, and the same old story is still being repeated.[9]

In an attempt to separate fact from fiction, it was considered that the first course of action should be to check what Fraser-Mackintosh had actually said against any historical documents relating to the estate which could still be traced. A surprising amount of information was gleaned

190

from available public records, the Register of Sasines being particularly useful. Details of property deals and family names and relationships were uncovered, filling many blanks in the history of the estate.

Quoting from an 'old deed', Fraser Mackintosh described the estate as,

'All and hail the lands of Culbin, comprehending therein the lands, mill, fishings and others underwritten, viz:- All and hail that part of the lands and barony of Culbin called the Mains of Culbin, with the manor place, houses, biggings, yards, orchards, tofts, crofts, and hail pertinents of the same; The Hill of Findhorn, with houses, biggings and pertinents, the ferme coble on the water of Findhorn, with liberties, commonties and privileges thereof, with the mussell scalp and salmon fishing and pertinents, as well in fresh as salt waters of Findhorn, commonly called the Stells of Culbin ....'[10] In similar vein the other properties were described as 'the lands of Macrodder *alias* Mirrietown; the lands of Aikenhead, *alias* Ranchkers ... the lands of Binn, *alias* Middle Binn ... the lands of Laick and Sandifield, the lands of Delaith, *alias* Delpottie with the mill of Delpottie, multures, and sequells of the said lands and barony of Culbin ... the manse of the Chapel of St. Ninian ... the lands of Earnhill ... the lands of Easter Binn ... and the said salmon fishing on the water of Findhorn, called the common stell or the Sheriff Stell....'

Many writers have fallen into the trap of quoting directly from this, and including 'houses, biggings, yards, orchards, tofts, crofts, doves, dovecotes etc.' with each property as listed. This was merely the standard phraseology used in the conveyancing of the period by a 'writer' who might not have seen the property and had to cover all eventualities in his list of the estate's assets. The Mains, or home farm, was by tradition the best farm on an estate, usually close to the proprietor's residence. No mention is made in any of the charters or sasines as to the annual rent or size of the Mains of Culbin, and it is therefore suggested that the phrase the 'Mains with the manor place' was also part of the conveyancing jargon of the period, and that the laird must have stayed at the farmhouse of Binn, 'of old called Middlebin'. An obvious mistake is the statement that the total area of the estate amounted to 3600 acres (1457 ha). In a footnote, Fraser Mackintosh explained that about 1865 the area of the sands had been measured and found to extend to 3600 acres.[11] Thus this figure was the total area of the sands and not the extent of the Barony in 1694.

As other documents connected with the Kinnaird family were uncovered, it became apparent that there were differences between the various lists of the estate's holdings. These arose from various causes — the misinterpretation of old handwriting, faulty translation from Latin, the copying of a list of properties from an old document when in the meantime some lands had been sold, the assumption that a named property was a farm, when in fact it was carseland and so on. Exploration in this quarter effectively reduced the productive part of the Culbin estate to Middle Binn, Laik and Sandifield, Delpottie with its mill, and Earnhill, plus the salmon fishings.

The most-quoted extract from Fraser Mackintosh's account is the rental for the year 1693,[12] which was supposed to show that the estate had sixteen farms producing a rent of £2720 Scots, plus 640 bolls of wheat, and similar amounts of bere, oats and oatmeal. A closer look at the rental shows that the list was not of sixteen farms but of sixteen tenants in six holdings, namely those listed in the previous paragraph. Of the three larger ones, Middle Binn supported five tenants, Delpottie and Laik four each, while Sandifield, Earnhill and Culbin Croft (presumed to be all that remained of Middle Binn after the sand blowing) had one tenant each. This raised the question of how much ground a single tenant worked in these days of traditional agricultural methods of the pre-improvement era.

Annual rents for Culbin Croft and Kintessack for the years 1733 and 1734 were quoted by Fraser Mackintosh for comparison with those of 1693.[13] These are extremely detailed and show the acreage held by each tenant, together with the rents paid in grain, money and kind. The grain rents of the period were approximately 1.6 bolls per Scots acre.[14] Figures for Kintessack showed each tenant had on average 4.4 acres. Using these figures, Earnhill covered 13.3 acres and Delpottie and Laik 19.4 acres each — a total of 52.1 acres. A plan of Moy estates dated 1776 shows the boundaries of Earnhill and Delpottie at that time enclosing 42 acres.[15] Both sets of figures indicate that the holdings were small.

From a wadset held by William Duff in 1682,[16] the Culbin estate included 'The 5 ploughs land of Binn, of old Middlebin', with a yearly rental of 90 bolls of bere — a very low figure for a 5-plough farm, and not much more than the combined holdings of Earnhill, Delpottie and Laik. (It should be borne in mind that farmers of the period had little or no knowledge of how to drain the land, and that what today appears to be soil suitable for arable farming might not have been workable in 1692.) This also suggests that there is need for the revision of the popular beliefs as to the size of the old Barony.

The other asset of the estate was the salmon fishings, and here the Kinnairds held the fishing rights along the left bank of the river from where it left Findhorn Bay to the sea — the Common Stell and the East and West Stells of Culbin (Fig.10.3). Various sasines in the period 1667-1677, when the Dawsons of Findhorn held a wadset on the Stells of Culbin, and the 1682 wadsets held by William Duff, show that the income from the salmon would produce a rent of some £750 Scots annually — a figure similar to the grain rents of the estates. A total annual income, depending on the price of salmon and grain at the time, could have been between £1300 and £1600 Scots.

The value of land in this period is commonly put at around twenty times

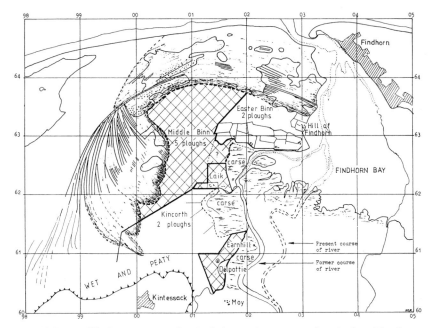

*Fig.10.3   Middle Binn positioned to include maximum area of agricultural land.*

the annual rent, with reduced values for deteriorating circumstances. The rental for 1733 quoted by Fraser Mackintosh calculates a '22-year purchase' of £10,872:15s:4d for Earnhill, Delpottie and Laik.[17] This uses a price of bere of £5 Scots per boll. Had this been 5 merks per boll, the value would have fallen to £7810. In 1673 William Dunbar of Kintessack held a wadset on Earnhill and Delpottie with its mill, against 8500 merks (£5667 Scots), while in 1682 William Duff held the whole estate, including the fishings on a wadset of 25,000 merks (£16,667 Scots).[18] In this latter case this is some ten to twelve times the annual rent. A twenty year purchase at the lower rent of £1300 per annum would put the value of the estate at £26,000. When the estate was finally sold in 1698 it fetched £20,259:10s:6d, a figure said to be some £6000 less than the sum due to William Duff and Sir James Abercrombie of Birkenbog, the only other preferential creditor.

The improvements in agricultural methods which were already under way in southern Scotland did not reach Moray until some 75 years after the destruction of the Culbin estate. This is of great importance when one considers that there had been a severe deterioration in climate throughout the 17th century, leading to several periods of famine.[19] The century saw the total abandonment of many upland farms, the rise in Scottish mercenary armies and the plantation of Northern Ireland. During the years 1691-1700 there were seven years with total crop failure and it has been suggested that up to 20% of the population of Scotland perished. This is the background against which we must weigh the 'highly cultivated fields with heavy corn; the rich meadows, dotted here and there with thriving herds and the extensive pastures with numerous flocks.'

The method of infield and outfield prevailed, with the agriculture being run on equal shares rather than for efficiency. Such subsistence farming, being aimed at providing a living for as many souls as possible on the land, was particularly vulnerable in a time of deteriorating climate. Taking into account the accepted crop-yields and rent structures throughout Scotland during this period, the 1693 rental looks ridiculously high if we are to agree that the Culbin estate was of a much smaller size than the popular accounts would have us believe. There then enters the possibility that the 'rental' was an attempt at some form of valuation, albeit incomplete.

### The Boundaries of the Barony of Culbin

Middle Binn was listed as being five ploughs (265 ha) in extent in 1682 and Easter Binn appeared in a sasine of 1625 as being two ploughs (106 ha)[20]. The adjoining property of Kincorth had a similar rating in the valued rent of the shire of Moray in 1667, and is also taken to have been about two ploughs in extent.

On the map of 1758[21] the lands of Binsness (formerly Easter Binn) cover approximately 53 ha, or half the original size of the estate, and if an additional 'plough' is added to the north of the 1758 field systems we have a representation of the old Easter Binn, lying between the river and the shingle ridges (Fig.10.3). Adding information from the 1776 plan of Moy, the carse lands, Delpottie, Laik and Earnhill can then be positioned. A good approximation of the boundaries of Kincorth can then be inserted on the east and south sides, and then the two plough size of the holding brings the western boundary against the Culbin more or less on the present day boundary.

Laik can then be positioned from the 1758 map as a 11 ha block, leaving room for Sandifield between it and Easter Binn. Sandifield was always mentioned in conjunction with Laik, and had one tenant against Laik's four. It has therefore been allocated 3 ha. Assuming the 'Mains of Culbin' to have been a conveyancing term, as argued above, the remaining 207 ha of the arable land between these boundaries and the shingle ridges has been allocated to Middle Binn. The additional 58 ha required to make up five ploughs has to overlap into the rougher ground on the shingle ridges.

The completed map (Fig.10.4) is in agreement with what documentary evidence has survived and satisfies the evidence on the ground. It reduces the sixteen farms to five and the 3600 acres to 735 (1457 ha to 298), an area only some 10% of the present Culbin Forest.

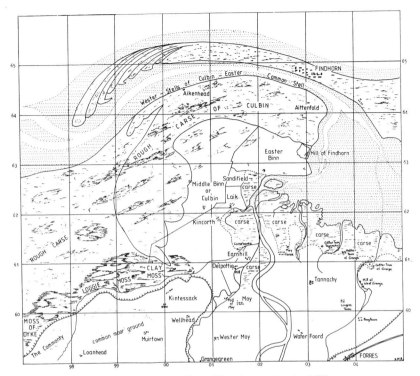

*Fig.10.4    The Barony of Culbin and neighbouring estates in 1680.*

## Buildings and Sand-Blowing on the Culbin Estate

With no building stone available between the rivers Findhorn and Nairn, and no roads or wheels to help them, the tenants and cottars on the estate built their houses largely of turf. The renewal of roofs and walls took up a considerable amount of time each year and, in addition, the 'feal' dykes round the infields had also to be maintained. Traditionally the turf from the rough grazing or carse lands was used for this purpose, and in the case of the Culbin the turf capping the old dunes on the shingle ridges was stripped, and bent grass pulled for thatch. This exposed the sand below to the wind. Turf was also needed for mixing into the middens to make compost, and while old roofs and walls were dumped there, much more was dug up. The amount of turf used up by a ferme toun for these purposes was surprisingly large, and in the case of the Culbin led to extensive sand-blowing. Descriptions by early travellers describe sandstorms in the area and Nairn Town Council periodically banned the digging of turf. In 1695 Alexander Kinnaird, the last laird of Culbin, appealed to Parliament for

195

a reduction in taxes as half of his estate had been overblown by sand. This led to an Act of Parliament being passed prohibiting the pulling of bent on coastal dunes.[22]

There is no doubt that the destruction of the estate was greatly accelerated by the turf-stripping. However, modern theories of sand-blowing point to inundation being a gradual process rather than the dramatic burial of the popular tale. The turf houses crumbled away to dust, but the remains of some were seen during the 1800's. Legend had it that the 'Manor House' also appeared from under a large dune and that its stonework was 'quarried' by neighbouring farmers. There is no record of this as such, but about 1920 sandstone blocks bearing parts of the family coat of arms were found, and during the 1930's, a complete outline of foundation stones was exposed a short distance to the north west of Kincorth.[23] Unfortunately no measurements or distances were recorded and today we are still uncertain of the position and size of the building.

### The Murrays of Culbin

The earliest possessors of the lands of Culbin on record are the family of Murray or De Moravia. In 1235 King Alexander II confirmed a grant of the lands of Skelbo in Sutherland to Richard de Moravia from his brother St Gilbert, bishop of Caithness.[24] Richard is the undoubted ancestor of the Murrays of Culbin. Lachlan Shaw considered him to be a descendant of Freskin de Moravia, and thus related to other families using this designation.[25] In this he has been generally followed, although D Murray Rose believed Richard to be a descendant of an earlier Richard de Moravia, supposedly a son of Angus, Earl or Mormaer of Moray, who rose against King David I in 1130.[26]

Freskin de Moravia, himself almost certainly of Flemish origin, was settled at Duffus in the time of David I. His descendant Hugh Freskin aided David's grandson, King William, against Harald Madaddsson, Jarl of Orkney, and was rewarded with the forfeited lands of Sutherland. When the Caithness clans again rebelled and murdered their bishop, Hugh's son William helped put down the rebellion and was made the first earl of Sutherland.[27] The new bishop of Caithness was Gilbert de Moravia, formerly archdeacon of Moray. Hugh Freskin granted him the lands of Skelbo and, as noted above, he passed them on to his brother Richard.[28] From the days of Richard onwards, although only scattered pieces of information survive, the family of Murray of Culbin can be traced until the early 15th century when their heiress Egidia (otherwise Giles) married Thomas Kinnaird, son and heir of Alan Kinnaird of that ilk.[29]

### The Kinnairds of Culbin

The family of Kinnaird had a Flemish origin in a merchant, Radulphus de Kynnard, who received lands in Perthshire sometime prior to 1184. The

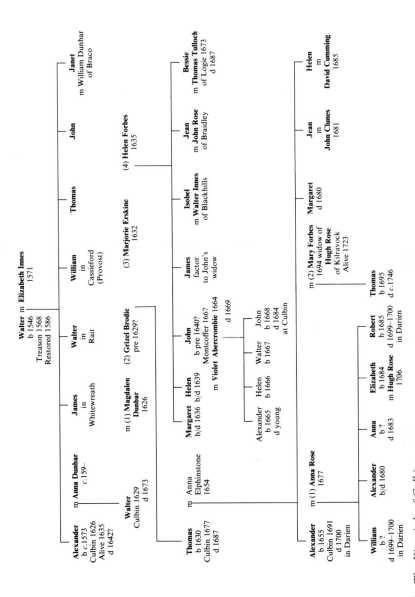

*Fig.10.5   The Kinnairds of Culbin.*

197

*Fig.10.6    Gravestone preserved in Dyke Church.*

family prospered and obtained other lands in the east and northeast coastal region of Scotland. When Sir Thomas Kinnaird married Egidia Murray, heiress of Culbin, their combined holdings of land were very extensive.

The early records of the burgh of Forres were destroyed, and while a few papers have survived from the first part of the 16th century, it is not until after 1575 that any information can be gleaned from that source. As a result the early history of the Kinnairds of Culbin is largely a table of the line of succession and a list of properties controlled. There is a marked increase in available information after 1575, and it then becomes possible to build up a more general picture of the Kinnairds as was done by Murray in his history of the family (see Fig.10.5).[30]

The picture he paints is one of a land-owning family which prospered for a considerable time, acquiring property and fishing rights, and was in a position to loan money to neighbours. Circumstances then changed, and over the last twenty years or so of the life of the estate, debts suddenly increased until in the end the whole of the Barony was sold off. Murray

198

also recounts several family feuds and escapades, some outwith the law. The tale would probably fit many families of the period; all, that is, save the overwhelming of the estate by sand in 1694. Murray's account is straightforward, linking together small pieces of information and episodes in the history of the family from the sources available to him. However, additional information uncovered, mainly from the Register of Sasines, the Parish Register of Dyke and Moy and from the records of other families, shows parts of his version of the family tree to be flawed. There had also been several deals involving the estate, of which he was unaware, some of which indicate that financial problems may have started as early as 1660. Some of these additional findings are discussed below.

In the church of Dyke there is preserved a gravestone found in a heap of rubbish in the churchyard around 1823. The stone is in good condition and bears the names of Walter Kinnaird and Elizabeth Innes (Fig.10.6). Under the coats of arms of the two families is the date 1613. Walter Kinnaird had married Elizabeth Innes in 1571, and they had six sons and a daughter. Murray presumed that Elizabeth Innes had died in 1613,[31] but the Register of Sasines showed she was still alive in 1629 but probably died before 1632.

In 1626 Alexander Kinnaird, Walter's eldest son, was served heir to his father, who must have been about eighty when he died. Murray states that Alexander died in 1630 and that his eldest son Walter married Grizel Brodie on 20th August 1629, having by her at least three sons and two daughters, and later marrying, as his second wife, Helen Forbes, widow of James Elphinstone of Barns, on 19th March 1644.

Pitfalls, however, await those who take for granted that the date of the charter of a son's succession to an estate was also the date of the death of his father, or that the date on which a wife was granted rents from the estate was the date of her marriage. At this range one can never be certain that every document has been uncovered. In a charter granted by Alexander Kinnaird in 1626 reference is made to a marriage contract between his son Walter and Magdalen Dunbar, daughter of Martin Dunbar of Grangehill.[32] Murray makes no mention of this Magdalen in his history of the Dunbars.[33] Walter and his second wife Grizel Brodie got the tenancy of Culbin in 1629, while Walter's parents were still alive. Provision was made for the parents out of the estate for their lifetime, and for Elizabeth Innes, Walter's grandmother.[34] Grizel Brodie died before 1632, as in that year Marjorie Erskine was named in a sasine as 'future spouse' to Walter Kinnaird, and with permission of Walter's father, was given rents from the estate.[35] On 12th January 1635, Helen Forbes received sasine of the lands of Culbin with permission of Walter's father. She was referred to as '... nunc sponse honorabilis viri Walter Kinnaird de Cowbin'.[36] Whether Walter actually married Marjorie Erskine is not clear.

The Parish Register for Dyke and Moy reveals a daughter born to Helen on 5th January of the following year who died when not quite three months old, and on 27th March 1639, another daughter, Helen, who died aged four months. In 1642 Walter Kinnaird received a charter of the estate of Culbin from King Charles I, and in 1644 Helen Forbes received sasine of her life-rent of part of the estate. This was a reaffirmation of the charter granted in 1635 when she married Walter, who after getting the 1642 charter (presumably on the death of his father), was now the feudal superior. 1644 was not, as Murray suggested, the date of their marriage. The chronological order of the births of Walter's family by his four wives, if four there were, is in doubt, but their names and histories can be traced. As can been seen from the accounts of this and other landed families, there seems to have been no difficulty for the lairds in getting new wives, but childbirth was more hazardous than the battlefield. What the prospects were for wives and infants in the squalor of the cottar houses, we can only guess.

One of the problems facing any landowner with a large family was the provision of lands for his sons and dowries for his daughters, particularly when finances were stretched. The original Kinnaird estate had been divided up in 1514, when the lands of Skelbo, Kinnaird and Naughton in Fife had gone to the eldest son, and Culbin alone had gone to the second son. In 1626 when Alexander Kinnaird had moved into Culbin, the family was still well off, with at least four of his five brothers being placed in farms of their own. When his son Walter had, in turn, to provide for his family of three sons and three daughters, money appears to have been much tighter. Whether this was due to the adverse effects of the deteriorating climate, we do not know. There are many records of his acquiring lands and fishings, and loaning money during the first 20 to 30 years of his tenure; but in 1660 he first sold off some land to set up his son John, then in 1667 we see for the first time, a laird of Culbin borrowing money using part of his estate as security. First the fishings were wadset, then some of the farms.

Walter Kinnaird died in 1673 and the estate lay in the hands of the crown because of non-payment of feu duties. His son Thomas could not gain possession until this was paid off. Thomas' brother, John of Montcoffer, had died in 1669 leaving a widow and three children. His lands were confirmed to Walter, the eldest son, with life-rent of the lands going to his widow. When his mother died in 1676, young Walter was only nine years old, and the estate was administered by his uncle James Kinnaird.

The boy's maternal grandfather, Sir Alexander Abercrombie of Birkenbog, had originally owned the lands, and he and his brother John now arranged to sell the farms to John's son-in-law, in spite of the questionable legality of such a deed. The proceeds, 10,000 merks, were then paid to Thomas Kinnaird of Culbin as the children's nearest relative, and the money was to be applied for their benefit. With this injection of capital there was a temporary improvement in Thomas' affairs. In 1677 his son married, he redeemed a wadset held on his fishings on the Findhorn, and he finally gained possession of his father's lands of Culbin after a delay of four years — presumably on the payment of the overdue taxes. He also paid certain moneys to his brother James as his share of the estate.

This period of opulence did not last long. There had been a shortage of peat for fuel for a long time in Lower Moray, and in 1680 Brodie tells of the Laird of Culbin stealing his peats.[37] From his diary it would appear that Brodie disapproved of the attitudes and behaviour of the Kinnairds — perhaps fueled by his support for the Covenanters, while the Kinnairds were staunchly Catholic. By 1682 the whole of the estate had been pledged, and no further loans could be raised. Murray states that Thomas Kinnaird died in 1691, but according to the Dyke Parish Register he died on 3rd July 1687, the 1691 date being when his son, Alexander inherited the estate. It is interesting here to note that when the estate was finally sold to cover the debts, young Walter, son of John of Montcoffer, was listed among the creditors who received nothing.

### The Last Kinnairds of Culbin

Of the early accounts of the final saga of the Kinnairds of Culbin, only brief and scattered versions exist — some conflicting, most inaccurate and all incomplete. Later accounts are almost all repeats of Bain's 1911 version; sometimes quoted verbatim but often with additional embroidery.

By the time of Alexander Kinnaird, the last laird, William and Mary had come to the throne, and Catholics in Scotland had lost their positions of privilege. Alexander had been in trouble over his support for the Jacobite cause, and in 1689 had been listed among the 'rebels' associated with Viscount Dundee, which was possibly one reason for the delay in his getting control of his father's estate. When he eventually gained possession, the disastrous harvests and encroaching sands put an end to any vain hopes he might have entertained of paying off his creditors. His dramatic appeal to Parliament in 1695 blossomed into the legend of the 'Buried Barony', and fired the imagination of writers into keeping the tale alive. Had it not been for the saga of the sands he would have vanished without trace, like so many other landowners of the period, who had to sell off their lands to cover their debts in this time of recurring famine and hardship.

What we can glean of his background points to his having been an unruly character and a wastrel. He had married Anna Rose in 1677, and after her death he married Mary Forbes, widow of Hugh Rose, 14th Baron of Kilravock in 1694. Murray describes the first marriage as childless and the second as producing one son, Alexander.[38] Examination of the Dyke Parish Register, however, shows that the son of the second marriage was christened Thomas. He was the 'orphan' who, according to the legends, was taken to Edinburgh by a faithful nurse. Murray rightly directs his readers to the history of the Roses of Kilravock in which it is stated that the laird of Culbin died in Darien and that Mary Forbes was still alive in 1715.[39] He also points out that her life-rent from her first husband's estate would have been more than sufficient to have kept the wolf from the door.

It is difficult to explain the failure of local authors to mention Alexander Kinnaird's family by his first wife, Anna Rose. In the Dyke Parish Register four children are recorded: Alexander, Anna, Elizabeth and Robert. At the place of the entry of Alexander's birth in the register, the page is damaged and discoloured. The almost illegible entry is non-standard, and was interpreted as also recording his death in infancy. Re-examination of the register offered the alternative suggestion that the entry was 'This child was born and baptised at Nairn'. In the family papers of the Roses of Kilravock, a William Kinnaird appears as witness to two deeds, being described in one dated 1696 as being son of 'Alexander Kynaird of Cowbin'.[40]

Mary Forbes had been the second wife of Hugh Rose of Kilravock and bore him six sons. On Hugh's death, his son Hugh by his first marriage succeeded as 15th Baron of Kilravock. From a letter written by Mary Forbes to her stepson Hugh in 1723 we gather that in 1698 she had been staying in Edinburgh with her second husband and family, after the sale of the Culbin estate.[41] She blamed her stepson for refusing to help them unless Alexander Kinnaird left her to fend for himself. She went on to say that as a result, Alexander and his sons (*in the plural*) had gone to Darien, while she returned north with her family of young Roses, presumably leaving young Thomas Kinnaird with relatives in Edinburgh. Prebble, in his account of the Darien Scheme mentions that the laird of Culbin and his son, Ensign William Kinnaird, died on the voyage, but unfortunately does not give the source of his information.[42] The youngest son of Alexander's first marriage, Robert, is not mentioned here or in any other document, but he could also have gone to Darien, although he would have been only fourteen years of age.

When young Thomas Kinnaird enlisted in the army, the 'recognition' by a relative which led to his being commissioned was more than chance. That relative was his half-brother Alexander Rose, the oldest son of Mary Forbes by her first marriage. He had had a successful career in the army, reaching the rank of Lt. Col. in Lord Molesworth's Dragoons, and in 1742 Thomas was listed as being adjutant to that regiment. Lt. Col. Rose died in 1743, but only an approximate date can be given for Thomas' death — c 1746. There is no record of his ever having married, and with his death the line of the Kinnairds of Culbin came to an end.

## Epilogue

While researching into his own connections with the Kinnairds of Culbin, John Kinnaird, then membership secretary of the Scottish Genealogical Society, noticed in one of that Society's publications the following inscription from Newtyle grave-yard, '1813 George Watson Esq., Bannatyne House w Jean Rose, sole heiress of ancient families of Moray and Kinnaird of Culbin'.[43] Elizabeth Kinnaird, the only daughter of the last laird, married a Hugh Rose in Nairn in 1706. Since her brothers apparently died without issue, only descendants of Elizabeth could claim this unique ancestry.

It is a fitting end to the tale that, in spite of the legends, neither the estate nor the family vanished without trace.

## Acknowledgements

The account of the history of the Kinnairds of Culbin has been greatly improved by stimulating discussions with John Kinnaird. I also wish to thank Kris Sangster for providing the sketch in Fig.10.6.

## Notes

1. J Martin 'The Buried Estate of Culbin' *Elgin Courant* 1860; 'The Sandhills of Culbin' *Forres Gazette* 1867; 'The Sands of Culbin' *Elgin Courant* 1875.
2. G Bain, *The Culbin Sands* (Nairn, 1922)
3. S M Ross 'Notes on the Development of the Culbin Foreland' *Bulletin of the Moray Field Club* (1974) 2.
4. P May, *A Survey of the River Findhorn* (1758) (Elgin Museum.)
5. C Fraser Mackintosh 'The Lost House of Culbin' in *Antiquarian Notes* (Inverness 1865); 2nd ed. (Inverness 1913) 331-42.
6. J Pirie 'The Sandhills of Culbin' in *Journal of the Excursions of the Elgin and Morayshire Lit. and Sc. Association* (Elgin 1884).
7. Seafield Papers (Scottish Record Office [SRO] GD/245/95).
8. J G Murray, *The Kinnairds of Culbin* (Inverness 1938).
9. Eg. M Harding 'A Time of Smothering Sands' *The Northern Scot*, Xmas 1986; and D P Willis, *Sand and Silence* (Univ. of Aberdeen 1986).
10. Fraser Mackintosh, *Antiquarian Notes* 333.
11. Ibid., 336n.
12. Ibid., 336-7.
13. Ibid., 337-8.
14. As calculated from the more detailed Kintessack rental of 6 March 1734 (SRO GD 248/80/6/5.)
15. *Plan of the Lands of Moy, 1776* (anon.), (Moray District Record Office, DGS/P1).
16. *General Register of Sasines* [*GRS*] (Morayshire) 29/3 pp.116, 127 (1682).
17. Fraser Mackintosh, *Antiquarian Notes* 338-9.
18. *GRS* (Morayshire) 29/3 pp.116, 127 (1682).
19. H H Lamb, *Climate, History and the Modern World* (London 1982).
20. *GRS* (Moray) 28/3 p.18 (1629).

21. Above, n.4.
22. The Soil Preservation Act, 1695 (*Acts.Parl.Scot.* ix, 452, c.54).
23. M Anderson 'The Culbin Sands' *Forres Gazette* 1938.
24. *Registrum Episcopatus Moraviensis* [*Moray Reg.*] (Bannatyne Club 1837), Appendix to preface, no.IV; see further preface p.xxxiii, note o.
25. Lachlan Shaw *History of the Province of Moray* 2nd ed. (Edinburgh 1827) 99.
26. D M Rose 'The Morays of Culbin, Kinnairds and Roses' *Nairnshire Telegraph*, 25 Jan 1925. [Roses's arguments do not convince. They are founded on a transumpt dated 1 Oct 1476 'of Ane Confirmatioun made be King David of Ane Charter concerning the said lands (Naughton) disponet be My Lord Murray to Richard of Murray his son, which wantis the date'. From this Rose suggests that Angus, Mormaer of Moray, must have been lord of Newton or Naughton in Fife and must have had a son Richard to whom he disponed these lands. There are several arguments against this scenario, not least that there is no independent evidence for the existence of this supposed earlier Richard; and also the fact that the Naughton interest later possessed by the family of Culbin (half the barony) appears to have been inherited through the marriage of the historical 13th century Richard de Moravia with Marjorie de Lascelles, heiress of the family of Lascelles which had previously possessed it - see G W S Barrow *Anglo-Norman Era in Scottish History* (Oxford 1980) 182 (ed.)]
27. For Freskin and his descendants see *inter alia Moray Reg.* intro. and J Gray, *Sutherland and Caithness in Saga-Time* (Edinburgh 1922).
28. Above note 24, and *Moray Reg.* Appendix to preface., nos.I-III.
29. J G Murray, *Kinnairds*. Despite the researchs of D Murray Rose and others, the history of the Murrays of Culbin in the generation or so before the heiress Egidia is not clear.
30. J G Murray, *The Kinnairds of Culbin* (Inverness 1938).
31. Ibid., 15.
32. Seafield Papers (SRO GD 245/95).
33. J G Murray, 'The Dunbars of Grangehill' *Forres Gazette*, 1938.
34. *GRS* (Moray) 28/3 p.223 (1629).
35. *GRS* (Moray) 28/3 p.337 (1632).
36. *GRS* (Moray) 28/4 p.596 (1635).
37. A Brodie, *The Diary of Alexander Brodie of Brodie* (Aberdeen 1863).
38. Murray, *Kinnairds* 35.
39. H Rose, *The Family of Kilravock 1290-1847* (Edinburgh 1858).
40. Rose Family Papers (SRO GD 125 Box 19).
41. Rose Family Papers (SRO GD 125/31; 125/14/3).
42. J Prebble, *The Darien Disaster* (Edinburgh l968).
43. Newtyle, grave 106.

A full account of the development and history of the Culbin Sands by Sinclair Ross is now available: *The Culbin Sands — Fact and Fiction* (Centre for Scottish Studies, University of Aberdeen).

# THE HISTORIC ARCHITECTURE OF MORAY
## Ronald G. Cant

In this paper the term 'historic architecture' has been taken, arbitrarily perhaps but conveniently, to cover the period from the early twelfth century onwards when Moray came to be effectively absorbed into the medieval Scottish kingdom, itself being integrated into a pattern of life developed in most parts of Europe in what has sometimes been called 'the medieval renaissance'.

In terms of organisation this pattern involved four major elements. First was the authority of the King of Scots based on royal castles like those of Elgin and Forres under such officers as constables or sheriffs. Second, associated with certain castles, were settlements of merchants and craftsmen that might (as at Elgin and Forres) develop into organised urban communities or *burghs*. Third, in the surrounding countryside, were the defensible dwellings of greater and lesser lords holding lands and authority directly or indirectly from the king and ultimately answerable to him. Fourth was the medieval church, an international organisation under the Pope but enjoying a certain autonomy in each of the countries in which it functioned and closely associated with these other elements at every level.

### Kings, Barons, and Burghers

Each element in this 'medieval order' had its distinctive building requirements. For the king control of the previously strongly independent regional dominion of Moray stretching from west of the River Ness to east of the Spey was secured by the building of castles (with associated sheriffs) at Inverness, Nairn, Forres, and Elgin. Beyond the Spey was another at Banff but in civil affairs most of the area there had little direct association with Moray until comparatively recently, while in the west Inverness became the seat of a different and more extensive authority. In ecclesiastical organisation, however, Moray survived to its full traditional extent as a diocese of the medieval church, identifiable from at least 1120.

It was, then, the castle of Elgin that became the chief centre of royal authority here from the 'conquest of Moray' by King David I in 1130; and with the selection of a site nearby as the centre of the diocese in 1224 its dominance in the life of the area became clearly paramount. Like most medieval castle sites that of Elgin made use of a natural feature, the 'Lady Hill', rising steeply to the south of the flood-plain of the River Lossie and commanding on its southern side a level plateau on which an associated burgh could be located. As first planned this seems to have formed a rectangular enclosure some 550 metres long by 250 metres wide with the Castle at its north-west corner and the burgher houses arranged along a single longitudinal street.

*Fig.11.1   Duffus Castle. Fourteenth century work on earlier motte. (E Beaton)*

At Forres there was a somewhat similar arrangement but with the castle at the west end, on a low hill protected by the Mosset Burn, and with the burgh enclosure forming a rough ellipse to the east. The arrangement is virtually that of the 'motte and bailey' so characteristic of defensive works of this period, the motte being a mound surmounted by a tower and the bailey an associated annexe on a lower level. Of this — but without any burghal provision — there is a remarkable example at Duffus north of Elgin (Fig.11.1), granted by King David in military tenure to Freskin, a Fleming already settled in West Lothian. The original structure, here as elsewhere, would probably be of timber — later replaced by stone.

In addition to great *fiefs* like Duffus, held by a family of such importance that it came to be known as the house of Moray or Murray, there were lesser military tenants. Of such a good example is another Lothian Fleming, Berowald, who held lands at Innes — from which his descendants eventually took their name — also a *toft* in the burgh of Elgin for 'knight-service' (but perhaps not in person) in the castle. Mingled with these 'incomers', however, were representatives of older indigenous families of some standing, holding their lands on ancient tenurial conditions with associated social relationships that affected the whole functioning of society — though of their dwellings we know little until a rather later period.

A particular problem in Moray for the descendants of King David I (Malcolm IV and William I) was the claim to regional authority advanced by descendants of the ancient *mormaers* or *earls*, and its association with a further claim to the crown itself by a more senior branch of the Royal house, so much so that it was only after 1200 that the new 'medieval order' became an irreversible fact of life here.

*Fig.11.2   Birnie Kirk. (Crown Copyright: RCAMHS)*

## The Medieval Church

In this process the king and his local representatives had a particularly effective ally in the church. As we have seen, a 'territorial' (rather than a 'personal') bishopric of Moray had emerged by the 1120's, but it was not until the early 1200's that it acquired a fixed base. Before this, apparently, the bishop made use of three churches in the neighbourhood of Elgin — Birnie, Spynie, and Kinnedar. The first of these may still be seen, almost in its pristine state, a simple *romanesque* structure of nave and chancel built of squared stone or *ashlar* (Fig.11.2).

Sometimes dated as early as 1130 or 1150, the church had a particular association with Bishop Simon de Tosni who arrived here in 1172 with authority from King William to extend to his diocese the system of tithes or *teinds* already in operation in southern Scotland by which one tenth of each year's produce was assigned to the church. Beginning at the diocesan level the arrangement was extended to districts associated with a major church or *minster*, as at Elgin and Forres, with subordinate chapels in the surrounding area. By the mid thirteenth century most of the latter had acquired 'parochial status'. And although Birnie alone can show a structure of the earliest phase of this development, Altyre has a small early gothic church complete apart from its roof, while the minster of Mortlach, though replaced as an episcopal centre by Old Aberdeen (c.1130), was rebuilt in a dignified gothic style c.1240.

The earliest surviving example of this more sophisticated form of design to be seen here is the sadly ruined abbey of Kinloss founded by King

*Fig.11.3   Elgin Cathedral. ( R W Billings )*

David for Cistercian monks from Melrose c.1150, but unlikely to have secured buildings of this quality until late in the century. In 1206 Bishop Brice de Douglas obtained authority from the Pope to establish a proper cathedral (and associated *chapter*) at Spynie, but before this plan could be fully implemented King William died (1214) and his successor Alexander II seems to have prompted the construction of a much larger building on a new site just to the east of Elgin.

This was the church of the Holy Trinity (the patron of the diocese for some time already), a cruciform structure the choir and transepts of which were inaugurated as Elgin Cathedral in 1224. Parts of the early fabric survive in the south transept gable and the lower stages of the western towers, the architecture a mingling of romanesque and early gothic details carved in ashlar by masons from southern Scotland but in walling otherwise of local traditional *rubble*. Yet the over-all concept as completed after a fire in 1270 was of more international provenance, the twin-towered nave with its double aisles of French inspiration and the extended choir and octagonal chapter-house English, but blended in a form wholly appropriate to its locality and function (Fig.11.3). Surrounding it was a walled precinct known as 'the College of the Chanonry', containing the manses of its associated clergy, maintained (to a regrettable extent) by the 'appropriation' of parochial teinds throughout the diocese.

Rivalling Elgin Cathedral in the scale and elegance of its component parts yet never completed to its original design was the Priory of Pluscarden founded for monks of the French Valliscaulian order by King Alexander II in 1230. But if the building in its present form derives much of its character from late medieval improvisations and modern restorations it is nevertheless one of the finest examples of a medieval abbey to be seen in Scotland, in a setting moreover of exceptional natural beauty.

**Climax and Decline of the Medieval Order**
The reigns of Alexander II (1214-49) and Alexander III (1249-86) formed a period of consolidation when the changes effected in Scotland, and Moray in particular, developed into a more homogeneous and harmonious pattern. In the two main centres of royal authority here, at Elgin and Forres, the timber structures of the castles would now be replaced by stone — in which the parish churches would have been built from the outset. But as burghal growth seems to have been relatively limited there would be no thought of replacing or enlarging them until a later period. Stone houses, too, were as yet a rarity and self-government concerned mainly with the regulation of trading activities by the merchant guild.

By the close of the thirteenth century the Comyns had erected the great stone-walled fastness of Lochindorb in Brae Moray and there are suggestions that the Morays or Murrays might have effected a comparable transformation of their motte and bailey counterpart in the Laich but more probably not until rather later. By this time the political situation in Moray, as in Scotland generally, had been profoundly altered by the succession crisis of 1290 and the attempted subordination of the northern kingdom to the English monarchy by Edward I and his successors. Although the attempt failed, the long struggle — in which Moray was crucially involved — weakened the ability of later Scottish kings to maintain control of their realm.

The situation was further complicated by the arrival of two new dynasties (though descended from the old royal house), that of Bruce from 1306 to 1371 and of Stewart thereafter. And while King Robert I had undoubtedly saved the independence of his realm, the redistribution of lands and authority that resulted from what was in part a civil war left problems that would endure for long thereafter. In the case of Moray, the title of Earl, with much of the associated lands and jurisdictions, was conferred on Thomas Randolph, one of King Robert's principal lieutenants, but at the expense of families like the Comyns who seized every opportunity to reassert their former influence. The chief failing of the Randolph family, however, was its lack of dynastic continuity, though under John Dunbar, Earl from 1372 to 1391, it made a magnificent addition to its castle of Darnaway in the great hall that has now been scientifically dated to this period, as discussed elsewhere in this volume.

By contrast, the greatest threat to the wellbeing of Moray in the later fourteenth century came from within the new royal house in the person of Alexander Stewart, brother of King Robert III, who in 1390, from Lochindorb, ravaged first Forres and then Elgin, so severely damaging the cathedral as to necessitate the reconstruction of the chapter house and central tower, with the loss of the three-spired profile that had been one of its finest features. His career is discussed in this volume by Alexander Grant. In 1424, however, a more effective period of royal government began under James I, and although the reigns of each of his like-named successors began with a minority, there was a steady growth in the power of the crown, especially under James II who in 1455 destroyed the threat of the house of Douglas in Moray as in southern Scotland, redistributing its lands to 'new' great lords like the Gordon Earls of Huntly and lairds associated with the royal service.

### Burghs, Churches, and Castles of the last Medieval Phase

The period 1400-1560 was marked by considerable development of the burghs. As these had originally been laid out on a fairly generous scale their later growth was not so much in area — though both Elgin and Forres expanded eastwards at this time — but in the character of their buildings. These were now increasingly of stone, of two main storeys, with 'crowstepped' gables, dormer windows, and *pends* leading through to *closes* at the back. Among the first of these was the Great Lodging of the king in Elgin, replacing the royal residence in the castle destroyed in the War of Independence. The Lodging would subsequently pass into private hands as Thunderton House but parts of the original fabric survive to this day. Otherwise most of the structures of this type still to be seen belong to the late fifteenth, sixteenth, and seventeenth centuries and will be discussed later.

In the centre of the High Street, adjacent to the parish church of St. Giles, was the Market Place and Tolbooth, the sturdy tower and spire of the last perhaps already in existence by this time. Most Scottish burghs continued to be served by a single church enlarged or re-built in this period — as would be necessary here in any event after the disaster of 1390. A severe gothic cruciform structure with unaisled choir and transepts, low central tower, and an aisled nave of five bays, the new St Giles would serve the community for four centuries and come to occupy a special place in its affections but had perhaps more character than elegance as an architectural design.

Little is known of the corresponding Church of St. Laurence at Forres, but the lower (stone) part of the old Tolbooth tower might date from this period, both communities having become 'royal burghs' with extensive powers of self-government under the crown in their town councils, merchant guilds, and craft organisations. As the larger urban centre Elgin also attracted such new religious orders as the Dominicans and Franciscans (Black and Grey Friars) who, unlike the more conservative monks, did not cut themselves off from contact with the ordinary world but wrestled with its problems. Both were in Elgin in the thirteenth century but their principal architectural legacy was the church of the revived Franciscan foundation of 1479, a simple but elegant structure admirably restored by John Kinross for the 3rd Marquess of Bute in 1896.

For the smaller communities of the countryside parish churches were of more modest character but when King Robert I's wife Elizabeth died at Cullen in 1327 he endowed a chaplainry in her memory, an example followed by other benefactors until in 1543 the whole group of clergy acquired corporate status as the provost and prebendaries of a 'collegiate church'. These 'chantry foundations' were characterised by special chapels and sepulchral monuments of remarkable elaboration. More representative, however, of country churches is the long plain building at Duffus (widened after the Reformation) with a fine vaulted porch of 1524 and, like several others in Moray, a kirkyard cross that may have served as a market centre.

These country churches depended much on the support of the local landowner whose primary concern, understandably, was with his own residence. Among the most important in Moray of the fifteenth century was that usually known as Gordon Castle, begun by the 2nd Earl of Huntly in 1479 for what was then becoming the greatest family of north-east

Scotland. Completed in the sixteenth century and largely re-built in the eighteenth, all that remains of its one-time splendour is a single gaunt tower six storeys high. By contrast the massive tower-house added to Spynie Palace by Bishop David Stewart in 1461-75 as a defence against this same Earl still forms part of the most impressive episcopal stronghold in Scotland. The Gordons themselves had another castle at Auchindoun to the east of Dufftown that for a century before its burning in 1591 completely dominated the short hill routes giving access to Moray from the east.

### Reformation and Renaissance

In 1560 a coalition of Scottish nobles favourable to a reform of the church, with English naval and military assistance, overthrew the government of the Queen Mother, Mary of Lorraine. Just two years before, in 1558, by the marriage of her daughter Mary Queen of Scots to the future King Francis II, Scotland had passed under French control from which it was now freed. And when the Scottish queen, after the death of her husband, returned to her own country in 1561 she found it impossible to alter this general situation. Although the Reformed Church failed to recover more than part of the parochial teinds, especially those appropriated to monastic houses, now mainly under the control of Protestant nobles, it was nevertheless the only church permitted to function in the land, and by 1600 its dominance was almost complete. In such places as the Enzie and the Braes of Glenlivet, however, geographical and political circumstances enabled the old faith to survive, precariously, over the next two centuries.

On certain fundamental issues, especially the functioning of the church at parochial level, the Reformers were at one, but on the nature of its higher government — whether by a form of episcopacy like that of England or a system of courts (generally known as Presbyterianism) — and its relations with the civil government there was controversy. With the details we are not concerned here but it may be noted that from the early 1600's to 1638, and again from 1661 to 1689, the polity of the 'established church' was Episcopal and from 1638 to 1661 and from 1690 onwards Presbyterian. In actual practice these alternations made little difference to the character of church buildings or their use, only a small element in the Episcopal party inclining in this period to services of a liturgical character like those in the Church of England.

Between 1560 and 1690, then, the typical parish church was the medieval building (or its nave) re-furnished so as to accommodate a 'congregation' gathered round the two focal points of pulpit and communion table. In larger buildings like St. Giles' Elgin *lofts* or galleries were inserted by the town council, guildry, and trades, and in country churches by the local lairds. In Moray the only completely new church to be built in this period was that of Drainie, grudgingly provided by the *heritors* of the parish in

*Fig.11.4   Balvenie Castle, Dufftown. Mid sixteenth century facade. (E Beaton)*

1654-71 but replaced in 1823 and, with its successor, unfortunately removed in 1952 for the extension of Lossiemouth aerodrome. Although of Reformed 'T-plan', its detail was gothic of which an even later example may be seen nearby in 'Michaelkirk' built in 1705 by the widow of Sir Robert Gordon of Gordonstoun as a mortuary chapel for her husband of whose architectural eccentricity another example may be seen in the famous 'round square' adjoining his mansion.

The Reformation was, in part at least, a product of the more general cultural renaissance that occurred in Europe in this period. The movement derived its name from the re-birth that it involved of the legacy of the ancient world. And as it developed first in Italy it was natural that Roman models should dominate its concepts of art and architecture. Such influences were apparent in Scotland by 1500 but it would be a full century and a half before they reached maturity with Sir William Bruce (c.1630-1710), architect of the first truly 'classical' buildings here.

In the intervening period, nevertheless, renaissance influences may be seen, not only in decorative details but in a desire, first apparent in the greater nobility, as they became better acquainted with the more relaxed and sophisticated manner of life of their English and continental counterparts, to live in buildings of a more horizontal or 'palatial' character. An early example of this, still impressive in ruin, is the new front added to Balvenie Castle by the 4th Earl of Atholl in 1547-57 (Fig.11.4). And if the lesser nobility proceeded with more caution, in such buildings as Brodie

*Fig.11.5 Coxton Tower. Early seventeenth century. ( R W Billings)*

*Fig.11.6    Innes House. Mid seventeenth century. ( E Beaton)*

Castle (1567) their interiors were both spacious and elegant. Thus when the Laird of Innes built his new house in 1640-53, although it maintained a strong vertical emphasis, its designer, William Aytoun, master mason of Heriot's Hospital Edinburgh, ensured that it was in essence a mansion, not a castle. And it is only necessary to compare it with the little tower, vaulted throughout and accessible only by an external ladder, built by another Innes at Coxton at this time, to see how different they are in character (Figs.11.5, 6).

In the burghs the greatly enhanced prosperity of the merchants and craftsmen was reflected in the handsome stone buildings that fronted their streets. If some of their details derived from such town mansions of the neighbouring nobility as Thunderton House in Elgin, enlarged by the Sutherlands of Duffus around 1650, the arcaded structures that came to line its High Street — of which three survive from the later seventeenth century — were highly original versions of a formula developed earlier in Edinburgh and Glasgow and ultimately of Italian origin as the designation *piazza* indicated.

**Georgian Elegance**

As the seventeenth century drew to a close, classical design, from being a comparative rarity, became the norm to which most buildings came to conform, if not in particular details, in the symmetry that was its most characteristic feature. In the higher reaches of this development were structures of considerable size and sophistication designed for great magnates by 'architects' familiar with stylistic developments elsewhere in Europe but themselves, for the most part, products of the indigenous building traditions of their own country. Among these were such well-established families as the Mylnes and the Smiths (from Forres), joined in the opening years of the eighteenth century by William Adam (1689-1748) whose influence would be continued for a further generation by his sons John (1721-92), Robert (1728-92), and James (1731-94). But despite the special respect in which they and others of the kind might be held, the distinction between 'architect' and 'builder' was sensibly blurred and some of the most pleasing designs of the period were by unrecorded master-masons.

While the parliamentary union of Scotland with England — following on the 'regal union' of 1603 — inevitably reduced the distinctive identity of the smaller country, and architects like Robert and James Adam and James Gibb or Gibbs (1682-1754) followed the nobility, politicians, and other Scots in making their careers mainly in the south, life in an area like Moray retained a vigorous identity of its own for some time to come. Nevertheless, as in previous periods, it was to be expected that innovations should come mainly from outside, albeit in response to local initiative. Among the most ambitious clients of the elder Adam was a *nouveau riche* family of Moray banker-politicians, the Duffs of Braco, who in 1730, in their ascent to the peerage (as Earls of Fife) commissioned the vast and ornate classical mansion of Duff House at Banff — deliberately outside the milieu in which they had risen to affluence. More representative, however, was the New House of Balvenie designed for them by James Gibbs in 1722 (but demolished in 1929).

Among surviving country houses of the ensuing period the most pleasing tend to be those of moderate size like the re-casting of Moy to a plan by John Adam (c.1762), Dalvey (c.1770), or Invererne (1818) (Fig.11.7), all near Forres. The three largest mansions are, by contrast, somewhat disappointing. At Gordon Castle little now remains of the enormously extended facade added by John Baxter in 1769 to the remodelled tower-house of its ducal proprietor and representations of it when complete suggest an 'unresolved duality' between horizontal and vertical emphasis. At Gordonstoun, the massive central block inserted between earlier wings in 1775 composes rather better and features impressively in the formal landscape in which it is set. At Darnaway the new building by Alexander Laing that in 1802-12 replaced the ancient stronghold of the Earls of Moray — apart from its great hall — includes restrained castellations in its external design, though more as a polite historical allusion than mere pretence, in a composition of some merit on its own account. In a class by itself is Robert Adam's severe (but appropriate) garden front of Letterfourie (1773).

As landed proprietors these great magnates and lesser lairds were

*Fig.11.7    Invererne House, Forres. (E Beaton)*

responsible for farm-houses, cottages, steadings, and doocots on their 'improved' estates, also for public roads and bridges, and (as heritors) for parish churches and manses. Among such a wide range of buildings, of such general merit, it is possible to mention only a few. Speymouth (on the Gordon Castle estate) has a handsome church and manse of 1732-3 and, nearby, the elegant farmhouse of Stynie. Other churches of merit are at New Spynie (1736, with details from its predecessor near the old episcopal palace), Edinkillie (1741, with manse of 1821), and a charming neo-gothic example at Rafford (Gillespie Graham 1826). Remarkably, however, the finest country church of this period is the Roman Catholic basilica at Preshome in the Enzie (1788-9), boldly anticipating the coming of freedom of worship in 1794-5 and a striking contrast to the discreetly unobtrusive 'sheepcote kirk' of 1755 at Tynet nearby or the college maintained at Scalan in Glenlivet between 1717 and 1799. Among bridges the most impressive are those over the lower Spey, at Fochabers (a four-arched design of 1804 but with two arches replaced by a larger single one, first in wood and then in iron, after the disastrous floods of 1829), and Telford's majestic metal span of 1814 at Craigellachie.

A distinctive activity of these 'improving landlords' was the founding of 'new towns' on a scale exceeding most parts of Scotland of the time, amounting as they did to some twenty in all. The earliest, Lossiemouth, was in fact of burghal origin, as the port of Elgin from 1698, though it was only in 1764 that it acquired its definitive plan, and its growth as a major fishing port owed much to the enterprise of the Branders of Pitgaveny, from 1830 onwards, in promoting the adjoining settlement of Branderburgh. Further west, at Burghead, a port of more varied character was developed from 1805 onwards by a group of neighbouring landowners headed by the enterprising William Young of Inverugie. East of the Spey,

217

*Fig.11.8    Fochabers Square. (Valentine Collection)*

the success of Port Gordon (1770) was less enduring and it was not until late in the next century that Buckie would become the busiest fishing port in Scotland.

These new towns were laid out on a rectangular plan of which that devised by John Baxter in 1776 for the re-sited (Gordon) burgh of Fochabers, with the parish church of 1798 at its centre, is the most impressive and best preserved (Fig.11.8). Larger and more successful as an urban venture is New Keith, first set out alongside Old Keith in 1750 by the Earls of Seafield (whose own particular new town of Cullen was not begun until 1820). An interesting feature of its plan is the prominence accorded to the Roman Catholic Church of St Thomas (William Robertson 1828-31, dome by C J Menart 1916), though the Parish Church of St Rufus (a towered gothic design by Gillespie Graham 1816-18) holds an appropriately commanding position in the open space between the old town and the new. Further south, other new towns at Dufftown (1817), Aberlour (1812) and Tomintoul (1775) provided centres for localities previously unprovided in this way, and if Archiestown (1760) was little more than a village, it had amenities singularly lacking in such places hitherto.

It was only to be expected that a comparable spirit of 'improvement' should show itself in the long-established burghs of Elgin and Forres, and though this would reach its climax in the ensuing period, it was now that Elgin acquired the three major buildings that still dominate its townscape — in the west Dr Gray's Hospital (Gillespie Graham 1815-19), in the centre a new St Giles' Church (Archibald Simpson 1825-28) (Fig.11.9), in the east Anderson's Institution (likewise by Simpson 1830-33). And if

218

*Fig.11.9   Elgin High Street: St Giles Church. (Valentine Collection)*

Forres has only one such for this period — Anderson's School (William Robertson 1823) — this has both elegance and charm. On Cluny Hill above, Nelson's Tower (Charles Stewart 1806) forms an impressive landmark for miles around.

**Victorian Variety**

Although architecture of the Georgian age was mainly of Roman derivation, it included Greek and Gothic designs, but these were as nothing to the self-confident variety of the Victorian age in town and countryside alike. And if building initiative of the preceding period had come mainly from the landed aristocracy of the countryside it was now most vigorously pursued by the merchants and manufacturers of the towns. This was particularly true of Moray, and at the present day the architectural character of its principal urban centres — Elgin, Buckie, Forres, Keith, and Lossiemouth — derives predominantly from this vigorous and accomplished age.

A further point of interest is the extent to which this spirit of self-reliance involved the employment of local architects. Foremost among these was William Robertson (1786-1841) whose practice was continued by his nephews A & W Reid and thence through their partners and successors J & W Wittet to the present time. The other major figure was Thomas Mackenzie (1814-54) who came to Elgin by way of Archibald Simpson's office in Aberdeen. If his own career was short — though brilliantly productive — his talents descended to his son and grandson, practising from Aberdeen until well into the present century.

Among Moray towns Elgin is now by far the largest but partly because of this it has sustained injuries to its character that make it less attractive than in the early years of this century. Buckie, by contrast, has suffered a

219

*Fig.11.10   Forres High Street: Tolbooth. (Valentine Collection)*

decline, and it is now arguably at Forres that the civic dignity of the Victorian age is to be seen to best advantage. Appropriately dominant in its High Street is the Tolbooth as re-built by William Robertson in 1838, its tower recalling the form of its historic predecessor (Fig.11.10). Nearby is the Italianate Falconer Museum (A Reid 1869) and opposite it the Town Hall, its imperial facade (by John Forrest 1901) masking Archibald Simpson's more elegant interior of 1829.

By the Victorian era denominations other than the established church, having achieved complete toleration, were concerned to provide places of worship of some architectural equality. In Forres, indeed, it was only in 1904 — beyond the Victorian era yet in a part-Victorian mode — that the Establishment would have in John Robertson's new Church of St Lawrence (replacing that of 1775), a building to compare with St John's Episcopal Church (as re-modelled by Thomas Mackenzie 1843) or the United Free High Church (now St Leonard's) by Ross and Macbeth 1901-3. Viewed from without the resulting assemblage of towers and spires is wonderfully impressive, and as all these buildings were in the main street and linked by others of good design, while the outer residential areas developed in this period were of equally high quality, the combined effect is one of the most pleasing townscapes of its kind in Scotland.

Unlike Forres, Elgin entered the Victorian age well equipped with public buildings (though William Burn's Assembly Rooms of 1822 would eventually be lost in 1970). To these were added in 1842 Thomas Mackenzie's Museum and in 1864-6 A & W Reid's Sheriff Court, each in its own Italianate manner. As in Forres, but on a grander scale befitting the county town, the central part of the High Street (on each side of St. Giles' Church) was lined with three-storeyed buildings for the conduct of its business activities, the Royal Bank of 1876 (by Peddie and Kinnear) being only the most outstanding. These were continued southwards, by Commerce and Batchen Streets, into the corresponding part of South Street and from 1840 onwards the area beyond (mainly in municipal control) was laid out for further extensions.

It was here that several of the churches and public buildings of Victorian Elgin would come to be sited. Already in 1824 a new gothic Episcopal Church of Holy Trinity had been built by William Robertson, skilfully closing the vista of North Street from the town centre. In the southern development an even more emphatic focal point was supplied by the spired South Church (a gothic design of 1852 by A & W Reid for a second Free Church to supplement the High Church of 1843). The Reids also provided the United Presbyterians (in 1858) with the towered building in Moss Street, still a feature of the Elgin townscape. Less ambitious but with a charm of its own is Thomas Mackenzie's Roman Catholic Church of St Sylvester (1844) at the head of Duff Avenue. Among public buildings of the area (all in Moray Street) were the new Elgin Academy of 1885, a classical design by A & W Reid, the huge baronial Town Hall, also of 1885, by A M Mackenzie (burned out in 1939 and later demolished), and the 'Richardson romanesque' Victoria School of Science and Art of 1890 by G Sutherland.

If much of the character of Victorian Forres and Elgin is derived from their churches, this is even more true of Buckie which has as its most prominent feature the twin-spired Roman Catholic Church of St. Peter (by A and W Reid and Bishop James Kyle 1850-7) (Fig.11.11). Of comparable merit, however, are the crown-towered North Parish Church (Duncan MacMillan 1880) and the fastidiously detailed All Saints Episcopal Church (Alexander Ross 1875). At Lossiemouth, too, the sturdy tower, white walls, and red roof of St Gerardine's Parish Church (Sir John Burnet 1901) seem entirely appropriate to its location and stand out dramatically in more distant views. The principal churches of Keith have already been described. But the most influential unifying factor here was provided by the strong architectural character of Mid Street in New Keith, and by two buildings in particular — the North Church (originally Free, by A & W Reid 1845-6) and the Institute with its elegant clock-tower (F D Robertson 1885-9).

Despite the proliferation of country mansions in the Georgian era, Victorian landowners had both the inclination and resources to add to their number or engage in massive reconstructions and extensions of earlier buildings. Among new designs architects of the locality were deservedly prominent, William Robertson's classical Aberlour (1838) being followed by Thomas Mackenzie's grandly romantic Drummuir (1847), and, as the century ended, by the baronial ostentation of what is now the Rothes Glen Hotel (Alexander Ross 1896). To this same general locality Robertson

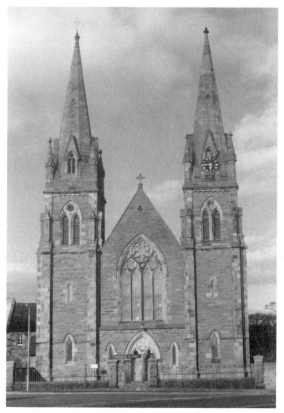

*Fig.11.11   St Peter's Church, Buckie. (E Beaton)*

also contributed a sympathetic addition to the charming little castle of Kininvie (1840) and Mackenzie a more grandiose enlargement of Ballindalloch (1847). But in all this activity David Bryce's majestic enlargement of Cullen House for the Seafield family from 1859 onwards must undoubtedly be accorded pride of place (Fig.11.12).

### Later Developments

The point at which architecture becomes or ceases to be 'historic' can never be precisely determined. It is nevertheless possible, well before the end of the nineteenth century, to identify certain ideas or inclinations that would undermine many of its assumptions and strongly influence the architecture of the succeeding age. What these tendencies had in common was a questioning of the self-confidence, at times verging on an aggressive ruthlessness, that characterised much Victorian activity. In one form this

*Fig.11.12   Cullen House. (Valentine Collection)*

produced the 'arts and crafts movement' promoted by William Morris in England but having influential support in Scotland. Among other things Morris advocated a more restrained and informed approach to the 'restoration' of works of former ages (especially churches) and to this end in 1877 founded the Society for the Protection of Ancient Buildings. By the 1890's, too, there were others who argued that architecture should be more simple and direct in its approach, an attitude that might incline them to such varied forms of expression as 'modernism', 'functionalism', and *art nouveau*, but sometimes to a sharing of sympathies with 'arts and crafts' exponents.

Influences of this kind are evident in the work of John Kinross (the restorer of Greyfriars, Elgin), as in his church at Chapeltown, Glenlivet (1897) and Cothall Cottages at Altyre (1900). And if Macgregor Chalmers' 'romanesque-transitional' church at Elgin (St Columba's 1906) is more traditional, it belongs to the same general group, likewise the new mansion house of Blervie near Forres in a simplified classical style by J D Dick Peddie 1906. And when the remarkable Edward S Harrison (1879-1979) came to build his own house of The Bield, west of Elgin, in 1930 (with J B Dunn as architect) it incorporated traditional features but in a commendably functional manner. In Elgin itself his distinguished services as Lord Provost are most fittingly commemorated by the arcaded Harrison

223

*Fig.11.13   Harrison Terrace, Elgin. (Crown Copyright: RCAHMS)*

Terrace, designed for the Town Council by John Wright (of J & W Wittet) in 1949 (Fig.11.13).

It says much for the stylistic awareness of architects here that this same firm was also responsible for the austerely 'modern' block of flats in Hay Street c.1930. And when a new Town Hall came to be built in the 1960's it was entrusted to a partnership of two of the most accomplished 'modernists' of the time, William Kinninmonth and Basil Spence.

**Bibliographical Note**
This article is a reconstruction — with the kind assistance of Elizabeth Beaton and Ian Keillar — of an illustrated talk (rather than a formal paper) given at the Forres conference of 1987. For this reason no detailed notes or citation of sources have been provided here. An admirably comprehensive survey of the whole range of buildings in the area, with a book list, may be found in Charles McKean's *The District of Moray: an illustrated architectural guide* published in 1987 by the Scottish Academic Press in association with the Royal Incorporation of Architects in Scotland.

Illustrations are reproduced by courtesy of Mrs Elizabeth Beaton, the University of St Andrews and the Royal Commission on the Ancient and Historical Monuments of Scotland.

# THE PATTERN OF MORAY BUILDING
## An introduction to traditional building materials and practices
### Elizabeth Beaton

**Introduction**

In 1962 a book was published in England that looked at buildings not through the eyes of the architectural historian, not for their ancient or modern associations, their illustrious family connections nor their style or plan form, but solely for the materials from which they were constructed and the sources from whence those materials came. This study revealed a rich heritage of visual interest, a wide variation of types and textures of walling and roofs and the reasons for these variations. The buildings included were mainly secular and ranged from the manor to the small cottage, from the medieval gatehouse to the suburban villa. Different types of stone, clay, brick, wood, plaster and metal all found their way into this study.[1] This paper attempts to identify buildings and their materials in similar vein in a small geographical area in north-east Scotland, taking into account the differences of history, communications and social pattern. Here too, examples are drawn mainly from the field of domestic architecture.

The District of Moray (Fig.12.1), combining since 1975 most of the old counties of Moray and Banff, is an area of geographical, geological and economic variety. The hills and plains, coast and glens that make up the varied landscape are also the source of different building materials and local building typology. Though there is a considerable survival of medieval fabric in the District, compared with other similar sized areas in the north of Scotland and some important 16th and 17th century tower houses such as Brodie Castle and Innes House (1640-53), the greater part of the traditional domestic buildings date from the later 18th and 19th centuries. These were times of great change; improvements in agriculture, expansion of the fishing industry and the increased circulation of money. Well into the 19th century most building, except for the affluent, was confined to local materials, but as roads improved so there was some modest expansion in range of transport. The greatest changes came in the later 19th century with the introduction of the railways, when materials from outwith Moray arrived in the district, competing with some local resources. As most of the surviving buildings fall within this period, from the late 18th century onwards, they serve as a mirror not only of building history, but also of some aspects of society, economics and communications. The growth of agriculture and change in farm buildings, the desire of the medium sized landowner for greater domestic style and comfort, the improvement in housing of farm workers, estate employees and fisherfolk, all this and more is mirrored in this network of building.

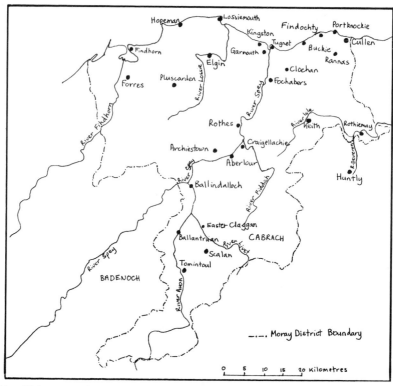

*Fig. 12.1    Map of Moray District.*

The word building is used in favour of architecture, for most cottages were constructed without plans by local people. Many larger houses erected before 1820 were designed by architects living and working far from Moray who may not even have visited the site nor had knowledge and experience of local building fabrics. Even the laird was limited to local resources unless he could dig deep into his pocket for transport, as at Innes House,[2] particularly if he lived away from the coast and seaborne goods. Though the architectural profession plays little part in this study, the letters and specifications of the architect William Robertson, who practised in Elgin from circa 1821 until his death twenty years later in 1841, do throw interesting light on choice, sources and quality of materials and the cost of their transport at a time when roads were expanding locally. So do the advertisements of entrepreneurs and tradesmen in the Elgin and Forres newspapers, circulating from the late 1820s.

There is, therefore, a local 'pattern' of building harmonising with the landscape until well into this century. It is hoped that the following notes,

226

if only tentatively, will echo Alex Clifton-Taylor's response to 'the visual aspect of our buildings, and the reason why they look as they do in one place, and perhaps so different only a few miles away'.[3]


**Stone**

The geological map of Moray shows that a wide variety of rock types occur in the District, providing a range of materials of varying type and quality for building purposes. The low-lying, more highly populated coastal fringe of the Laich was well provided for by having extensive outcrops of good quality sandstone. Inland there are some scattered exposures of granite, while along the coast from Buckie to Cullen the rocks are mostly flaggy schists and gneisses, constituting an inferior building fabric. Each have their own texture and some were better than others to quarry, tool and with which to build.

In lowland Moray outcrops of sandstones of Upper Old Red Sandstone age were widely quarried along the ridges from Alves to Elgin, with very large workings at Newton and in Quarry Wood. This stone is creamy yellow to pale pink in colour and the textures vary from pebbly, through gritty to fine-grained varieties. As these sandstones are well cemented, they could be dressed to smooth ashlar and were suitable for carving and decorative tooling. Beds of finely laminated stone also occur but are poorly cemented, wearing badly if used as facings; some of these split well and were utilised as roofing slabs.

Along the coast between Burghead and Lossiemouth there were many quarries working in the sandstones of Permo-Triassic age, which also outcrop on the ridge at Spynie and on the top of the hill at Quarry Wood. This is generally a more even-grained and firmer textured sandstone of a pleasing pale yellow colour; the harder varieties were much sought after for facings and decorative work and were dearer than those that were softer (Fig.12.2).

These quarries in lower Moray achieved a considerable reputation far beyond Moray. In 1746 there were thirteen quarries between Burghead and the Broad Hythe, where the planned village of Hopeman was established in 1812. Clashach quarry, east of Hopeman, had its own jetty, and was used, no doubt, by some or all of the 'five large boats with six people in each ... employed in transporting stones from quarries to different parts of the country'[4] in the 1790s.

In Elgin, many fine public buildings, villas and cottages are constructed from these sandstones. The medieval cathedral is outstanding and of national importance, if now a roofless shadow of its former glory. The three remaining late 17th century arcaded merchants' houses in Elgin High Street have harled rubble walls, utilising cheaper stone, but well-tooled columned arcades and margins (Fig.12.3). The austerely classical St. Giles

*Fig.12.2    Cullen Home Farm, 1816. Decorative tooled Moray sandstone dressings with local schist rubble walling. (Crown Copyright: Historic Scotland)*

Church[5] is executed in smoothly finished sandstone ashlar with fine joints and restrained carved detailing.

In villages such as Lossiemouth, Hopeman and Burghead, use was naturally made of the stone from nearby quarries. Forres, on the other hand, is situated equally distant from the sandstone quarries of Hopeman, Nairn and Newton and stones from the last two sources are difficult to tell apart, though there is no difficulty in identifying those from the coastal quarries. The Forres High Street is lined with shops with dwellings above, churches and other buildings, all executed in sandstone with a variety of different textures and tooling. With the nearest quarries all being at roughly the same distance, transport charges from each would have been similar; however a few buildings show what might have been a compromise. They have been built of the massive (high grade) Moinian gneiss from the New

*Fig.12.3 Braco's Banking House, Elgin, 1694. Harled rubble, tooled and polished sandstone ashlar dressings; sandstone slab roof.*

Forres quarry on the outskirts of the town, while the dressings are usually of Hopeman sandstone. The gneiss is very hard and difficult to work and is currently quarried for roadstone. The gables of the buildings have been constructed with rubble while the frontages are of evenly dressed blocks of the same gneiss. This stone is dove grey with a slight pink tinge and contrasts well with the yellow sandstone.

South of Elgin, in Speyside and east to Keith, granite of various types was the principal building fabric. The large granite mass of Ben Rinnes and the smaller one at Rothes, are coarse-grained biotite granites, similar to that of the Cairngorms. There are no records of quarries of any substance ever having been opened for this stone. Granite *in situ* is generally very deeply weathered and there is considerable luck in uncovering fresh material. Loose stone from such sources soon disintegrates but some fresher materials could be found as water-rounded blocks in the River Spey or amongst the glacial erratics and fluvio-glacial debris which littered the countryside. These were gradually cleared to create fields during agricultural improvement and were exploited as building material, forming a useful source of random rubble of varied colour and texture. Of such is the walling of mid-18th century Arndilly House, near Craigellachie, though the dressings are of tooled granite; here later additions can be identified by the use of more easily handled sandstone ashlar margins. The original

*Fig.12.4    124 Land Street, Keith, circa 1900. 'Aberdeen Bonding'; pale grey granite pinned with dark whinstone wedges. (Crown Copyright: Historic Scotland)*

granite quoins are very pleasing though the work involved in their prep-aration must have been arduous.[6] In Rothes the mainly 19th century houses and cottages are fronted with roughly squared pink, brown and white granite, most of which splits reasonably well on the horizontal plane but which leaves rough fractures at the vertical edges. These fractures are masked by contrasting dark pinnings or 'Aberdeen Bonding',[7] making a decorative virtue out of necessity. Similar walling is found in Keith and Rothiemay, both sited reasonably near the Avochie granite quarries. This is a pale grey stone which contrasts well with dark pinnings, making a distinctive frontage to otherwise simple houses (Figs.12.4, 12.5).

At Keith, however, there is a separate, small outcrop of granite in which the town had its own quarry inside the burgh, subsequently infilled and built over. Many of the earlier houses in the town were built of this stone which is a drab yellow-brown in colour. It is an unusual type, being in the form of a coarse schist; it is this schistosity which has made the stone easy to work.

In the Knockando, Ballindalloch and Archiestown area the granite is red, pink and yellow. As random rubble it creates an attractive walling; when tooled and laid in a chequered pattern and further pinned with dark bonding it is almost exotic. The finest examples date from the late 18th

230

*Fig.12.5   124   Land   Street, Keith.   Detail   of masonry.   (Crown Copyright:   Historic Scotland)*

*Fig. 12.6   Cairnfield House, 1802. Actinolite schist rubble cherry-pointed with fragments of slate from same geological beds; tooled local granite dressings (later harling extreme right). (Crown Copyright: Historic Scotland)*

*Fig.12.7    2 East Street, Fochabers. Random rubble laid in courses developed from local clay building technique.*

*Fig.12.8    70 High Street, Fochabers, 1828. Mixed tooled rubble with painted joints; tooled sandstone dressings.*

232

century and are in Archiestown. The Cottage, a single storey house of circa 1790 with unusual advanced pavilion wings, has a red and yellow granite chequered frontage, while Old St. Andrews in The Square combines these same coloured blocks with dark pinnings. The stone is very hard and its preparation costly in human and economic terms.

Where squared blocks of stone are slightly uneven, the practice of 'galleting' (the word *galet* is French for water worn pebble) or 'cherry-pointing' is carried out. Small pebbles or chips of stone or slate are pressed into the masonry joints, either to strengthen the mortar course or to level up irregularities. Though strictly functional, the practice is also ornamental, particularly where there is a contrast of colours in the materials used. At Letterfourie House[8] the blocks of pink granite used on the north entrance front are levelled and decorated with tiny polished black pebble studs while the humbler red sandstone Bogmuir School (mid 19th century, now disused) has its broad mortar courses cherry-pointed with slips of black slate; mid-later 19th century Burgie Mains House has its frontage of yellow-brown sandstone similarly treated. Galleting is never used with ashlar, for the joints are too fine 'but even were this not so, galleting is too rustic a process to consort with such elegance'.[9] (Fig.12.6).

Courses of mis-shapen random or field rubble are infilled or caulked with smaller pieces, locally known as 'cherry-cocking'. This is a very old practice which has continued well into this century. Amongst early examples are the walls enclosing the garden at medieval Pluscarden Abbey and the park walls at Rothiemay House, occupying the site of Rothiemay Castle.

Nowhere in Moray is the variety of stone for building more in evidence than in Fochabers. Established from 1769 onwards by the fourth Duke of Gordon to replace the old village inconveniently sited nearer the castle, the town has a neat grid plan devised by the Edinburgh architect, John Baxter. The immediate neighbourhood is not blessed with good building stone and the variety of materials and methods of usage are of considerable interest. Small stones, gathered from field or river, are laid as random rubble, there are chequered walls of mixed pink, brown and white granite, red sandstone from Stynie and yellow-brown sandstone from Elgin, which became easier to obtain after the fast flowing River Spey had been bridged in 1810. The tradition of clay building in the immediate hinterland of the lower Spey, when the clay mix was laid in courses (a practice elaborated later in this paper) which dried out before the next lift was added, has been adapted to a mixture of small stones and mortar, the lifts regularised and defined in height by the tooled ashlar long and short corner dressings. The line between one lift and another is clearly visible, notably in some Gordon Castle estate houses at nos. 2, 4 and 6 East Street (Fig.12.7) and a row of late 19th century cottages (also Gordon Castle estate) in Bogmuir.

Fulton House, 70 High Street, dated 1828 (Fig.12.8), and 24 High Street

*Fig.12.9   16 Bogmuir, near Fochabers, 1828. 'Clay and bool' cottage; note hori-
zontal lines indicating the courses, each of which was allowed to dry out
before the next addition. Corrugated iron roof replaces former 'clay'
thatch. (Crown Copyright: Historic Scotland)*

of circa 1870, both have frontages of squared mixed pink, grey and brown
rubble with tooled sandstone margins, giving individuality to the frontages
and variation to the principal street where the regular building line with
simple 2-storey, 3-window elevations could otherwise be monotonous. The
public buildings, such as John Baxter's Bellie Parish Church of 1797 which
is the centre-piece of the village square and the Episcopal Chapel (facing
it one block to the north) designed by Archibald Simpson in 1834, are of
the finest ashlar. The impact and importance of these churches is brought
about not only by their architecture and siting but also by the quality of
the materials of which they are constructed.

## Clay

In certain parts of Moray, principally in the parishes of Urquhart, Bellie,
Speymouth, St. Andrews Lhanbryde and Rathven, all in coastal districts
near the outflow of the River Spey to the west and Cullen to the east, there
is a scarcity of good building stone. Here, as in similar areas elsewhere in
Scotland and England, clay has been exploited as a walling material.[10]
Clay or mud, with chopped straw, heather or bent grass (vegetable matter
prevented cracking during shrinkage) was worked to a stiff consistency
before being laid in courses on a boulder foundation. Each course was
allowed to dry out before the next was raised.(Fig.12.9) Dressed stone of

varying quality (according to means and resources available) was used for windows and door openings, and at the corners. Providing the walls were kept dry with an outer coat of lime harl or regularly lime washed, this was a durable and warm walling. Though mainly used for single-storey cottages, in 'the populous village of Garmouth .... The houses, many of them three storeys high, are built of clay, kneaded up with straw, in a frame (shuttering) as practised in the South of France'.[11] Though the use of shuttering is mentioned for these houses which exceed single storey height, many cottages appear to have been constructed without this aid.

A variant where the clay mix has added round stones from the river or shore, known as 'bools', was called Auchenhalrig work from the name of a hamlet in Bellie parish. The following description, written in 1812, on the use and preparation of Auchenhalrig work, is worth quoting at length:-

'This work is built of small stones and mud, or clay, mixed with straw. The proportions of these materials required to make a rood of thirty-six square yards, are nearly as follows, viz. about thirty cart loads of stones, ten cart loads of clay or mud, and twenty-four stones weight of good fresh straw. When the clay is strong and tough it will require fully three cart loads of sharp water sand. The mode of preparation is thus — if the mud or clay is lumpy, it must be reduced with a mallet, mixed with the sand, and made pretty thick with water: the straw is then equally strewed over it, trampled with the feet and wrought from one side to the other; until the whole is of proper consistency for admixture with the stones.

In building any kind of stones will answer; even stones from the channel of a river, which are generally round, are preferred by some workmen to any other. They ought not to be larger than a workman can with ease put upon the wall; and though much smaller, they are perfectly sufficient; indeed, large stones are improper, as they prevent the mud from consolidating, and, by consequence, diminish the strength and durability of the walls, which are of much the same breadth as those built with stone and lime: twenty-two inches are sufficient for a wall of seven feet high: if higher, they should be two feet thick, carried up perpendicularly the same as other walls, and care should be taken never to build more than two or three feet of height in any one part in the same day: if raised more, the wall is apt to swell, for which there is no remedy but to pull it down, and rebuild. To prevent accidents of this nature the work is so proportioned to the number of hands employed, as to admit of three or four days for each division to dry, before more is put upon it. In order, therefore, to keep two men constantly at work, one building and another preparing the mud, a wall to the extent of about forty feet going on at one time is requisite. Where there is any joisting for grain lofts, etc. there should always be a wall plate of wood one and a half inches thick laid below the joists, and their ends brought within six inches of the outside of the wall: a similar plate is also necessary below the feet of the couples.

235

*Fig.12.10    Cowfurach, near Broadley. 'Clay and bool' revealed. (Crown Copyright: Historic Scotland)*

*Fig.12.11    Hopeman, circa 1900. Clay thatched cottages; the centre cottage is in process of being re-thatched and the underlay of divots is clearly visible. Note clay slurry on roof of left hand cottage.*

These walls are equal to the weight of any roof commonly put on mason work, either slate, heath, mud and straw, or stob thatch. If done with mud or stob thatch there should be a good heath brush laid on the wall head to bear up the straw, and to carry the rain over the walls, as nothing is so injurious as rain falling into the face, or getting into the middle of the wall.

In the course of two or three years after being built, the frost has generally such an effect upon the mud on the outside of the walls, that it falls off, leaving the stones (which are covered with it when newly built) quite bare. Whenever the walls begin to appear in this state, they should be harled over with lime properly mixed with pure river or sea sand pretty rough; and that the inside walls of barns and grain lofts may be sufficiently close and smooth, it is strongly recommended to do them over with a thin coat of plaster lime, which adheres firmly to the mud. Thus finished, the Auchenhalrig houses are, out and inside, as ornamental as those built entirely of stone and lime mortar'.[12]

As at Cowfurach, Rathven, the 'bools' are laid in neat rows (Fig.12.10): in a shed on Longhill Mill, Urquhart, they are in a herring-bone pattern. Most of the cottages at Kingston-on-Spey, built initially at the end of the 18th century to house workers in the ship building and timber industries there and at Garmouth, are of clay and bool. The material was used for simple linear steadings at Bogmuir and considered in 1820 for a 'Square of offices' to be built at Edom, Pluscarden. Here the farmer, Mr. Bain, when advertising for tenders for the work, stated that he would provide the materials but 'as it is not yet decided whether the offices will be of Mason or Achainhalrig (sic) Work, Contractors are requested to estimate for these different works separately'.[13]

Clay was used also for internal party walls. It was daubed over a wooden frame and straw or grass suspended from horizontal lathes or sticks and was widely used in Moray, even in houses of superior status. 'Braco's Banking House' (1694), High Street, Elgin, an arcaded merchant's dwelling, had such internal walling; an excellent example divides the attic from the stairwell at Pittensair, St. Andrews Lhanbryde, a beautifully detailed small house built for himself by the master mason, James Ogilvie, in 1735.

Clay was added to thatch in the clay building areas of Moray. Bundles of wheat, rye or oat straw (in that order of preference) were pinned to an underlay of turf divots daubed with a clay mix (Fig.12.11). After thatching the roof was washed over with a clay slurry which kept the thatch firm and only a strip of wood was required to hold it down at the eaves which were frequently re-enforced with a strip of heather thatch, a tougher material which protected the vulnerable wallhead.[14] Rye was grown expressly for thatching on some farms well into the 1930s.[15]

At Rannas, Rathven, a series of stone pegs project from the gable end of the 18th century implement shed (now slated) indicating that the roof

*Fig.12.12   Implement shed, Rannas, near Buckie, 18th century. Projecting stone
'pegs' for retaining thatch. (Crown Copyright: Historic Scotland)*

was originally thatched and secured to these pegs by ropes (probably of
twisted straw). This is a West Coast and Highland practice (where the pegs
are of wood) and the sophisticated Rannas example begs the question as
to whether it was also widespread in Banffshire (Fig.12.12).

**Bricks**
Clay is also the raw material for bricks and pantiles. Early bricks were
moulded and then fired in field kilns near the clay pits, a process that
became industrialised in due course. Brick and tile works were established
at Tochieneal, near Cullen by John Wilson in 1841:[16] at Lochside, Spynie,
William Priest set up The Morayshire Drain Tile and Pottery Works in
1847,[17] while by 1850 there were the 'Brick and Terracotta Works' at
Craigellachie on or near a site formerly known as Mudhouse. This name
soon changed to the appropriately industrialised version of Brickfield.
Craigellachie not only offered 'Brown ware domestic pottery' and bricks
but also 'drainage material, chimney cans, chimney vent linings, water
sewerage pipes, flower pots, roof tiles etc..'[18] Pantiles proved popular as a
roofing material in the expanding seatowns which grew fast during the
mid-19th century fishing boom and, to some extent, on smaller farm
steadings and agricultural cottages, for they were usually less expensive

Fig.12.13 *Cullen House walled garden, 1788. Brick with Moray sandstone dressings and wallhead chimney stack (some stacks served glasshouse and mural heating ducts, some were ornamental). (Crown Copyright: Historic Scotland)*

than slates but had a longer life than the cheaper thatch. Some pantiles were slightly porous, particularly on the exposed coastal sites, but this was remedied by a coating of pitch, causing the undulating roofs to take on a pleasing and characteristic black sheen. The availability of chimney cans indicates the gradual passing of the 'hinging lum', the mud daubed canopy which drew the smoke directly to a square, likewise mud coated, chimney; sewerage pipes suggest an improvement in sanitation, at least in the homes of the more prosperous, if an unlikely facility in rural cottages. Bricks were not much used as house walling, though a terrace of brick houses on the Dufftown Road in Craigellachie testify the local product: these houses would not merit a passing glance in the brick lined streets of English towns, but are noteworthy in north-east Scotland.

Bricks really came into their own for their thermal qualities as lining to large stone walled gardens. Their heat retention capability encourage the growth and ripening of fruit on wall-trained trees. The construction of these gardens was one aspect of the expansion of the greater (and also the lesser) country house and its estate from the mid-18th century onwards. Dockets for thousands of bricks appear among the building accounts for the large walled garden at Gordon Castle, constructed between 1803-4. These were supplied at 14/- per thousand by John Thow, Brick Macker (*sic*).[19] The slightly earlier but equally grandiose garden at Cullen House

*Fig.12.14    Cullen House walled garden, 1788. Detail of close jointed ashlar; also bricks laid in 'English garden bond', 4 rows of 'stretchers' alternated with 1 row of 'headers'. (Crown Copyright: Historic Scotland)*

was designed by James Playfair in 1788: it has solid brick walls (except for the north facing aspect of one wall) with fine sandstone ashlar corner stones and copes from Moray. The raw material for the bricks probably came from somewhere on the estate near 'Clay Pots' bridge and were moulded into bricks and then fired on site (Figs.12.13, 12.14).

Conversely bricks help retain cold. The biggest icehouse known in Scotland was built at the mouth of the Spey at Tugnet in 1830[20] to serve the rich salmon fishings of the River Spey belonging to the Dukes of Gordon. Ice was collected during the hard weather and stored in subterranean or semi-subterranean vaults and withdrawn as necessary as packing for salmon sent to the expanding urban markets of the south. At Tugnet there are six large vaulted chambers, entirely lined with brick.

Clay tiles were much in demand for field drainage, a vital factor in agricultural improvements and land reclamation during the late 18th and 19th centuries. Early field drains were stone lined but this practice was superseded by the cheaper, mass-produced earthenware pipe for which there was considerable demand.[21]

**Turf**

The pliable nature of turf, besides its thermal qualities, made it the usual covering for the vaulted roofs of icehouses in Moray as elsewhere in Scotland. The three long parallel rounded roofs of the icehouse at Tugnet

240

*Fig.12.15    Gordon Castle park wall, 1814. Rubble with turf cope.*

are still covered with this material. Even for so illustrious and wealthy an estate as Gordon Castle, the use of a turf cope was considered satisfactory for the park walls, which run for several miles in length and were constructed of local rubble schist in 1814 by William Logie who charged respectively £35.10.2d and £31.12.2d for lengths of 145 and 150 feet.[22] Suitable stone for coping would have had to be brought to the site from a considerable distance at some expense while the turf was readily available, growing in the park in the process of being enclosed (Fig.12.15).

At a more humble level, turf was sometimes the walling material for the upper part of cottage gables besides the foundation for thatch. Remains of turf gables are to be found in deserted upland settlements such as Croft of Scalan in the Braes of Glenlivet and at Lyne in Strath Avon.

### Concrete

As Walker has pointed out 'mass concrete is a logical extension of the solid clay wall technique and concrete houses and sheds are often found in areas of clay construction'.[23] There are some examples of use of this material in garden walls and sheds in Garmouth, probably dating from 1886 onwards with the arrival of the railway.

The Banffshire coastal railway was largely responsible for another use of concrete and the establishment of a late 19th and early 20th century vernacular tradition in the seatowns which is still very much alive today. Villages such as Findochty and Portknockie grew and expanded as fishing prospered, wealth increased and the standards of housing improved. Inferior quality schists were available for rubble walling but there was no

*Fig.12.16   Seafield Street, Portknockie, circa 1900. Rubble walling with painted
concrete angle and window dressings, cornices and lintels; also flared
concrete chimney copes. (Crown Copyright: Historic Scotland)*

local good quality quarried stone for dressings and margins. With the
coming of the railway in the 1880s it was possible to bring in concrete
with which to cast on site the component parts such as chimney copes,
skewputts, dormer finials, shaped door and window lintels, and blocks for
use as window jambs and corner stones. Concrete, however, is drab and
engendered the almost universal practice of surface painting, a custom
that frequently spreads to the entire house front, even masking alterations
and heightening of earlier cottages from single to two storeys. The square
blocks used as dressings for corners, door and window openings, when
painted have created the 'long and short' contrasting detailing which is
very much part of the street scene in these settlements, so much so that
where earlier cottages originally had simple stone margins, these sometimes
have painted 'blocks' superimposed on the window surrounds to keep up
with fashion. Add to gaily painted margins and long and short work the
defining or 'stroking' of masonry joints with fine white brushwork, and the
frontages take on a colourful appearance which has earned the Banffshire
coastal villages the nickname of 'Tartan Tounies'. Cullen seatown, Findochty and Portknockie (Fig.12.16) are particularly colourful.

**Lime**
Lime for mortar and agricultural use was extensively quarried along the
outcrop running from Sandend (Banff-Buchan) through Keith, Dufftown
and Tomintoul and there were innumerable quarries along this line, many

masons having their own particular workings. Today only one remains, the Richmond quarry at Dufftown.

## Slates
'Scotch slate' is often considered synonymous with the better known West Highland slates but Moray and Banffshire have been well endowed with this durable roofing material. The earliest surviving stone roofs are not of slate but of sandstone. The Rannas aisle (1612) at Rathven and Coxton Tower, St. Andrews Lhanbryde (dated 1644 but probably somewhat earlier) both have sandstone blocks slotted into the upper face of their vaulted roofs, laid so as to form a flush, sloping surface to throw off the rain. There are unusual roofs on two Moray dovecotes, at Pittendreich and New Spynie, both dating from around 1600. On both these simple rectangular buildings the roof is supported by two pointed masonry arches rising from the wallhead carrying the large overlapping sandstone slabs. There is no ridge to either of these dovecotes, the slabs meeting at the apex; the square pigeon glovers or cupolas are also constructed of these slabs. On Braco's Banking House, Elgin (1694) similar but thinner over-lapping sandstone slabs are laid conventionally on rafters, held in place with wooden pins. The material for this roof is said to have come from Leggat's quarry, New Spynie, which is probably true for a few discarded slabs suitable for roofing still lie scattered around this abandoned site in Quarrywood. This is an area where finely laminated Upper Old Red Sandstone occurs which is poorly cemented and therefore splits easily.

Some mica schists of the Moin series in western Moray could be split for roofing slates. A quarry at Kellas, five miles south-west of Elgin, was mentioned by the Earl of Fife's factor when reporting progress on repairs to Pluscarden Abbey in 1822.. 'I yesterday contracted for roofing in that part of the Abbey under the repairs ... which after a great deal of competition I got done for £485 .... We have some hopes of getting slate for it in Kellas which would reduce the expense a little but this is by no means certain, 'tho' if they can be got I think they would look well being of a dark sparkling colour and not so light in colour as the Enzie slate is'.[24] In neighbouring Rafford parish in 1798 there was 'a slate quarry on the estate of Clunie, let out by the tenant of that farm to quarriers, at the rate of 3s 4d the 1,000 untrimmed slate';[25] in 1840 this quarry 'was not exhaustd but now not used'.[26] Further east on the banks of the Knockando burn at the similarly named Clune Lodge (now demolished), a disused slate quarry was noted in 1914.[27] Many of these small upland open slate quarries were of little commercial use but served local requirements, like that near the Grouse Inn on the Cabrach where there is a 'slate quarry of light grey colour on the Hill of the Bank; there being little demand for the slates, the quarry is not in lease. They are not sold, but given gratis'.[28] There are many abandoned farms and crofts in the hills of upper Banffshire. What

*Fig.12.17   Fochabers. Slates from Tarrymount quarries laid in diminishing courses.*

is remarkable about these houses and steadings is that they remain reasonably sound for many years because they have durable slated roofs. The landscape is therefore largely spared the depressing sight of roofless ruins that are all too evident in similar depopulated areas where thatching was the traditional roof, requiring constant renewal.

At Rothes it was reported that there were 'quantities of mica slate imbedded (*sic*) in rocks of granite';[29] this may be the roofing material of the 18th century dovecote at Orton and the bothy abutting the walled garden nearby. Bands of schist (Dalradian series) produce extensive beds of a brown slate with a silvery mica sheen on the hillside of Cnoc Fergan in Strath Avon which were widely used in the area. An early example of the use of this material consists of a few slates embedded in the wallhead of the roofless 16th century Blairfindy Castle at Minmore. Graded Cnoc Fergan slates laid in diminishing courses make a very handsome roof, blending with and complementing local masonry. A particularly good example is on the 1844 former Free Church manse and steading at Claggan. The last known occasion when this slate was quarried was in the early 1930s when it was used to roof The Bield, Elgin, at the express desire of the owner, the late Lord Provost E S Harrison.[30]

Several slate quarries existed in the vicinity of Dufftown in 1836 though a slater, repairing a roof of this fabric in the 1970s, commented that 'Dufftown slates were sick in the head' meaning that they slightly soft and broke at the point where they were holed for nailing.[31]

Finally extensive quarries were sited at Tarrymount, Upper Allaloth and Oxhill in the Braes of Enzie near Clochan, Buckie. These belonged to the Duke of Gordon while Slateheugh, south of the Hill of Maud, was the property of the neighbouring Sir James Gordon of Letterfourie.[32] Slates from the Enzie group were widely used in Fochabers and their warm, brown tone marks them out from the deep grey Aberdeenshire and purple or grey Welsh slates also used in that village (Fig.12.17). Oxhill slates and slabs were specified for the roof and dairy floor respectively of the new Bellie manse being built in Fochabers in 1822-3[33] and from Tarrymount for the same purpose for the new wing at Cairnfield House in 1825.[34]

These Moray and Banffshire slates were all fairly thick and consequently heavy. With improved roads, bridges and transport, they met with considerable competition. From the 1830s the quarry masters of the Aberdeenshire quarries at Foudland and Gartly were advertising their wares in the local newspapers and at the same time the recently opened Caledonian Canal facilitated the carriage of slates from Ballachulish and other West Highland sources. The final death-knell came in the later 19th century with the railway which brought in lighter, thinner and cheaper slates from Wales.

**Wood**

Locally grown oak figures as building material for medieval Duffus Castle, for which Sir Reginald de Chen received a grant of two hundred oaks from the royal forests of Darnaway and Longmorn in 1305.[35] Of this woodwork nothing remains in the roofless stone motte and bailey moated fortification, but the splendid medieval hammer-beam roof of Randolph's Hall at Darnaway Castle survives to rank as one of the most important of its kind in Scotland, and is discussed elsewhere in this volume. Even if no other castle in the area achieved quite the sophistication of carpentry as at Darnaway, in a district so rich in castles and tower houses there must have been a wealth of panelling and carved wooden fittings. Some ecclesiastical work, such as the Laird's loft in Cullen old church, dated 1602 and incorporating re-used material, and the 1684 pulpit from old St. Giles', Elgin (now in St. Columba's Church, Moss Street, Elgin) indicate that both wood and the skill to work and carve it were available locally from early times.

Either oak or pine would probably have been the material for cruck blades. Cruck construction, when pairs of curved timber trusses, resembling the wishbone of a chicken, were set up in line to support the roof of a building, eliminating or at least substantially reducing the need for load bearing walls. The cruck blades were placed on a stone foundation or plinth, infilled to wallhead height with turf, wattle daubed with mud or with rubble, and thatched with heather or straw; the weight of the heavy roof was then transmitted directly to the ground by the cruck trusses. Thomas Dick Lauder illustrates skeletal cruck framed cottages standing ruined and desolate in the receding flood waters of the River Findhorn in 1829 at Broom of Moy, the greater part of their turf walling carried away by the 'Great Spate'.[36] A single jointed cruck blade has recently been

*Fig.12.18  Buckie.  Banffshire seatown  panelled front  door  with characteristic  convex  centre  rail. (Crown  Copyright: Historic  Scotland)*

revealed in a close in the centre of Elgin, evidence that cruck framed dwellings were an urban as well as a rural tradition in Moray.[37]

In the 18th and 19th centuries, timber from the pine forests of Rothiemurchus and Strathspey was harvested in considerable quantity and was highly regarded for its quality throughout Scotland. Some of it found its way into houses in the immediate area. Good examples of mid-18th century raised and fielded panelling box beds, doors and cupboards are at Ballantruan in Strath Avon and Croughly near Tomintoul. Logs were floated down the Spey to the yards at Garmouth and Kingston-on-Spey for use in the boat building industry in these locations and for distribution elsewhere. The increase in house building from the mid-18th century onwards and the desire for a higher standard of domestic comfort amongst the landowners and merchants provided opportunities for good quality house carpentry. Excellent examples are found in the merchants' houses in Findhorn, which was the port of Forres and the entrepot for the immediate neighbourhood, notably at Kilravock which has a wide wooden staircase leading to the panelled first floor parlour. Elegant slender turned balusters grace the curved stairwell and landing of 124 Findhorn. In Forres

*Fig.12.19    Easter Claggan, Inveravon. Blacksmith crafted iron door handle (probably late 18th or early 19th century).*

itself the domestic quarters of John Cumming, merchant and banker, are 'over the shop' in his fine High Street premises built circa 1820. The public rooms have good decorative plaster ceilings, beaded and sometimes bowed panelled doors, reeded dados and panelled window shutters.[38] Fochabers exploited the raw material that was logged downstream past the village from the Duke of Gordon's forests in Rothiemurchus and there is an overall high standard of house carpentry in the village. In mansions built by landowners in the neighbourhood, such as Cairnfield[39], Orton[40] and Arndilly[41] the panelling and carved overdoors achieve an elegance equal to many a metropolitan counterpart.

In the late 19th century and well into the 20th, increasing prosperity in the Banffshire seatowns encouraged house building; many of these gaily painted homes are fitted with good panelled front doors, some with a characteristic convex centre rail (Fig.12.18). Weatherboarded fishing stores and fish curing kilns are also a feature of the coastal villages. Hexagonal wooden paving blocks, sawn to reveal the grain, were manufactured at Urquhart's saw mills (Mills of Forres). Besides local demand they found a market in London in the 1840s.[42] The pend at 94 High Street, Forres is still paved with these attractive and serviceable blocks.

247

*Fig.12.20    South Lodge, Ballindalloch Castle, 1850. Ornate wrought-iron door hinge. (Crown Copyright: Historic Scotland)*

## Iron

As elsewhere, wrought-iron fittings such as yetts, window bars, door handles and hinges, were used in Moray. An early dated example of local blacksmith's work is the 1739 door latch fitted to the plank and stud door at the Peterkirk, Duffus. Iron was mined during the 18th century at the Lecht, near Tomintoul and a bloomery, to process the ore, has been identified at Ballindalloch.[43] Possibly it was this local source of iron that generated characteristic hand wrought door handles found in Strath Avon between Tomintoul and Ballindalloch, with a heart shaped plate at each end of the curved handle with which to attach the fitting to the door (Fig.12.19). At Scalan, in the Braes of Glenliver (just over the hill from the Lecht mine) the 1767 former Roman Catholic seminary has a neat door latch with a cross cut in the simple traceried door plate. This tradition of crafted door fittings continued into the 19th century; the South Lodge at Ballindalloch Castle[44] has a studded plank door with long ornate strap hinges on which the blacksmith has incised a diamond pattern to match the diamond-headed fittings (Fig.12.20). In the main, however, iron would have been brought in by sea or carrier from the south for the use of blacksmiths[45] and also cast-iron goods from such well known sources as the Carron Iron Works. Some local blacksmiths combined 'imported' cast items with their work; for instance the spearhead railings enclosing the garden at The Cottage, Archiestown, were locally made but the urn finials

*Fig.12.21    Aberlour House, 1837. Fine Moray sandstone in Speyside. (Crown Copyright: Historic Scotland)*

capping the intermediate stiffeners were cast and purchased elsewhere as a component part.

Though Carron and Banff are outside the scope of this paper, it is worth noting that the products of James Fraser's blacksmith's shop and foundry in Banff found their way to prestigious locations in Moray, notably the steel fire grates in the dining and drawing rooms of Letterfourie House.[46] Besides being of shapely and cunning design, these are decorated with incised flowers and one is signed by Fraser. The same firm designed and made carriage gates for the Quarry Gardens entrance to Gordon Castle in 1825.[47]

**Conclusion**

The early 19th century improvements in communications, canal, road and rail, brought changes in the distribution of building materials, very slowly at first but in due time sufficient to eliminate the use of nearly all local fabrics. The effect of the opening of the Caledonian Canal in 1822 in relation to the movement of slates from west coast quarries has already been mentioned; conversely Moray sandstone made an appearance in Fort William by means of this waterway.[48] Roads improved and bridges were built (the bridging of the River Spey at Fochabers in 1810 was of particular importance) so horse drawn transport could cover wider distances. By the 1850s the railway network reached Moray, its own pioneer line from Elgin to Lossiemouth linking with the trunk route between Aberdeen and Inverness. The much prized Moray sandstone, which had previously mainly been exported by sea, was now beginning to be used further inland. In 1833 William Robertson, architect, hoped that Bishop James Kyle might find sufficient funds to use this material on the entrance porch and baroque belltower that fronts the Roman Catholic Chapel at Huntly, a town where the local building stone was a hard grey granite.[49] Four years later the same architect used his favourite 'white freestone' for the austerely classical mansion of Aberlour House commissioned by a Jamaican nabob, Alexander Grant (Fig.12.21). After the Highland Railway penetrated Speyside in 1863, quite modest houses could have decorative cast-iron balusters fitted to their staircases (chosen from catalogues) rather than locally turned pine — but the use of the same pine spread wider throughout Moray and in the late Victorian period was the fashionable wood for house carpentry in the increasing number of villas in the expanding suburbs of Forres and Elgin, and the substantial new farmhouses in the countryside.

Concrete and paint, already cited, proliferated in the growing seatowns, where new houses were roofed with lighter Welsh slates coming from the south by rail. Stone continued to be used for walling until well into the 20th century, though the skills that quarried, tooled and carved this fine material gradually diminished as demand slackened. By the last quarter of the 20th centry the concrete block and roofing tile, aluminium window frames and plastic rainwater goods had arrived to stay, by the expanding road and shrinking rail networks, putting an end to the general use of local building materials and traditions.

## Acknowledgements

I am grateful to Mr David Alston, Dr Ronald Cant and Mr Sinclair Ross for their constructive help and advice in the preparation of this paper, and also to Captain Ramsay of Mar for permission to quote from the Duff House (Montcoffer) Papers.

Illustrations are reproduced by courtesy of the following: Fig.12.11, the Keeper of Manuscripts, University of St. Andrews Library with assistance from Elgin Library; Fig.12.19, The School of Scottish Studies with help from Dr. Margaret Mackay; Figs.12.2, 4, 5, 6, 9, 10, 12, 13, 14, 16, 18, 20, 21, Historic Scotland (Crown Copyright).

### Notes

1. Alec Clifton-Taylor, *The Pattern of English Building* (1962, revised ed. 1972).
2. *Ane Account of the Familie of Innes* ed. C Innes (Spalding Club 1864) 166-172; R G Cant, *Old Moray* (1948) end cover page. Innes House was designed by 'William Aitoun Maister Maison at Heriott' who was paid £26.13.4d (Scots money) for 'drawing the forme of the house in paper'. Sir Robert Innes kept precise accounts of the building of his house in Moray from 1640-1653; these included stone from Covesea which was transported by sea to Speyslaw, the nearest point to Innes, at between three and four times the price of the stone

itself. Iron came from Leith, wood from Glen Moriston and 'twantie two thowsand skleatts' from Caithness. The slater was paid for 'theaking' (thatching) 'my houss', the verb being then synonymous with slating. I am grateful to Dr R G Cant for drawing my attention to these accounts.

3. Alec Clifton-Taylor, *Pattern of English Building* 28.

4. *The Statistical Account* [*Stat.Acct.*] (1792-3; edd. Witherington and Grant, 1982, xvi) 493. I am grateful to Mr Sinclair Ross for information on the number of mid-18th century quarries between Burghead and Hopeman and for evidence of stone being transported from the Moray coast to Dunrobin, Sutherland. See also note 2 above.

5. Archibald Simpson, architect, 1828-9.

6. Arndilly House, circa 1770; additions William Robertson, 1826; remodelled by Thomas Mackenzie, 1850.

7. Considerable use of this building practice is to be found in Aberdeen.

8. Robert Adam, architect, 1773. Charles McKean, *The District of Moray, An Illustrated Architectural Guide* (1987) 124-5.

9. *Pattern of English Building* 53.

10. For detailed coverage of clay building and clay thatch see Alexander Fenton 'Clay Building and Clay Thatch in Scotland' in *Studies in Folklife presented to Emyr Estyn Evans* ed. Desmond McCourt (1970) 28-51. Also Bruce Walker, *Clay Buildings in North East Scotland* (1977).

11. Thomas Dick Lauder, *An Account of the Great Floods of August* 1829 (1830, 3rd ed. 1873) 241.

12. D Souter, *General View of the Agriculture of Banff* (1812) App., 9-11.

13. *Elgin Courier*, 28 May 1830.

14. Alexander Fenton 'Clay Building and Clay Thatch' 40-41. Until the cottage finally collapsed circa 1980, there was an example of clay thatching at Fernyfield, Urquhart.

15. Pers. comm. the late Miss Isobel Brown, Dipple, 1977.

16. *The Wilsons, a Banffshire Family of Factors* ed. Andrew Cassels Brown (1936) 58-9.

17. *Elgin Courier*, 31 December 1847.

18. *Elgin Courier*, 13 and 27 December 1850.

19. Scottish Record Office GD 44/51/389/11.

20. 1830 datestone was mistakenly re-cut to read 1630 circa 1975. The 1830 date was noted by the Inspector, Historic Buildings, during his survey in 1965. In any case the date 1630 is too early for commercial salmon fishing on the scale operated at Tugnet.

21. Alexander Fenton, *Scottish Country Life* (1975) 18-20.

22. Scottish Record Office GD 44/51/39. Discrepancies in cost per footage of walling are probably due to variable carriage costs of material according to distance from source of rubble stone.

23. Bruce Walker, *Clay Buildings* 10, 16, 17.

24. Duff House (Montcoffer Papers), MS 3175/vol. 11, Aberdeen University Special Collections. Letter from John Lawson, Elgin, to the Earl of Fife, 18 June, 1822. At this date Pluscarden Abbey was owned by the Earl.

25. Anon. *Survey of the Province of Moray* (1798) 163.

26. *New Statistical Account* [*NSA*] xiii (1842) 242.

27. *Northern Scot*, 2 May 1914.
28. *Stat. Acct* xvi, 116.
29. *NSA* xiii (1842) 229.
30. James B Dunn, Architect, 1930-32, though the design of this house was largely that of the owner, E S Harrison, who directed the building after the death of the architect prior to completion.
31. *NSA* xiii (1836) 107. Dufftown slates are more calcarious and therefore slightly softer.
32. Ibid., (1842) 248.
33. Scottish Record Office GD 44/37/39. The architect was probably William Robertson.
34. National Register of Archives (Scotland), Gordon of Cairnfield Papers, bundle 150. William Robertson, architect.
35. W Douglas Simpson, *Duffus Castle and Church*, HBMD Guide (1951).
36. Thomas Dick Lauder, *Account of the Great Floods* pl.34.
37. Elizabeth Beaton 'Cruck Blade, Elgin, Moray' *Vernacular Building* xii (1988) 14-15.
38. 107-111 High Street, Forres. Besides being a successful merchant John Cumming was agent for the British Linen Bank. Premises appear on Wood's map of Forres, 1823.
39. Robert Burn, architect, 1799-1804; wing, William Robertson, 1825; minor additions, R B Pratt, circa 1930. National Register of Archives (Scotland), Gordon of Cairnfield Papers, bundles 131, 150, 185, 211.
40. Dated 1786 and 1848, drawing room and dining room wings by William Robertson, 1826. Though the mansion is mostly gutted internally the drawing room retains its fine dado, overdoors etc.
41. See note 6 above.
42. *NSA* xiii (1842), 172. No evidence of the use of 'oaken splinters or spoors' (shingles) has been identified in Moray, but as with paving blocks, the raw material was locally available. Balnagown Castle, Ross-shire, was roofed with these in 1668 (W MacGill, *Old Ross-shire and Scotland* (1909-11) 123, 192). Many building traditions in Easter Ross have similarities with those in Moray.
43. Information per Mr Ian Keillar, lecture SSNS, Forres, 1987.
44. Thomas Mackenzie, architect, 1850.
45. See note 2 above.
46. See note 8 above.
47. Scottish Record Office GD 44/51/391/100. The bill for 'ornamental gates' was £68.19.11d. There are no longer gates at the Quarry Gardens Lodge.
48. The former Ben Nevis Low Level Observatory, Achintore Road, Fort William (now Glentower) has tooled sandstone margins and dressings, most of which have been painted. These dressings are said to have come from Moray via the Caledonian Canal. Sidney Mitchell, architect, 1889.
49. Scottish Catholic Archives IM 18/3/5 and IM 18/2/8 (both 1833).

# NAMES IN THE LANDSCAPE OF THE MORAY FIRTH

## W F H Nicolaisen

At the very outset, I would like to draw your attention to the exact wording of the title of this presentation — 'Names in the Landscape of the Moray Firth' — for it has been chosen with more than usual care. Titles anticipate and make promises; they summarise and raise expectations; they some-times tease and woo us. Above all, however, they open gates to paths of intellectual exploration at the end of which the mind should be comfortably satisfied. It is for all these reasons, but especially the last, that titles should be as accurate and as directional as signposts, for the sake both of those who shape them and of those for whose guidance they are intended. Otherwise their paths and ours will diverge from the very beginning.

Now that I have made you, the reader, disturbingly title conscious, you are entitled to know the reasons for this unusual preface. Why all this wordiness? Mainly to highlight the three major terms contained in the title — names, landscape, and Moray Firth — because these not only carry the greatest semantic freight but also represent the three key concepts of this discussion. They orient with regard to subject matter, setting and location or, put more simply, to the what, how and where. Let us briefly consider these points in reverse order.

It seems self-evident that, in a review of the place names of Moray, somehow the notion of Moray has to be one of its major shaping com-ponents but the question is: Which of the several possible Morays is it to be, since all of them are different in historical significance or spatial extent, or both? Is it to be the province, the diocese, the synod, the district? Is it to have largely historical, prehistoric, or ecclesiastical connotations, to express a nostalgic hankering after, or regret for, the passing of a com-paratively recent administrative unit for which the name Moray had been revived earlier this century to replace the pair Elgin and Forres, or is it to acknowledge the current political status of the mauled district within the Grampian Region, i.e. what Donald Omand has called the 'new Moray'?[1] In order not to be bound by the implications of any of these several Morays, I have added the generic Firth to the name Moray, thus making most of that estuary's southern shore and the more or less immediate hinterland my bailiwick for the purposes of this essay. The northern delineation of the area to be surveyed is therefore unmistakable whereas its western, eastern and southern boundaries largely coincide with those of the former counties of Nairn, Moray and Banff.

The second semantically pregnant term — landscape — has also been chosen with deliberate care. After all, a title such as 'Place Names on the Moray Firth' or even 'Place Names in Moray' would have been quite an adequate successor to those used in past toponymic presentations to this

Society by Ian Fraser, Gillian Fellows-Jensen and myself. The word 'landscape', however, is to serve as a reminder that place names are not only embedded in language but also in the world out there. It would be misleading to regard names exclusively as the product of mental processes, and it is therefore understandable that some publications treat and present them, together with flora, fauna, rock formations, etc., almost like natural features, regarding the onomastic characteristics of a given area in more or less the same way as the botanical, zoological and geological ones, and not as past human footprints. There is, indeed, something almost 'natural' about the belongingness of names and their persuasive appropriateness. After all, it is through the process of naming, the speech act of identification, that we structure the actual world outside our minds as it offers itself to us, thus taming, mastering and domesticating a potentially threatening wilderness and turning it into a familiar habitat which we tend to call 'landscape'. There is no landscape without a network of names or, from the point of view of the creative act of naming, names make a landscape. It is therefore inevitable, because essential, that the word 'landscape' should appear in our title.

That the term 'names' is also part of it, is probably even more predictable as it points to the very subject matter to be explored, the 'what' of the triad. Naming is a ubiquitous activity; as far as we know, human beings everywhere and at all times have named and will go on doing so as long as man or woman draws breath. Names are so much more than lexical items with certain peculiar additional properties; they are a matter of survival, of orienting oneself in the world, and, for this reason, are as important as food, drink and shelter. Names never occur singly — this would be a *contradictio in adjecto* — but in their individuating function relate to other names through contrast, through juxtaposition, through stratification, thus forming onomastic fields which are ever-changing and ever-readjusting. To have a name is to be, but never in solitude. Without names we are lost.

A title like 'Names in the Landscape of the Moray Firth' therefore attempts to open a window on the toponymically structured, or perhaps rather the toponymically articulated, landscape of a region defined somewhat loosely and yet not without discernible boundaries. Harnessing this title for this essay is consequently an act of appropriation, a desirable closing in on the essence of 'Moray', whatever that may be these days; only the people of Moray can decide that.

Naturally, there are several ways of going about this business. Over eighty years ago, Donald Matheson, in his *Place Names of Elginshire*,[2] now thoroughly out of date and even in its own days highly suspect, chose the acceptable, though deceptively disruptive, device of listing names in alphabetical order, his sole purpose being, consonant with the main tenor of name scholarship in his time, the ferreting out of the so-called 'meaning' of the names included in his alphabetical list. This approach assumes that it is possible, indeed incumbent upon us, to reduce names to the words they once were,[3] and that the restoration of such original meaning or etymology is the prime purpose of name studies. It completely ignores, or at least obscures, the fact that names — whether derived from words, other names, or from arbitrary sound sequences — at the very point of naming acquire a content independent of all lexical needs and considerations, and that it is this content and not their etymologies that allows names to function viably in our efforts at effective communication. Nevertheless, the recovery of lexical meaning and of linguistic affinities is, of course, when carried out with competence and circumspection and with due regard to all the available evidence including early spellings and modern pronunciation, an essential first step, a *sine qua non* in all onomastic research, a kind of linguistic archaeology. It is, however, not the be-all-and-end-all; nor should such a fundamentally lexical procedure be confused with a thoroughly onomastic approach which recognises and exploits the status and function of names as names.

More recently, in 1976, in his contribution to Donald Omand's *Moray Book*,[4] Donald Macaulay, bringing his considerable expertise as a Celtic scholar and his skills as a native speaker of Gaelic to bear on his investigation, chose to present the bulk of his material in several discrete categories, such as references to settlement, land division and fields, crops, domestic animals, 'activities', churches, and topographic elements, like water, raised ground, low ground, 'valleys', as well as non-domestic animals and birds, vegetation, shape and size, and colour. Such classificatory approach takes it for granted that the etymology of each name thus classified has been satisfactorily established; it is therefore a kind of second step, the findings of which, when described in this fashion and systematically analysed, go a long way towards making good use of place names as linguistic fossils and towards employing them in the reconstruction of past landscapes. If Donald Macaulay had not chosen to do this so recently, I might well have decided on such an approach for this investigation, but there is no need for this kind of duplication.

The third frequently practised and very fruitful method in the study of place names also starts with the supposition that the first step in establishing reliable etymologies has already been successfully taken and that the names in question have been made lexically transparent, not just semantically but also with regard to, for example, their pronunciation and their morphology. Instead of focusing on the several distinctive categories of meaning involved, as in Donald Macaulay's treatment, it attempts to make constructive use, on the one hand, of the linguistic features of names and, on the other, of their onomastic properties. Taking into account the well-known fact that names, because of their virtual independence of lexical meaning, their desemanticisation, so to speak, often survive when words do not, this method tries to place names and their elements in their relevant distribution patterns in time and space and, subsequently, to derive from these patterns information regarding the historical stratification of languages in a given area and the geographical scatter of settlers speaking the languages in question. This, mostly historical, orientation to name studies underlies, for instance, my own book on *Scottish Place Names*[5] which, like Donald Macaulay's chapter, was also published in 1976. Again, it would be inappropriate to reiterate in detail its conclusions concerning Scotland as a whole and the Moray Firth area in particular but it may be helpful to sketch out, with a few strokes of a broad brush, the picture as it emerges from the place-name evidence. The discussion of principles and methods without the use of illustrative examples is a pointless enterprise.

Leaving aside for a moment the fascinating question of the possibility that the Celts may not have been the first Indo-Europeans to have reached these shores,[6] there cannot be any doubt that the region to the south of the Moray Firth was once settled by non-Gaelic speaking Celts whom we know as the Picts and whose linguistic connections were with southern Scotland and Wales and ultimately with the Celtic areas of the Continent, rather than with Ireland. According to that great Celticist, W J Watson, there are, or once were, fifteen names beginning with the generic *Pit-* in Banffshire, twelve in the county of Moray, and one in Nairnshire.[7] These names quite clearly form part of the larger area in the Scottish east and north-east in which compound names containing this generic can be found, from the Firth of Forth northwards. As has been demonstrated convincingly, *Pit-* is the modern reflex (practically all the earlier name spellings use a form *Pet-*) of a Pictish word for a portion of land derived from an early Celtic \**petia* and therefore, in a roundabout way, via Latin, is cognate with our modern English word *piece*.[8] It is not found in the British Isles anywhere outside the area once settled by Pictish-speaking Celts, although it would be erroneous to assume that all the names in this group were actually given by Pictish speakers themselves. Many of the specifics in these names are, in fact, Gaelic.[9] Some of these may have been translated or adapted from Pictish but the majority of them must go back to speakers of Gaelic who had adopted *pit* or *pet* as an element suitable for the naming of places, especially of farm-like settlements. This is certainly true of Moray as Donald Macaulay has shown[10]; he cites *Pitchaish*, *Pitchroy*, *Pircraigie*, *Pittendreich*, *Pittensier*, *Pitgaveny*, *Pitglassie*, and *Pittyvaich*. *Petty* also belongs here. It is unlikely that these names were given much before the tenth century from when on Gaelic-speaking settlers became well established in what had been Pictland. Such dating is supported by the dearth of ecclesiastical names beginning with *Kil-* (Gaelic *cill* 'church, churchyard') which seem to have become less fashionable or productive about the time the Gaels entered Pictland.[11]

256

Other names which have survived from pre-Gaelic times are *Aberarder*, *Aberchirder* and *Aberlour* all of which contain river names as their specifics, and possibly *Fochabers*. Unlike *Pit-*, Pictish *aber* 'a river mouth or confluence' does, of course, occur in southern Scotland and also in Wales[12] but this wider distribution only emphasises the point that Pictish is not likely to have been as different from the Celtic languages south of the Firth of Forth which Professor Jackson calls Cumbric,[13] or from the Brittonic ancestor of Welsh, Cornish and Breton as the evidence of the *Pit*-names when viewed in isolation might lead one to conclude. *Pluscarden*, despite the shift of stress to the first syllable, also contains an element which places it alongside the *Aber*-names, a topographic term now represented by Welsh *cardden* 'thicket, brake'.[14] The area which has our attention was therefore once thoroughly Pictish, and we must assume that Pictish in this part of the world was a Celtic language, unlike the linguistic situation north of the Moray Firth.

As already indicated, these Pictish-speaking Celts on the south side of the firth were overrun and succeeded by Gaelic-speaking Celts from about the ninth century onwards. The incomers speaking this language not only utilised elements of the onomasticon, or name vocabulary, of their Pictish predecessors, like *Pit-*, but also brought with them and applied their own toponymic terminology. Chief among the generics used in settlement names and found wherever Gaelic speakers once settled in Scotland are the terms *baile* 'homestead' and *achadh* 'field'.[15] The landscape south of the Moray Firth yields many examples of both as, for instance for *baile*, *Balblair, Ballachurn, Ballanlish, Ballanloan, Ballenteem, Balgreen, Ballindalloch, Balnacree, Balnaferry, Balnageith, Balvenie,* and many others, and, for *achadh, Achfad, Auchenhalrig, Auchindown, Auchingoul, Auchintoul, Achnahannet, Auchnarrow, Auchness,* and others. Just as this area was once solidly Pictish, so it participated fully in the Gaelic settlement which followed. In fact, it can easily be shown that the presence of Gaelic here for about a thousand years has left an indelible mark on the toponymic palimpsest of our maps. In view of this extended and extensive influence, it is not surprising that this stratum is distinctly stratified within itself, the last places in our area having been named possibly around the beginning of this century. There are hundreds, if not thousands, of names to vouch for such a claim. These incorporate a plethora of Gaelic generics and specifics including many of the most classical ones such as *blár, ceann, torr, tom, allt, beinn, cnoc, dún, druim, aodann, leitir, gleann, inis, inbhir, ráth, árd, barr, clac, cúil, lann, loch, logach, mágh,* and the like. Most of these, like their Pictish counterparts, have in the course of time become semantically opaque to speakers of Scots or English who have gradually turned into the dominating linguistic force but the lexical opacity of these names has not in any way detracted from their staying fully functional as names. While meaning is no longer accessible, the all-important content still is, however much it may change from time to time and from person to person.

So much, or so little, for the Celts. As far as speakers of Germanic languages are concerned, there is, again in contrast to the region north of the Moray Firth,[16] no place-name evidence to indicate that any Scandinavians ever held sway over our area.[17] The Cromarty and Beauly Firths seem to have stopped even the boldest of them. Like the Romans before them, the Norsemen apparently never lived long enough in the Moray landscape to contribute to its articulation. As is to be expected, however, there is now a sizable crop of descriptive English names well anchored to the ground, such as *Berryhillock, Birkenbog, Cairnfield, Drybridge, Limehillock, Lintmill, Longmanhill, Marypark, Milltown, Newmill, Oakbank, Sandend, Whitehills, Broomhill, Househill, Lodgehill, Piperhill, Tradespark, Bogmuir, Cooperhill, Ferry Road, Grange, Imperial Cottages, Linkwood, Mouiton, Newton, Silver Sands, Westerfolds, Whiteinch, Whitemire*, and so on. These are now all names of settlements and are lexically, on the whole, quite transparent. We know what they mean as words. They are, therefore, the kinds of names that name scholars in the past, and sometimes even in the present, have often regarded as pedestrian, boring and not worth bothering about, and have consequently been accorded left-handed comments such as 'meaning self-evident'. From a purely etymologically oriented approach to name studies, this may well be true but this lack of etymological challenge does not make them less valuable and functional or worthy of study than names whose meaning is now obscure and has to be recovered through complex and lengthy procedures, if it can be recovered at all. When Donald Macaulay comments on the name *Dyke*[18] that it probably means simply *dike*, there is that very kind of disappointment in his comment. I am myself not at all disillusioned by names like *Dyke* for I still want to know when and why they were first given. Because so many of them were coined so late and originally referred to rather minor features in the landscape, the recorded evidence for them is often almost non-existent, or at least scanty and hard to find. For example, in my extensive search for early spellings for my *Dictionary of Scottish Place Names* I have yet to find reliable documentary evidence for about half the names just listed, the 'self-evident' ones. They are thus among the most elusive toponymic material one comes across and are often traceable only in very local sources. In contrast, names which have come down to us from the Middle Ages or some other earlier period are usually so much better documented.

Another category of such comparatively recent names which, according to the language of the namers, can only be called English but which have local historical and genealogical, sometimes very personal, connections with this area, are those of the various ports and towns planned and developed from the seventeenth century onwards. Instances would be:

*Dufftown*, founded in 1817 by James Duff, fourth Earl of Fife; *Gardenstown*, founded in 1720 by Alexander Garden of Troup; *Macduff* which was erected a burgh of barony for the Earl of Fife in 1783 and whose earlier name had been *Down* (1683); *Branderburgh* where Colonel Brander of Pitgaveny built a house for himself in 1830; *Castle Grant* which replaced *Freuchie* and *Ballochastell* when the Regality of Grant was erected in 1694; *Gordon Castle*, the old *Bog of Gight* (older *Geith*), named about 1685; and *Gordonstoun* which came into being when Sir Robert Gordon, from 1636 on, purchased such places as *Ogstoun, Plewlands, Ettles*, etc. to form the estate; Grantown-on-Spey, a town planned by Sir James Grant of Castle Grant in 1776; or *Cummingstown* whose proprietor, Sir William Cumming Gordon, planned it as a village in 1805. As a foreign intruder from south of the Border comes *Kingston* which, it is said, was created in 1784 by two Englishmen from Kingston-upon-Hull (even in Hull they don't call it Kingston anymore).

A related group consists of names like *Portessie* which became a fishing station in 1727; *Portgordon*, founded in 1797 by the fourth Duke of Gordon; *Portknockie*, founded in 1677; *Portsoy* which became a burgh of barony for Ogilvy of Boyne in 1550; and even *Lossiemouth*, the harbour of which was constructed in 1698 and for which our earliest record is from 1702, and *Buckie* which grew out of several separate villages. Names like these, despite their obvious Gaelic antecedents, are largely post-Gaelic echoes of coming to terms with the riskful ambiguity of coastscapes, offering onomastic promises of shelter and haven and livelihood for those in peril on the sea.

These two groups of names are excellent examples of how the toponymic ingredient of our landscapes is forever changing and how the onomastic field changes with them. Landscape has historical structure as well as current existence.

That this process of change is not yet complete and will, to some extent, continue for ever, is demonstrated not only by the several distillery names made famous to thirsty imbibers of the water of life all over the world, but also by such seemingly mundane names as *Ballindalloch Station*, opened on July 1, 1863; and closed November 1968; *Alves Station*, opened on March 25, 1858, and closed on November 7, 1966; *Dava Station*, opened on November 1, 1864, and closed on October 18, 1965; *Dunphail Station*, opened on August 3, 1863, and closed on October 18, 1965; and *Fochabers Station*, opened October 23, 1893, and closed on March 28, 1966.[19] Although these stations do not exist anymore, having mostly fallen prey to Dr Beeching's axe in the sixties, the small settlements so named still do, but their content has changed. In all these instances, the originally appropriate generic — *station* — obviously no longer applies but the name persists, fossilising toponymically a way of locomotion now no longer in need of stopping places in these locations. Who says that only the ancient has its fascination? We are still adding to the palimpsest that will one day be deciphered by our puzzled descendants.

It is also worth remembering that, in addition to or intermingled with, the official or standard place nomenclature there is the vernacular one that has never been recorded on any map and probably never will be. There are *Foggy* and the *Douce Borough*, and further east there are the *Broch* and the *Blue Toon*, and I understand that no self-respecting native would ever call *Gardenstown* anything but *Gamrie*. This unofficial vernacular consists of alternative names, often nicknames, in non-standard or dialect forms, of additional names, of local pronunciations, but also of names in other languages like Gaelic. Mainly these operate in a different socio-linguistic register and are therefore appropriate under particular circumstances, in particular company, and as, largely informal, responses to particular stimuli. They have hardly been seriously studied at all because of their non-official popular associations but are a rich source of information for a differently articulated vernacular landscape that supplements, parallels or replaces the official one.

There is one more important point I would like to make: We have already seen that *Kingston* is an individual, possibly an intrusive, transferred name but sometimes, perhaps due to the motivation or the ability to innovate imaginatively or for other reasons, groups of names or nomenclatures are transferred, and with them whole landscapes. If W J Watson is right, such transference happened on a grand scale when Gaelic speakers first settled in this area.[20] The names which he groups together in support of such a claim are *Banff* which literally means 'sucking pig' but as *Banba* was also a name for Ireland; *Elgin* which as a Gaelic locative case *Eilginn* could be connected with a diminutive of *Elg*, another ancient name for Ireland; *Boyne* and *Boyndie* which have equivalents in Ireland; and especially *Findhorn* (*Fionn-Éire* 'white Ireland') which was *Invereren* in 1187-1203, the mouth of the *aqua de Eren*. Linking this with *Strathdearn* (*Stratheren* 1236) and *Auldearn* (*Aldheren* 1238) = *Allt Éireann* 'Ireland's Burn', he postulates a district name *Eryn* 'Ireland', and if his interpretations are right this would indeed be a remarkable accumulation of names reinforcing each other in their direct links with the country from which the settlers or their ancestors had ultimately come. The problem I have with this cumulative evidence, despite my great admiration for Watson as a scholar, is that it is very difficult to reconcile such a wholesale transfer with the several river names in question. I have been studying river names for almost forty years now, and instinct tells me that they do not behave in this way. Animal names for rivers such as *Banff* are quite common in the Celtic world, and *Boyne* and *Boyndie* might well have been created independently. For the second part of *Findhorn* and *Auldearn*, as well as the related *Deveron*, an original river name is more likely and much points in this direction, i.e. of *-horn, -earn* and *-eron* representing ancient river names meaning 'flowing water'. If this explanation is acceptable, one might further suggest that this older name belonged to a pre-Celtic Indo-European stratum to which the river name *Nairn* probably also goes back.[21] In addition, although an etymology is hard to establish, the name of the *Spey* may also belong here; a meaning 'hawthorn river' which Watson proposes for the most important river in the region is difficult to substantiate.

Whatever the explanation, it is highly probable that the Celtic people who settled in *Moray*, Gaelic *Moireabh*, the old *Murebe* or early Celtic *mori-treb-* 'seaboard settlement',[22] may well have found other people already there whose language was very much akin to their own. *Moray* itself has an honourable, ancient history as a name but one would like to dig deeper. Unfortunately, the evidence that has come down to us does not allow much more than speculation, for even place names, that wonderful inheritance from several linguistic pasts, are not inexhaustive in their provision of knowledge, and there comes a point in prehistory at which even names cease to speak and only things still have a voice.

No doubt there were topographic features asking to be named, no doubt there were namers equipped and willing to name them, no doubt as a result there were names, maybe not as many as today but still enough to create a landscape; but maps were only in people's minds, and the ears that heard them in oral tradition have long been unhearing. Names, those eloquent, informative witnesses for the last 3000 years or so, at that point offer nothing but silence.

**Notes**

1. Donald Omand (ed.), *The Moray Book* (Edinburgh: Paul Harris, 1976).
2. Donald Matheson, *The Place Names of Elginshire* (Stirling: Eneas Mackay, 1905).
3. See W F H Nicolaisen 'Names Reduced to Words?: Purpose and Scope of a Dictionary of Scottish Place Names' in *Scottish Language and Literature, Mediaeval and Renaissance* edd. Dietrich Strauss and Horst W Drescher (Frankfurt am Main: Peter Lang, 1986) 47-54.
4. Donald Macaulay 'Place Names' in Omand, *Moray Book* 248-263.
5. W F H Nicolaisen, *Scottish Place-Names: Their Study and Significance* (London: B T Batsford, 1976).
6. Ibid., 173-191. Also: W F H Nicolaisen 'Die alteuropäischen Gewässernamen der britischen Hauptinsel' in *Beiträge zur Namenforschung* 8 (1957) 211-268; 'Great Britain and Old Europe' in *Namn och Bygd* 59 (1971) 85-105, 'Thirty Years Later: Thoughts on a Viable Concept of Old European Hydronomy' in *Festschrift für Johannes Hubschmid zum 65. Geburtstag* edd. Otto Winkelman and Maria Braisch (Bern; Switzerland 1982) 139-149; and 'Old European Names in Britain' in *Nomina* 6 (1982) 37-42.
7. William J Watson, *The History of the Celtic Place-Names of Scotland* (Edinburgh: William Blackwood & Sons, 1926) 407.
8. Nicolaisen, *Scottish Place-names* 152.
9. Ibid., 154.

10. Macaulay 'Place Names' 249.
11. Nicolaisen, *Scottish Place-names* 143.
12. Ibid., 164-165.
13. See, for example, Kenneth Jackson 'Angles and Britons in Northumbria and Cumbria' in *Angles and Britons* ed. Henry Lewis (Cardiff: University of Wales Press, 1963) 60-84.
14. Nicolaisen, *Scottish Place-Names* 158-159.
15. Ibid., 136-143.
16. See Ian A Fraser 'Norse and Celtic Place-Names Around the Dornoch Firth' in *Firthlands of Ross and Sutherland* ed. John R Baldwin (Edinburgh: Scottish Society for Northern Studies, 1986) 23-32, esp. 29-31.
17. A name like *Surradale* is a newcomer not recorded till the nineteenth century. I am grateful to Mr. Ian Keillar, Elgin for this information.
18. Macaulay 'Place Names' 260. *Dyke* is, on the other hand, a curiosum in so far as one would not expect an English name of such importance to have been recorded in the twelfth century in this part of the country. Is it possible that an English or Scandinavian loan-word in Gaelic was employed when this name was coined?
19. This information has been provided by the late Mr. Norris Forrest, Aberdeen.
20. Watson, *Celtic Place-Names* 228-232.
21. Nicolaisen, *Scottish Place-Names*, 187.
22. Watson, *Celtic Place-Names* 115-116.

# List of Abbreviations

The abbreviations used in this volume follow mainly the conventions adopted by the *Scottish Historical Review.*

| | |
|---|---|
| *APS* | *The Acts of the Parliaments of Scotland,* edd. T Thomson and C Innes (Edinburgh 1814-75). |
| CBA | Council for British Archaeology. |
| *ER* | *The Exchequer Rolls of Scotland,* edd. J Stuart and others (Edinburgh 1878-1908). |
| *ES* | *Early Sources of Scottish History 500 to 1286,* ed. A O Anderson (Edinburgh 1922, and reprint 1990). |
| HBMD | Historic Buildings and Monuments Division. |
| *Moray Reg.* | *Registrum Episcopatus Moraviensis* (Bannatyne Club, Edinburgh 1837). |
| *Njal's Saga [NS]* | *Njal's Saga,* trans. M Magnusson and H Palsson (Harmondsworth 1960). |
| | *Njal's Saga,* ed. Magnus Finnbogasson (Reykjavik 1944). |
| *NSA* | *The New Statistical Account of Scotland,* 15 vols. (Edinburgh 1845). |
| *Orkneyinga Saga [OS]* | *The Orkneyinga Saga,* trans. with intro. and notes by A B Taylor (Edinburgh 1938). |
| | *Orkneyinga Saga. The History of the Earls of Orkney,* trans. with intro. by Hermann Palsson and Paul Edwards (Harmondsworth 1978). |
| | *Orkneyinga Saga,* ed. F Gudmundsson (Islenzk Fornrit, Reykjavik 1965). |
| *Pop.Arch.* | *Popular Archaeology.* |
| *PSAS* | *Proceedings of the Society of Antiquaries of Scotland.* |
| RCHM | Royal Commission on Historical Monuments (England). |
| RCAHMS | Royal Commission on the Ancient and Historical Monuments of Scotland. |
| *Reg.Mag.Sig. [RMS]* | *Registrum Magni Sigilli Regum Scotorum,* edd. J M Thomson and others (Edinburgh 1882-1914). |
| *RRS* | *Regesta Regum Scottorum,* edd. G W S Barrow and others (Edinburgh 1960-). |

| | |
|---|---|
| *SHR* | *Scottish Historical Review.* |
| *SGS* | *Scottish Gaelic Studies.* |
| SRO | Scottish Record Office. |
| *Stat.Acct.* | *The Statistical Account of Scotland*, 21 vols. (Edinburgh 1791-9; new edition 1975-). |